T0275992

Emerging Pervasive Information
and Communication Technologies (PICT)

Law, Governance and Technology Series

VOLUME 11

Series Editors:

POMPEU CASANOVAS, *UAB Institute of Law and Technology, Bellaterra, Barcelona, Spain*

GIOVANNI SARTOR, *European University Institute, Florence, Italy*

Scientific Advisory Board:

For further volumes:
http://www.springer.com/series/8808

Kenneth D. Pimple

Editor

Emerging Pervasive Information and Communication Technologies (PICT)

Ethical Challenges, Opportunities and Safeguards

 Springer

Editor
Kenneth D. Pimple
Poynter Center
Indiana University
Bloomington, IN, USA

ISBN 978-94-017-8434-4   ISBN 978-94-007-6833-8 (eBook)
DOI 10.1007/978-94-007-6833-8
Springer Dordrecht Heidelberg New York London

Printed on acid-free paper

Springer is part of Springer Science+Business Media (www.springer.com)

Acknowledgments

This book is the culmination of a long process of collaboration, grant writing, workshops, and more collaboration. A central event was a 2-day workshop entitled Ethical Guidance for Research and Application of Pervasive and Autonomous Information Technology (PAIT), March 3–4, 2010.[1] The workshop was supported by the National Science Foundation (grant number SES-0848097), the Poynter Center for the Study of Ethics and American Institutions, and the Association for Practical and Professional Ethics.

The views expressed in this volume are those of the authors and do not necessarily represent the views of the National Science Foundation, the Poynter Center, the Association for Practical and Professional Ethics, or Indiana University.

I am pleased to acknowledge[2] the invaluable contributions of

- Donald F. "Rick" McMullen, who introduced me to pervasive technology and some of its ethical implications;
- Richard B. Miller, Director of the Poynter Center, and Glenda E. Murray, the Poynter Center's Program Associate, for intellectual, logistical, and moral support;

---

[1]For details on the PAIT workshop, see http://poynter.indiana.edu/pait/.

In preparing this book, I chose to de-emphasize autonomous technology, which played an important role in the workshop, primarily in the form of robots and military applications. Robots and computer-controlled weapons appropriately receive a great deal of attention in the mass media as well as academe, but less dramatic technologies that are profoundly changing our everyday experiences – often in ways that are not only hard to detect but, in many cases, deliberately hidden – tend to get short shrift. This is why I dropped the A from PAIT and inserted the C, thus overtly adopting a widely used term – information and communication technology (ICT) – that also emphasizes the connectivity (communication capabilities) of P/ICT.

I am indebted to Joe Herkert, who impressed upon me the importance of the C in ICT, a lesson I was slow to learn.

[2]Many of the named individuals belong in more than one category; these are mentioned in the category in which they made the greatest impact.

- Brian Schrag, then Executive Secretary of the Association for Practical and Professional Ethics;
- the members of the PAIT Planning Committee: Colin Allen, Anthony F. Beavers, Katherine Connelly, Joseph Herkert, Deborah Johnson, Nancy J. Obermeyer, Michael S. Pritchard, Marianne Ryan, Katherine D. Seelman, Kalpana Shankar, and Katie C. Shilton;
- Julia A. Pedroni and Sandra Shapshay for joining me, Rick McMullen, Nancy Obermeyer, and Kalpana Shankar on a panel at the 2009 APPE annual meeting;
- the 36 participants at the March 2010 workshop and the three featured speakers, Fred H. Cate, Helen Nissenbaum, and Noel Sharkey;
- Yoshi Kohno, who met with 16 potential contributors to this volume and gave a public lecture at Indiana University on October 20, 2010;
- Keith W. Miller for organizing a PAIT-related panel at the 2011 APPE Annual Meeting at which he, I, Michael Davis, and Charles W. Huff presented;
- other scholars and practitioners too numerous to mention who have supported this project in a variety of ways;
- and, of course, the contributors to this volume.

Indiana University Bloomington   Kenneth D. Pimple

Contents

Abbreviations

AHIMA   American Health Information Association (7)
AHRQ   Agency for Healthcare Research and Quality (7)
ARRA   American Recovery and Reinvestment Act (7)
CDC   Centers for Disease Control and Prevention (U.S. agency) (3)
CDSS   Clinical Decision Support System (7)
CENS   Center for Embedded Networked Sensing (9)
CFP   Certified Financial Planner (2)
CFTC   U.S. Commodity Futures Trading Commission (2)
CMS   Centers for Medicare and Medicaid Services (7)
CPOE   computerized physician/provider order entry (7)
CSTE   Council of State and Territorial Epidemiologists (3)
DCI   direct computer interface (7)
DHHS   (U.S.) Department of Health and Human Services (7)
DJIA   Dow Jones Industrial Average (2)
DNR   Do Not Resuscitate (6)
EHR   Electronic Health Record (7)
ELSI   ethical, legal, and social issues (of a project) (9)
ETF   exchange-traded fund (2)
GPS   Global Positioning System (2, 8)
HFT   High-Frequency Traders (2)
HIE   Health Information Exchange (7)
HIM   Health Information Management (7)
HIPAA   Health Insurance Portability and Accountability Act (7)
HIT   Health Information Technology (7)
HUD   heads-up display (8)
ICT   information and communication technology (7)
NAPFA   National Association of Personal Finance Advisors (2)
PDV   Personal Data Vault (9)

Numbers in parenthesis correspond to the chapter(s) in which the term is used.

PHR	Personal Health Record (7)
PPACA	Patient Protection and Affordable Care Act (7)
PPR	participatory privacy regulation (9)
SEC	U.S. Securities and Exchange Commission (2)
VID	values in design (9)

Chapter 1
Introduction: The Impact, Benefits, and Hazards of PICT

Kenneth D. Pimple

1.1 Background

Consider:

- Facebook has more than one billion (1,000,000,000) active users.[1] If it were a country, it would be the third most populous in the world (behind China and India, ahead of the United States).[2] Not even China has as much personal information about its residents as Facebook has about its users.
- If the Egyptian government had used the locational technologies in mobile phones to find and "neutralize" leaders of the Twitter/Internet uprising, dictator Hosni Mubarak might still be president and the revolutions in Libya and elsewhere – the so-called Arab Spring (Toumi 2011) – might not have happened.
- As populations age, non-professional caregivers (adult daughters and sons) will increasingly turn to inexpensive, Internet-connected sensing and communication devices to keep tabs on their elderly parents. The elders will appreciate being able to stay in their own homes longer and the caregivers will have additional peace of mind – at some cost to the elders' privacy.

---

[1] "More than billion monthly active users at the end of December 2012," according to Facebook Newsroom. From http://newsroom.fb.com/content/default.aspx?NewsAreaId=22 (accessed February 8, 2012).

[2] The World Factbook's July 2012 estimates lists China with a population of about 1.3 billion; India with about 1.2 billion; and the U.S. with .3 billion. From https://www.cia.gov/library/publications/the-world-factbook/rankorder/2119rank.html (accessed February 8, 2013).

K.D. Pimple, Ph.D. (✉)
Poynter Center, Indiana University Bloomington, 618 East Third Street, Bloomington,
IN 47405-3602, USA
e-mail: pimple@indiana.edu

K.D. Pimple (ed.), *Emerging Pervasive Information and Communication Technologies (PICT)*, Law, Governance and Technology Series 11, DOI 10.1007/978-94-007-6833-8_1,
© Springer Science+Business Media Dordrecht 2014

The common thread is a concern with ethical issues surrounding emerging technologies for which, for ease of reference, we use the term "pervasive information and communication technologies" (PICT). This collection of original chapters is united by this thread and theoretically informed by *anticipatory ethics* – "ethical analysis aimed at influencing the development of new technologies" (Johnson 2010: 590). Anticipatory ethics treats technology as one aspect of a *socio-technical system* (Johnson 2011: 66) comprising physical machines, the software that runs them, the companies that make them, the people who use them, the electric companies that power them, the coal mines that supply the electric companies, the banking system that enables coal mine owners to pay coal miners, and so on. The point is that physical devices depend on a large social and technological infrastructure to be useful, usable, and meaningful: Without electricity, cell phone towers, Wi-Fi hot spots, and the like, our smartphones are just expensive paperweights.[3]

New technologies that achieve widespread popularity can change social practices in unintended ways. The invention of oral contraceptives – the pill – provides a particularly dramatic example. Introduced in the United States in 1960, the pill did not just give women greater control over reproduction, but also had an impact on "women's health, fertility trends, laws and policies, religion, interpersonal relations, family roles, women's careers, gender relations, and premarital sexual practices" (Tyrer 1999). In socio-technical systems, social practices – what we do in daily life – inspire technological innovations, which in turn change social practices.

PICT is variously termed ubiquitous computing (or ubicomp), pervasive computing, everyware, and ambient intelligence (AmI). The four adjectives – "ubiquitous," "pervasive," "every(where)," and "ambient" – highlight the expected omnipresence of these devices, being embedded in just about anything and found just about anywhere. "Ambient" also implies the subtlety of the devices; they will often be invisible and their functions undetected by the casual observer. "Ambient intelligence" applies particularly to artificial intelligence (AI) devices, but AI capabilities are not excluded by the terms "ubiquitous" and "pervasive."

Not highlighted in these terms, but certainly important to the power of PICT, is connectivity. It isn't just that PICT devices are everywhere, but also that the data collected can go anywhere. While it is useful for my physician to have easy access to my hospital records and vice versa, by the nature of the beast many other people have legitimate access to the same data streams; furthermore, the data is transmitted by the Internet and resides on a number of servers in different locations, setting the stage for illegitimate and malicious access. My health data could be pooled with other datasets to create a huge dataset that reveals otherwise unknown facts about my life, behavior, preferences, and predilections. Connectivity gives PICT the capability to know all and reveal all.

---

[3]There was a time when many people believed that computers would usher in the paperless office. If that state ever comes about, the paperweight – a rudimentary technology, to be sure – will disappear.

PICT technologies (a) perform multiple functions, including collecting, storing, distributing, analyzing, and acting upon information (b) collected by intentional human input, passive receptors (motion detectors, surveillance cameras), active receptors (drones, robots), and amalgamation of data from separate sources. Often the information is a side-effect of deliberate human activity: Every Internet search leaves a trace to be exploited by legitimate advertisers, but also, potentially, con artists and oppressive governments. Similar traces are created by social networking (Facebook, Twitter, etc.).

Two major concerns in PICT for end-users, policy makers, social scientists, and especially those who develop, design, deploy, and market PICT technologies are deception and privacy. When people use a technology for one purpose (chatting with friends) and the information they share goes to a third party (advertisers), those people have arguably been deceived just as surely as if their telephones had been tapped, and their privacy just as thoroughly invaded. PICT technologies are ripe for malicious exploitation if they are not carefully designed.

Perhaps more importantly, and much more subtly, the collection of massive amounts of private information makes possible the wide-spread manipulation of the behavior of whole populations – such as late-night watchers of "TV Land, the basic cable network devoted to reruns of old programs" (Rutenberg 2012). The Obama campaign

> [culled] never-before-used data about viewing habits, and combin[ed] it with more personal information about the voters the campaign was trying to reach and persuade than was ever before available, ... allow[ing] Mr. Obama's team to direct advertising with a previously unheard-of level of efficiency. (Rutenberg 2012)

The effectiveness of this strategy is credited by many for Obama's success. It seems likely that a similar strategy could allow organizations with other goals, such as passing specific legislation, to energize or demoralize a few hundred key voters. It could be argued that such targeted advertising undermines democracy by giving disproportionate impact to a relatively few votes.

Many PICT technologies take action only when initiated by a human, or as a response to strictly defined circumstances more-or-less after the fashion of a smoke detector. Others, however, take actions based on their own analysis of complex, quickly changing, or multiple streams of data, as in high-frequency trading (Chap. 2). In some cases these systems raise issues beyond privacy and deception to serious physical, social, and economic harms. AI systems are increasingly making life-and-death and/or multi-million-dollar decisions without direct human intervention or adequate supervision.

The tendency of computer technology to proliferate at an exponential rate – as stated in Moore's Law, computer capacity doubles every 2 years – suggests that both the benefits and hazards of PICT will become substantial soon. If the hazards are not addressed in advance of, and along with, the implementation of PICT, the prospect of correcting the trajectory and solving problems will be dim. To a certain degree, the ethical concerns raised by PICT can be summarized in a question: Will the technologies serve us, or will we serve the technologies?

1.2   Contents

The chapters in this book address a variety of topics related to PICT, but certainly not all of them. For example, PICT is sure to be used at an increasing pace for espionage and military applications. Our focus is on technologies that ordinary people are likely to encounter in everyday life. Military use is dramatic, which means it gets more press than more mundane technologies. We believe that it is vitally important for ordinary people to understand the everyday technologies that are quietly – often covertly – changing their lives.

The book begins with three case studies (Chap. 2) of actual recent events that highlight key aspects of PICT. Chapters 3, 4, and 5 tackle surveillance from three different angles, but together provide a primer on the ethical issues involved. Chapters 3, 6, and 7 focus on health care, an area of significant growth for PICT. Chapter 8 considers a particular type of PICT – augmented reality – and reveals its far-from-obvious ramifications. Chapter 9 provides a different kind of case study as a social scientist describes her experience working with technologists developing PICT with the goal (successfully achieved) of making ethics a design goal. Chapters 10 and 11 focus more narrowly on ethical guidance for PICT.

Chapters 2 through 11, organized in six thematic sections, are described below.

1.2.1   Real-World Cases

In Chap. 2, "Three Case Studies," Donald R. Searing and Elizabeth A. M. Searing describe and analyze in depth three real-world PICT-related events, using the framework of the sensor-effector system model. This model describes three distinct, fundamental aspects of ICT systems:

1. *Sensors*, such as motion detectors, cameras, microphones, etc., gather, store, and transmit data about the world outside the system.
2. *Effectors* make changes to the outside world by, e.g., turning other devices on or off, sounding an alarm, or causing a car's anti-lock brake system to pulse.
3. *Decision modules,* or control systems, process the data provided by the sensors and send action commands to the effectors.

Home heating-cooling systems provide a familiar example of this system. The sensor is a thermometer, the furnace and central air conditioner are effectors, and the decision modules are the thermostat's settings.

Each of the three cases concentrates on one component of this model.

The first case concerns global positioning systems (GPS) – sensors that provide users information on their location and how to get from point A to point B – as used by ordinary people and shows that over-reliance on technology can have fatal consequences.

The second case concerns the Stuxnet computer virus, an effector apparently devised by the United States and/or Israel to infect Iranian computers. The goal was to take control of centrifuges used by Iran to purify plutonium for use in atomic weapons. The virus was designed to make the centrifuges run too fast or irregularly, thus damaging or destroying the sensitive, expensive machines.

The third case concerns the so-called "Flash Crash" of May 2010. This is an example of a control system gone out of control and demonstrates how complex systems can cause significant harm (in this case financial harm) in a very short while.

The authors' clear presentation and sophisticated ethical analysis of the cases bring considerable insight into the cases themselves, but also to wider issues in pervasive information and communication technologies. Their three cases are examined again, from a different perspective, in Chap. 10.

1.2.2   Surveillance, of Sorts

The chapters in this section explore three aspects of one of the most promising and most disturbing functions of PICT. Technologies that can collect, store, transmit, analyze, and act upon data about the location, movements, behavior, and habits of individuals and masses of people have been in use for many years, but they are becoming smaller, less expensive, more powerful, and capable of increasingly sophisticated analysis.

An interesting example is the effort by the city of San Francisco to monitor the status of every parking spot with a meter. Drivers using smartphone apps can find empty spaces, and the cost of parking can be adjusted automatically to reflect supply and demand: Where available parking spots are rare, the price goes up – and vice versa (Richtel 2011; Cooper and McGinty 2012). The system promises to reduce the amount of time people spend cruising for parking spots and reduce wasted gasoline.

In Chap. 3, "Health Information in the Background: Justifying Public Health Surveillance Without Patient Consent," Lisa M. Lee does not address specific pervasive technologies, but a field in which PICT has the potential to be extremely useful and frighteningly intrusive.

The field of public health is dedicated to protecting the health of populations (as opposed to individuals). For example, when a contagious disease is detected by or reported to public health officials, steps can be taken that might forestall an epidemic. The earlier the outbreak is detected, the better the chance to slow or stop its spread and the fewer victims will suffer. This work is undeniably morally praiseworthy. But the most effective strategies for detecting health threats at an early stage often involve surveillance of the health status of the population, typically without the knowledge or specific consent of the population being monitored. Thus, as Lee describes, tension exists between two fundamental values – human health and individual privacy – and these must be reconciled.

Lee gives a brief overview of the history of public health surveillance, the complicated process involved in the protection of public health, and the state's legal responsibilities in promoting public health. She describes the clash of values in depth, as well as the ways in which medical ethics (governing doctor-patient relationships) is inadequate for guiding public health research and action. In particular, she calls on the great philosopher John Stuart Mill, one of the key proponents of a liberal society – that is, one in which government interference with individual freedom must be stringently justified and absolutely minimized – to show that, in spite of a common misreading of his work, Mill would almost certainly defend the moral value of public health surveillance.

Lee's chapter ends with a detailed outline of a policy that would adequately balance the needs of the public for health protection against the right to privacy. The provisions of the policy are well-considered, comprehensive, and worthy of careful consideration.

In Chap. 4, "Surveillance in the Big Data Era," Mark Andrejevic examines the implications of collecting massive amounts of data about as many people as possible, ideally everyone in a relevant population (a city, state, country – perhaps the entire world). As Andrejevic explains, the data is not of interest because of its content, but because of the patterns it reveals.

Consider the efforts of the FBI or the New York City police force to anticipate and prevent terrorist attacks. The most common police approach is to identify suspects after a crime has been committed and, in some cases, put one or more suspects under surveillance until enough evidence is collected to warrant an arrest. In such cases, a suspect's telephone calls, e-mail messages, and other activities might be intercepted, recorded, and analyzed. The content might show that the suspect is communicating with other known terrorists or has purchased material for building bombs. Content matters.

In preventing terrorist attacks, however, waiting for the crime to happen is not an option. Analyzing the *content* of the Internet usage of everyone in New York City is impossible, but analyzing the *patterns* of Internet usage – and especially *changes* in patterns – is possible and straightforward, as least relative to computerized content analysis.

Traditional police surveillance was targeted, confined to a handful of already-identified suspects. In the era of Big Data, surveillance will be (is) comprehensive, but not as intrusive as one might think. Although it's creepy to consider how many security cameras are tracking my whereabouts, it isn't as disturbing as it would be to learn that my e-mail was being read.

The era of Big Data is propelled not only by *in situ* technologies such as security cameras and ATMs, but, perhaps more importantly, by smartphones. Using an app to find a parking space in San Francisco could leave a trace of activity – one's location at a certain time – that could be used by police and, more often, by businesses interested in predicting and shaping one's buying behavior. Thus we become accomplices in our own constant, pervasive surveillance.

Andrejevic sketches the turning point from targeted to populational surveillance, explores the implications of this shift, identifies six key characteristics of Big Data monitoring, and proposes four ethical principles to guide the use of Big Data. His treatment of this generally unfamiliar and conceptually demanding type of surveillance is clear and engaging. The implications of his work are wide-ranging.

In Chap. 5, "We Know Where You Are. And We're More and More Sure What That Means," Francis Harvey introduces us to the power of combining locational and relational data, where the latter includes data about the relationships between activities, things, and people. He starts with a real-life case, also mentioned in Chap. 4, that shows how stores infer from women's purchases that they are pregnant and, based on this inference, send them advertisements for pregnancy and infant products. In at least one case, a teenager's father learned of her pregnancy when she received such advertisements.

Harvey provides a quick overview of the history of geography's study of locations and spatial relationships, citing, among other examples, how John Snow pinpointed a single water pump as the main source of a cholera epidemic in London by analyzing where cholera victims lived in relation to water sources. As many as 500 people from the same neighborhood died from cholera in 10 days, with the largest number of deaths from those living nearest that particular pump. When the handle on the water pump was removed, thus rendering the pump inoperable, the epidemic was contained (Crosier n.d.).

The chapter also explains three distinct phases in working with geographic information – data collection, data processing and analysis, and data presentation. Each of these phases has implications for the use and accuracy of data. Harvey describes the two basic forms of geographic analysis – quantitative and qualitative – and their combination, which he calls "hybrids of surveillance."

The chapter closes with descriptions of four different hybrids of surveillance. The first is a case concerning a study of behavioral changes in a minority group following the terrorist attacks of September 11, 2001; the second is a discussion of some of the ways in which the combination of location and personal data can violate privacy and confidentiality; the third mentions the uses and abuses of Radio Frequency ID tags (RFID); and the fourth introduces the concept of Geoslavery, or using locational data from one's mobile phone to instill fear, thus controlling one's movements.

1.2.3 Health Care

People born in the post-World War II baby boom of the United States, Canada, the United Kingdom, much of Europe, Australia, and New Zealand are entering or approaching retirement age just as PICT is emerging. The confluence of a large increase in the number of elderly with the availability of innovative technologies promises a revolution in elder care in the next few years. The chapters in this section focus on health care and elder care, describing some of the benefits and risks that PICT will bring and the ethical challenges they will pose.

In Chap. 6, "Preserving Life, Destroying Privacy: PICT and the Elderly," Cynthia M. Jones carries forward the seemingly ubiquitous theme of privacy and the invasion of privacy, but with a tight focus on the uses and abuses of PICT in elder care. Independent-minded baby boomers, who grew up in an era when nursing homes were generally thought to be as bad as prisons (at least in the United States), are likely to insist on staying in their own homes as long as they possibly can. PICT will almost certainly play a part in their extended semi-independence, as will their adult offspring-caretakers. When an elder's health and mental capacity deteriorates, her or his ability to stay at home will require compromises.

Jones also discusses other concerns that interact with privacy, including *competency*, or the capacity to make informed, rational decisions, a capacity which often diminishes with advanced age; *autonomy*, or the right to make one's own decisions without undo interference; and *paternalism*, or the responsibility of competent guardians to make decisions for wards of any age who have limited competence. When competence fails, paternalism is often required of well-meaning, respectful caregivers, and the patient's autonomy must be sacrificed to preserve health and life.

The use of PICT for elder care is also complicated by the difference in attitudes toward new technologies between younger and older generations: The elderly are more hesitant to make use of new, unfamiliar technologies than are their younger caregivers. In particular, professional caregivers who have special training in new technologies are naturally invested in making the most of the technologies. The probability of tension between caregiver and patient is high.

Jones illustrates with compelling examples the tensions between elders who want independence and their offspring-caretakers who want to protect their parents.

In Chap. 7, "When Cutting Edge Technology Meets Clinical Practice: The case of e-Health," Katherine D. Seelman, Linda M. Hartman, and Daihua Yu offer a comprehensive review of the many technologies, benefits, challenges, and ethical issues being raised by various efforts to bring health care into the Internet age. The authors provide their own e-Health socio-technical system model and review other models, providing numerous case studies to illustrate known challenges raised in health information technology, technology vendors, law and regulation, and clinical practice.

There are few institutional relationships more fraught than medical care. The intimacy between the health provider and the patient stands in stark contrast to the impersonality of insurance companies and hospitals. The most private of personal information, including taboo and illegal behaviors, become data, stored in vast depositories with the personal, ideally secret information of thousands of other persons, and can be accessed by hundreds.

However, in many cases, a health provider's easy access to intimate knowledge about a patient can save the latter's life. Technologies that aid diagnosis can be invaluable, but they can also lead to carelessness if health care providers depend on them too much or uncritically. Excellent technology can be a boon, but the interdependent units of the socio-technical system of health care are not always developed at the same pace and with the same care: A perfect algorithm can be defeated by a bad user interface, or by inadequate user training.

As in most situations, continuing cost-benefit analysis is vital to the ethical and practical success of e-Health. The complexity of such analyses, however, is rarely more complicated and difficult.

1.2.4 Augmented Reality

In Chap. 8, "Ethics and Pervasive Augmented Reality: Some Challenges and Approaches," Bo Brinkman discusses augmented reality – an emerging family of technologies that act directly on a user's senses through special glasses, earphones, or even gloves, to present realistic digital or virtual objects in alignment with the real world. Imagine wearing a headset that allows you to talk with your virtual assistant (Siri of the future) and see her walk beside you, so realistic that you are startled when she walks through a telephone pole.

Brinkman observes that such devices have the potential to become truly pervasive. Augmentation applications for smartphones are already available; one can look "through" a smartphone – actually, look at the image on the phone's screen captured in real time by the phone's camera – and see virtual labels on objects in the field of view. Such labels might give the addresses of buildings, the nature of businesses, or alerts about congested traffic ahead. If these and other rudimentary applications of augmented reality become adequately popular, more sophisticated applications are sure to follow.

Just as augmented reality will change the way we see the actual world, it will also change the way we *look* at the actual world – "look at" as in "understand the meaning of" – in at least two ways that Brinkman examines in depth. The first is an exploration of some of the metaphors that organize and give legal structure to our understanding of privacy. Brinkman offers the example of e-mail, which was consciously created using the metaphor of postal mail of the sort that has existed for centuries. The similarities between physical mail and virtual e-mail are therefore obvious and compelling, but the differences are many and significant and have the potential to change our legal understanding of concepts including ownership and privacy.

The second example has to do with property rights, in particular the right to display signs on one's property and the right to have an unobstructed view from one's property. When it comes to physical billboards, for example, the legal and ethical questions are fairly settled. But what happens when digital signs are superimposed over physical signs by augmented reality? Or when digital signs are superimposed on an existing, sign-free vista?

Brinkman's discussion is clear, subtle, and challenging. He makes an excellent case that the ethical and legal implications of augmented reality technologies should be carefully considered before – or at least as – they become pervasive.

1.2.5 Ethics and Design

In Chap. 9, "This is an Intervention: Foregrounding and Operationalizing Ethics During Technology Design," Katie Shilton describes her own 2-year experience working with a pervasive technology laboratory. Shilton is not a technician, but a social scientist, who was hired to help promote privacy, security, and other ethical values. She was a participant-observer, taking part in the life of the lab while simultaneously observing and analyzing the lab's people and their activities, including the decision-making process during design. She characterizes her work as a "values intervention."

Shilton describes several of the lab's projects and the constraints or enhancements that ethical considerations added to the process. Some of the projects involved the use of mobile phones to track, record, and analyze the physical location, movements, and activities of volunteers. The aims of the projects differed, but they were all intended to benefit the volunteers, the community, or both. Shilton and the other lab members identified as key social values privacy; consent and participation; equity; and memory and forgetting. These values were translated into principles and operationalized in technical features of the experiments.

In addition to describing the work of the lab and her role in it, Shilton characterizes three factors that contributed to successful interventions – changing the conversation to include social values; contributing in particular ways to technology development; and motivating values-based changes to technologies under development.

Shilton's work is not unique, but such interventions are all too rare. Her detailed description of her work and the work of the lab, along with her conclusions about the value and practicality of values interventions, should inspire other working groups to seek out and work with humanists and social scientists who, like Shilton, can help spotlight ethical issues and resolve them during the design process.

1.2.6 Ethical Guidance

The two chapters in this section provide ethical guidance specifically for PICT devices. The first chapter applies to PICT a more general moral framework designed to cover all computing artifacts, while the second was created with PICT in mind.

In Chap. 10, "Applying 'Moral Responsibility for Computing Artifacts' to PICT," Keith W. Miller briefly recounts the development of a remarkable document, then applies the document's precepts to PICT.

"Moral Responsibility for Computing Artifacts" is comprised of a three-page statement of five precepts offered "as a normative guide for people who design, develop, deploy, evaluate or use computing artifacts" (Ad Hoc Committee 2010: 1) followed by a half-page statement on how the document can be revised. Miller wrote the first draft and invited numerous scholars to assist in revising and improving it.

In just over 7 months, the document went through 27 versions and was endorsed by 50 scholars (Miller 2010).

"The Rules," as the document is informally called, is intended to apply to all computing artifacts and, as the title implies, makes a strong statement about collective and personal responsibility. Perhaps the main target of The Rules is the so-called problem of many hands: When many people are involved in creating, deploying, or using an artifact, it can be difficult to determine who is to blame when something goes wrong – and it's probably harder to assign moral blame than technical blame. The Rules make it clear that ducking responsibility is not a morally defensible option.

Most of Miller's chapter is dedicated to applying The Rules specifically to pervasive information and communication technologies, including the three cases discussed in Chap. 2. His thoughtful exegesis clarifies and expands on an already clear and concentrated document. Miller's examples of PICT devices and the applications of The Rules to them are instructive and persuasive.

Finally, in Chap. 11, "Principles for the Ethical Guidance of PICT," I endeavor to provide a short but comprehensive list of principles to guide the development, deployment, and use of PICT devices. The chapter begins with a discussion of kinds of ethical guidelines, ranging from one-sentence maxims like the Golden Rule and the Categorical Imperative that are presented as a summary of all morality to, on the other end of the spectrum, detailed compilations of morally required and prohibited behaviors like the 600-plus rules in the Hebrew Bible[4] which address many quite specific actions, such as eating birds and locusts (Leviticus 11: 13–22).

Between these two extremes, principles offer limited guidance of middling specificity. For example, "don't tell lies" is a generally accepted moral principle that provides adequate guidance for many, probably most, circumstances, but is of little help in a subset of circumstances in which telling a lie will (or is expected to) promote a moral good more important than honesty, such as the protection of innocent human life.

Having established the place of principles in the range of moral guidance, I describe the principles articulated in The Belmont Report, a foundational document in the practice of research using human subjects in the United States. The Belmont Report may be the most influential principle-based document in existence and is certainly a model of an effective work in practical ethics.

I then discuss social conditions under which the moral principles that I offer would be essentially meaningless. For example, when the prevailing moral ethos is "might makes right," the principle "do not lie" only means "do not lie unless you can get away with it."

Finally I offer eight principles for PICT in the hope of guiding behavior but, more importantly, in the hope of stimulating careful consideration and further development of principles and other forms of guidance for this promising and threatening sphere of contemporary and future life.

---

[4]Called the Old Testament by Christians.

References

Ad Hoc Committee for Responsible Computing. 2010. *Moral responsibility for computing artifacts: Five rules*. Available at https://edocs.uis.edu/kmill2/www/TheRules/. Verified 8 Feb 2013.

Cooper, Michael, and Jo Craven, McGinty. 2012. A meter so expensive, it creates parking spots. *New York Times*, March 15. Available at http://www.nytimes.com/2012/03/16/us/program-aims-to-make-the-streets-of-san-francisco-easier-to-park-on.html. Verified 8 Feb 2013.

Crosier, Scott. n.d. *John Snow: The London cholera epidemic of 1854*. Center for Spatially Integrated Social Science. Available at http://www.csiss.org/classics/content/8. Verified 8 Feb 2013.

Johnson, Deborah G. 2010. The role of ethics in science and engineering. *Trends in Biotechnology* 28(12): 589–590.

Johnson, Deborah G. 2011. Software agents, anticipatory ethics, and accountability. In *The growing gap between emerging technologies and legal-ethical oversight: The pacing problem*, ed. Gary E. Marchant, Braden R. Allenby, and Joseph R. Herkert, 61–76. Dordrecht/New York: Springer.

Miller, Keith W. 2010. *Moral responsibility for computing artifacts: The rules* (index page). Available at https://edocs.uis.edu/kmill2/www/TheRules/. Verified 8 Feb 2013.

Richtel, Matt. 2011. Now, to find a parking spot, drivers look on their phones. *New York Times*, May 7. Available at http://www.nytimes.com/2011/05/08/technology/08parking.html. Verified 8 Feb 2013.

Rutenberg, Jim. 2012. Secret of the Obama victory? Rerun watchers, for one thing. *New York Times*, November 12. Available at http://www.nytimes.com/2012/11/13/us/politics/obama-data-system-targeted-tv-viewers-for-support.html. Verified 8 Feb 2013.

Toumi, Habib. 2011. Who coined 'Arab spring'? *Gulf News*, December 17. Available at http://gulfnews.com/news/gulf/who-coined-arab-spring-1.952310. Verified 8 Feb 2012.

Tyrer, L. 1999. Introduction of the pill and its impact. *Contraception* 59(1 Suppl): 11S-16S (January). PMID: 10342090. Available at http://www.ncbi.nlm.nih.gov/pubmed/10342090. Verified 8 Feb 2013.

Chapter 2
Three Case Studies

Donald R. Searing and Elizabeth A.M. Searing

2.1 Introduction

Case studies can help one get a better understanding of an unfamiliar topic and the extent of its related ethical and conceptual issues and concerns. The area of emerging technologies known as pervasive information and communication technologies (PICT) includes a number of seemingly disparate issues and technologies. Analyzing a sample of real-world examples of these technologies, how they behave, and where they are headed can bring substantial clarity to this broad and novel field.

To properly grasp the effect of the emerging PICT systems in their full breadth, it is first important to define the types of technologies that fall under this broad umbrella. The key word in the acronym, in our opinion, is *pervasive*. *Pervasive* indicates that we are looking at a phenomenon that completely suffuses a world and all aspects of the lives of the inhabitants in that world. In this book, the pervasive phenomenon being examined is that of information and communications technology; as you read this, pervasive technologies are creeping into every aspect of our lives, such as mobile telephones, computers, the Internet, robotics, and automation. These technologies have had a significant effect on the way we live our lives already, and trends indicate that we are moving in the direction of even greater penetration and integration of these technologies into our everyday experience. The constant cost reduction and capacity growth in the basic units of computation represented by Moore's Law means that more and more capable technology is finding its way into ever more inexpensive devices, essentially putting a computer in everything with which we interact and in every environment we

D.R. Searing, Ph.D. (✉)
Syncere Systems, Lawrenceville, GA, USA
e-mail: desearing@synceresystems.com

E.A.M. Searing
Andrew Young School of Policy Studies, Georgia State University, Atlanta, GA, USA

K.D. Pimple (ed.), *Emerging Pervasive Information and Communication Technologies (PICT)*, Law, Governance and Technology Series 11, DOI 10.1007/978-94-007-6833-8_2, © Springer Science+Business Media Dordrecht 2014

inhabit. This computing capacity is amplified by the interconnectedness provided by the ever-present network that wirelessly flows through the radio spectrum all around us.

The world is in the fairly early stages of the spread of these technologies, and one could argue that there is a long way to go until the word *pervasive* would truly be appropriate to describe it; however, the exponential nature of the growth being experienced indicates that pervasiveness, in the truest sense of the word, is coming sooner than one might think. The case studies included below focus on recent events that presage the true extent of where the technology is going to take us and give us a glimpse of what issues are being brought to the forefront by the technologies they represent.

2.2 Functional Decomposition

It is important, before we look at an area as broad as the PICT technologies, to unpack the words used in its definition and build a structure for the space we are going to represent with the cases being discussed. From an engineering standpoint, we can use the process of functional decomposition to break this area and its technologies into their constituent pieces and examine the effects of those pieces on their contextual socio-technical systems to get a starting point to examine the overall emergent behavior of the system as a whole. The framework we will be using here for this decomposition is that of the basic sensor-effector system model commonly used in agent design architectures.

The sensor-effector system model describes a common pattern found in nature and in most technological designs. Its approach decomposes a system into sets of interconnected sensors, effectors, and the decision modules that connect them. A sensor is a component that perceives an aspect of the world surrounding the system. An effector is a component that affects the world surrounding the system in some manner. The logic in the decision modules converts the signals from the sensor into signals that drive the effectors to some action.

The most commonly used example of a designed sensor-effector system is the heating system in a house. The thermostat mounted on the wall contains a thermometer (sensor) and a control system, while the furnace is the effector. The thermometer *senses* the temperature in the house, and the furnace turns on to *effect* a change. The control logic in the thermostat compares the difference between the desired and the measured temperature and turns on the furnace to change the environment and thus a future measured temperature. When there is no difference between the desired and measured temperature, the logic in the thermostat turns off the furnace, thus removing the effect driving the change in the system. The temperature will then naturally drop and the cycle will repeat.

The sensor-effector model can be used to describe natural systems as well. Living organisms can be expressed as sensor-effector systems, as can larger-scale phenomena such as climate. Even the simplest forms of life exhibit this type of behavior. Bacteria sense chemical concentrations in their environment and use their various methods of locomotion (effectors) to move to a more advantageous location (e.g., one with a higher concentration of nutrients, or one with a lower concentration of chemicals toxic to the organism). Trees and plants sense light and grow (effector) toward the area of greatest intensity.

Using this model, the concept of PICT systems can be broken into the slightly more compact concepts of pervasive sensors, effectors, and control logic. Pervasive sensors imply a world where the many types of sensors available in our technological repertoire are found throughout all aspects of our lives and environments: physical, virtual, and mental. One can imagine a world where every aspect of our lives is under constant multi-modal scrutiny no matter where we are. The Internet gives us a good starting point for considering the issue of constant surveillance in a more tangible fashion as we examine our experiences and relationships (open and hidden) with companies like Google (which tracks our searched terms, email, and site visits to create detailed marketing profiles for their customers) and governmental agencies like the National Security Agency (NSA) in the United States (which monitors our online communications) (Bamford 2012). Pervasive monitoring is not only a concern in our online world, but in the physical world as well, as evidenced by the proliferation of cameras in the public places of the major cities of the world (e.g., London, Chicago). These two examples hint at another aspect for us to consider in our analysis: the pervasiveness of the technology may affect us differently or advance at different paces in each of those worlds. Google's and the NSA's pervasive monitoring efforts are currently focused on the virtual or online world of the Internet, while the city police's surveillance cameras are focused on the real or physical world. The mental world is another world that is increasingly becoming available to technological sensors, though not quite at the rate of the other worlds. It bears consideration, though, because recent advances in tools such as the fMRI indicate that the mental world of each of us may, one day soon, be as accessible as the other worlds already are to surveillance. The ethical implications and issues surrounding this type of surveillance, both real and virtual, are examined more closely in a number of other chapters later in this book.

The case study related to pervasive sensing in this chapter takes a different tack on the issue of pervasive sensors. It focuses on the changes in the behaviors of the inhabitants (agents) of the system when useful sensors become pervasive. The specific sensors being considered are the global position system (GPS) handset and the mobile communication technologies. The case and its analysis touch primarily on the implications of living in a world where the sensor technology has become pervasive enough to make most users completely dependent on it and subject to severe consequences when the technology fails or does not work as anticipated.

Worlds in which technological systems can affect all of the inhabitants and their behaviors and environments fall under the pervasive effectors umbrella in our conceptual model. Pervasiveness is the key here, as technological systems already provide control in many areas of our lives (e.g., the thermostat discussed earlier). The increasing penetration of networked computational units into our real-world objects increases the risk that currently non-threatening objects can become more dangerous or more open to allowing others to cause us harm. For example, over the last several decades automobiles have become increasingly computerized and networked. The computerization was undertaken to provide benefits such as additional safety (e.g., stability systems, anti-lock brakes, air bags), improved performance (e.g., fuel injection controllers), and convenience (e.g., OnStar, climate control, tire inflation sensors, entertainment systems). Though most of us do not realize it, our cars are in essence rolling data centers, full of computers, sensors, and network components, but lacking the basic protections that would be expected of an actual online data center (e.g., firewalls, encrypted communications protocols, intrusion detection devices). It has recently been demonstrated that a malicious person could take advantage of this lack of security to take control of someone else's car and cause it to unexpectedly brake, flash its lights, unlock its doors, and display messages to the driver through the instrument cluster (Koscher et al. 2010). The pervasiveness of the computing systems throughout the mechanical systems in the car gives those systems unprecedented intentional and unintentional abilities to cause physical effects and damage. This cross-over of the effects from the virtual to the physical world is a tell-tale characteristic of the systems that fall into the pervasive effector category.

This example of the computerized automobile also gives rise to another aspect for consideration when looking at these pervasive technologies. Besides the sensor-effector considerations and the multiple world considerations, one must also look at the intentionality of the harmful effects caused by the technology. In the example of pervasive effectors demonstrated in the automobile, it should be apparent that none of the systems provided in the car was provided with the intention to cause harm. They were furnished to provide additional safety, performance enhancements, and occupant convenience and comfort. The dangers came from the unforeseen uses of the system by a malefactor to cause harm to the car, its occupants, and others nearby. While it may be fairly easy to see how intentionally building a system to cause harm to its occupants would be subject to moral sanction, there is more room for debate in claiming that a failure to provide adequate safeguards against the possible misuse of the technology by malefactors is also subject to a similar level of moral opprobrium. The example case below focuses on both these aspects of intentionality while examining the deployment of the Stuxnet virus – the first computer virus generally recognized as designed specifically to cause real-world damage outside of a computer system (Brenner 2012) and the first generally regarded as an attempt at cyberwarfare between nations or their proxies (Farwell and Rohozinski 2011; Gross 2011).

The pervasiveness of control logic is a bit more difficult to see as a taxonomical category, due to the fact that the logic is not useful without its associated sensors and effectors. So, to imagine this world of pervasive control logic, one needs to imagine a world of pervasive systems, each using its sensors to fire its control logic and actuate its effectors. These systems can have varying levels of autonomy depending on the amount of oversight and involvement of a user in the control logic and the setting of system goals. Systems with greater levels of autonomy are more likely to be pervasive since they are not limited by a population of users who direct them. Thus, this last category of the taxonomy can be taken to be focused on the pervasiveness of autonomous systems and agents. Pervasive autonomous systems are also subject to the multiple worlds and intentionality aspects outlined in the other category above, and all of these aspects will be considered in the third case study in this chapter. In May of 2010, the stock markets in the United States experienced an approximately 20-min period, now known as the "Flash Crash," where trading in a number of derivatives and stocks experienced an unprecedented drop in value followed by a mysteriously quick recovery. In the ensuing investigation, we observed that the calamity was driven by the unanticipated interactions between automated trading systems that were operating properly in pursuit of their programmed goals.

2.3   Lost in Death Valley – Sensor Pervasiveness

2.3.1   The Case[1]

In the summer of 2009, a mother, son, and their dog set out on a camping trip in the mountains and deserts west of Las Vegas. The woman had just recently moved to the Las Vegas area to take a nursing job, and she wanted to spend some quality time with her son while exploring her new environs. She had informed her family that she and her son would be camping for the weekend at a popular free camping site near the south end of the Death Valley National Park in California. They set off for the weekend in their SUV with enough supplies (including water) for the trip and a GPS system to help in the navigation from their home to the camp site.

As they crossed through a remote part of southern Death Valley, the woman's GPS system instructed her to turn off the paved road onto a road that was little more than a dirt trace barely suitable for any sort of vehicle. Following the instructions on the GPS, she continued down the road despite its condition. The road got progressively worse, with deeper sand and larger rocks, and eventually one of the tires on the SUV went flat. She stopped and changed the tire, and then continued down the road following the directions being provided to her as any traces of an actual road disappeared. Several miles further down the track, the SUV passed over an animal's den, collapsing it and hopelessly miring the car in sand and dirt up to the axles.

Once her car had become immobilized, the woman attempted to call for help, but her mobile phone was well outside of the range of any towers that could provide it connectivity. The family used their weekend's provisions to stay alive as they first hiked unsuccessfully to find help or a mobile phone signal and then resigned themselves to wait near the car with the hopes that someone would eventually pass by and find them.

---

[1] Based on information provided in the August 8, 2009 Associated Press story, "11-Year-Old Boy Dies After Mom Says GPS Left Them Stranded in Death Valley."

Not hearing from the mother and son for four days, her extended family members called the authorities to report them missing. They provided the search and rescue teams that were assembled with the location where the woman and son were to be camping, and air and ground search and rescue teams went out looking for them. On Thursday, a full five days after the woman had left on her trip, a park ranger noticed tire tracks heading off the main road onto an abandoned mining road, and upon following the tracks for a few miles discovered the evidence of the tire change. He continued following the tracks until he found the family's stranded SUV with the mother frantically signaling him. By this point, the mother and dog were severely dehydrated and the son was dead from the combination of the heat (daytime highs at the time had reached 111 °F) and lack of water. Upon being questioned after her rescue, the mother insisted that the GPS had directed her down that road.

2.3.2   Analysis

There are two pervasive technologies that are at work in this case: the GPS system and the mobile telephone. These two technologies have become indispensable in many people's lives. The mobile phone gives its users constant connection and availability to communicate with friends, coworkers, and family, not to mention emergency authorities when necessary. The GPS unit gives users the navigation information they need, and in fact many smartphones have GPS systems built into them. Users of these technologies have become habituated to always knowing where they are and where they are going, and having ready contact with everyone in their lives at all times. The technology works wonderfully, until it doesn't, and that transition can be sharp and unexpected. Both systems require continuous contact with their base stations (cell towers for mobile devices, and the constellation of GPS satellites for the GPS unit) and both technologies become useless when they are taken out of the range of their larger system context. Mobile phones lose their connectivity in rural areas and in areas with geographies or structures that block signals, or when they are intentionally turned off (e.g., on commercial aircraft flights). Additionally, as many discovered in New York on September 11th, 2001, the cell networks don't always have the capacity to service everyone if there are high volumes of calls or if critical infrastructure (towers, cables, etc.) has been damaged. GPS systems work poorly in areas where the view of the sky is limited, including inside buildings, parking structures, and tunnels. For the continuously-connected generations, it can be difficult to function normally in areas where these tools lose their reference signals and cease functioning properly.

Both the behavior of the users and the structure of the worlds they inhabit have been changed by the ubiquity of these technologies. The mobile phone has essentially eliminated the public pay phone. Thus, its sheer ubiquity has removed the alternatives that would be the fall-back options when the mobile systems fail or cease functioning in the expected ways. Additionally, people's behavior has changed as a result of the new technology. The idea of never being out of contact with friends, family, and authorities provides a sense of security. If one's car breaks down, emergency services are a quick call away. Coordination between people, such as in finding a meeting place, is now done in real-time while walking towards the proposed location and each other. These are tasks that in a pre–mobile telephone world had to be planned out in advance and thought through before commencing the activity. Now they take place in an ad hoc fashion while on the move. These types of ad hoc planning sessions fall apart completely when the enabling technology becomes unavailable, and our world has removed many of the fall-backs we once had which would allow for a less "digital" boundary between functioning and failure.

With the changes in the world and the behaviors of its inhabitants, we do not find it out of the ordinary that the woman in this case would head out on a camping trip feeling secure in the presence of her enabling technologies. If trouble arose, the cell phone would be there to call for help, and besides, the GPS unit would keep them out of trouble by leading them to and from their destination. But this case illustrates that these assumptions can be deadly and that the limitations of the technology, while widely known (everyone has had their phone drop out of signal at some point), can be easily forgotten by the casual user, especially when it comes to considering a back-up plan. Experts in the areas of hiking and mountain climbing will often bring back-up gear, and in the most forbidding of locations, emergency beacons that can allow search and rescue teams to locate them. Experts do not assume that their activities will be non-threatening, and they better understand the risks inherent in what they are doing and take suitable precautions. In the past, getting to many remote locations in the wilderness required being an expert or having one as a guide, and it is this that has changed with these enabling technologies. Casual users are finding themselves in locations only experts would have gone in the past. Their device-enabled lack of fear allows them to push out into areas previously only accessible to prepared experts, leading to tragedies such as the one described above. In these areas, remote dirt tracks that would give pause to an expert in a normal SUV now are driven on because the GPS unit directs it and the casual explorer does not second-guess the device or necessarily understand that the trail in front of them is beyond the capabilities of their vehicle.

So, it is understandable that the socio-technical system of the users and their environment has changed, but it begs the question of just who in this case is responsible for the tragedy that befell this family. The GPS unit is a tool containing the necessary relativistic algorithms to locate the unit in space, a set of maps in memory that scroll to the location indicated by the sensors, and route-planning algorithms that provide directions to the user based on the current and desired locations.

Designers of the Devices

GPS is a non-autonomous tool, so the responsibility for its behavior must continue to fall upon its developers. These developers provided the algorithms and provided the data used in the mapping system, which in this case first indicated that there was a road where there was not one, and then directed the user onto it. The inclusion of roads that no longer exist on these maps is of great concern to the rangers in Death Valley National Park, who have subsequently lobbied the map data providers to remove these old roads from the maps of their park (Clark 2011). Dangerous incidents related to outdated maps and modified user behavior are not just an American phenomenon; there is a documented case in Spain where a GPS system directed a driver down a road into a reservoir that had been in place for over 20 years (Tremlett 2010).[2] The designers of these systems understood that maps do change and most if not all GPS units are capable of receiving map data updates online or through other means. What they failed to do, in the authors' collective opinion, is put in place the safeguards that would (1) prevent the bad data from being entered into the system and (2) ensure that no one could use the system without the updated data. They failed, not surprisingly, to anticipate the types of changes that would occur in the socio-technical system of users and their tools when this new technology was provided to them and did not build in these sorts of safeguards.

Beyond the data provided, the route-planning algorithms aren't required to be designed to prevent routes from being planned down all manner of roads. Most units not only contain information that there is a road but also have access to the properties of the road in terms of speed limit and road type (divided highway, multiple lanes, paved or unpaved, etc.). When navigating between destinations near major roads or interstates, it has been the authors' experience that the GPS systems do take road attributes into account, but it has also been our experience that when away from major roads, the directions can become increasingly focused on getting from one point to another and less focused on the quality of the roads being selected in the routing. The planning algorithms should not include unsuitable roads as connections between destinations for all types of routing or should allow the user to configure the types of roads they are comfortable traversing. Recent patents show that these algorithms are moving in the direction of being more cognizant of the dangers of the routes they are suggesting and allowing users to input the criteria used for their route planning (Herbert 2012). Of course in the changes discussed in the article cited, Microsoft's algorithm, which gives the user the ability to set their GPS unit to avoid "bad" (i.e., crime-ridden) neighborhoods in its directions, trades in our current set of moral concerns for an even more contentious set involving the labeling of neighborhoods as "bad".

Users of the Devices

Aside from the developers of these systems, who else bears responsibility for the use of these technologies? The users of the technologies should logically be a second set of responsible parties in this analysis. The users of these technologies get into trouble when they cede too much of their judgment to the devices, and that is driven

---

[2]Chapter 8 by Bo Brinkman looks at additional issues that will arise in the approaching world of augmented reality, where the data being blindly relied upon contains more than just simple mapping data and the user's perception of reality itself comes into question.

by a lack of understanding of the devices and their limitations as well as a misplaced balance of trust in the device's judgment over their own. As stated earlier in the analysis, expert users are experts due to their understanding of the underlying risks in the undertaken activities. Casual users do not always understand the dangers that they are putting themselves in, and in a pre-GPS and mobile phone–enabled world would not have been as easily capable of putting themselves into the situations they now find themselves in. That being said, the tragedy outlined above was not only a result of a user of these risk-enabling technologies going outside of their safe zone of travel. It was also a failure in the judgment of the user of the system in following the directions uncritically. The user in this case continued down a path that in all reports was obviously not a passable road and left no sign of trying to turn around even after her tire was damaged.

In the Spanish case, the user was driving late at night and unable to see the reservoir (Tremlett 2010). That death seems to us to be less the responsibility of the driver than of the designers of the system that lacked updated map data.

It is the change in our behavior due to the pervasiveness of these technologies that was not necessarily foreseen by the designers of these systems. The original users of the GPS systems were the military and others who were experienced in using older systems (e.g., LORAN) – in other words, expert users. The system worked so well, though, that additional civilian demand for its services lead to its inclusion into more and more devices and thus brought its power into the hands of the casual user. These users saw a useful feature added to their car's electronics or to their mobile phone and they changed their behaviors accordingly. Now they would never be lost, never need directions, and with their phone would always be in contact with others who could help them when they needed it. And they were correct: When used in well-covered cities and metropolitan areas, the devices work quite well. The danger comes, as it always does, on the fringes of these areas, where signals fade out and roads become less maintained.

The resolution to this problem is going to come from both of these responsible parties – the designers and the users. The GPS systems are going to get smarter, the map data is going to get better through the efforts of those responsible for the maps and even through the efforts of those who maintain wild areas such as the rangers in Death Valley. The failures of the GPS navigation systems will serve to ensure that the next generation of devices will contain some of the safeguards outlined above to prevent future incidents. Of equal importance, though, is the continued understanding that these enabling technologies require additional user training as they become easier to use. This seems counter-intuitive, simpler devices requiring more training, but the users of these technologies must be alerted to the fact that these devices are not foolproof and have limitations that may endanger their safety. Additionally, the training should have the primary function of alerting users that these devices may alter their behavior and lead them to discount the risks being taken.

With the lessons learned from these GPS-related tragedies, the GPS designers are building in more safeguards, and through exposure to these sorts of cases, the users are at least more cognizant of the types of issues that might arise. But, this change in behavior is not limited to only this type specific type of technology (Brennan 2010;

Denning et al. 2009). These types of enabling technologies and the perception of increased safety they engender commonly trigger risk compensation and actually drive the increases in risky behavior. The designers of these types of systems should be aware of this phenomenon and commensurately design appropriate safeguards. The users must also bear responsibility for understanding the nature and the limitations of the devices to which they are entrusting their safety.

2.4 The Worm Turns – Effector Pervasiveness

2.4.1 The Case[3]

In April 2010, scientists in Iran were finally beginning to implement their plans to enrich their store of uranium ore to isotopes usable in their plans for future power generation and possibly nuclear weapons research. They had run afoul of the United Nations and the International Atomic Energy Agency (IAEA)[4] in the past and the work was being done in a number of separate underground facilities deep in the heart of the country. These facilities consisted of great halls that contained hundreds of computer-controlled, high-speed centrifuges that were used to separate the more useful heavier isotopes of uranium from the lighter ones. The process requires precise control of the speed of the centrifuges, and Iran had purchased top-of-the-line motors from Finland and controllers from a manufacturer in Germany known for its quality and precision.

As the initial runs of the centrifuges completed, the scientists noticed that the expected output from the cascade of centrifuges was not being achieved. Additionally, the centrifuges were failing at a rate greater than was expected. The problems continued to hamper the effectiveness of the program as investigations began into what was causing the failures.

In June, an anti-virus researcher in Europe found an interesting worm infecting some of his client's computers in Iran that appeared to use a number of novel mechanisms to spread itself and had a large, apparently non-functional payload. It was given the name Stuxnet, based on a sample of text found within the compiled code of the virus (Gross 2011). Further research continued at a number of anti-virus system providers and they discovered that the payload was not inert, but it was a highly targeted attack aimed at an industrial controller used in high-speed motor

---

[3]The case is based on a very detailed narrative of the timeline provided in (Gross 2011) and information provided in a number of IAEA reports such as (IAEA 2009). Both are excellent reading and we would highly recommend the interested reader seek them out for more details regarding the events surrounding this case.

[4]The IAEA is charged with verifying Iran's compliance with a number of UN resolutions related to their nuclear program. See the February 19, 2009 report for details of the resolutions and non-compliance (IAEA 2009).

controls manufactured by a specific German company. Additionally, the trigger for the payload would only execute if certain other conditions were met: The controller must be operating within a certain target range of parameters and must be in a system that contained a combination of frequency converters built by certain Finnish and Iranian manufacturers (Gross 2011). When the payload was triggered, the worm was designed to cause the frequency converters used to control the high-speed motors to cycle unpredictably and remain unable to hold a specific speed within a certain RPM range. A second prong of the payload would then modify the logging systems in the controllers to report that a constant speed actually had been maintained (Gross 2011). All of the speed cycling would cause premature wear in the motor and eventually cause the failure of the system well inside of its normal expected lifespan while leaving no trace in the system logs as to the cause of the wear.

Researchers concluded that the code was likely aimed specifically at the cascades of uranium enrichment centrifuges being deployed in Iran based on the trigger conditions and the effects of the worm. Secretive Iran had not publicly admitted to any issues at this point with their centrifuges, but satellite observations indicated to other countries that something was going wrong at the enrichment facilities as the centrifuges were being replaced at a higher than normal rate.

Speculation began on the source of this highly targeted worm, and based on certain code metrics (size and complexity of the payload, the languages and libraries used, and the constructs and patterns followed), the advanced nature of the exploits (four vulnerabilities in software that had not previously been exploited were used for propagation), the evidence of the use of a stolen code-signing certificate (Gross 2011), and the precise targeting, most researchers came to believe that the worm was created by professional software developers likely in the employ of the intelligence services of the government of the United States or Israel. As of this writing, though, neither state has officially admitted to having played any role in the development or deployment of the worm, though recent leaks provided to the *New York Times* seem to lend additional credence to that conclusion (Sanger 2012).

2.4.2 Analysis

The Stuxnet worm is not the first attempt at attacking the computers of an opposing or hostile state, but it is apparent evidence of the escalation both of the severity of such attacks and of the intention of harm inherent in them (i.e., the intention is now to target systems that control physical effectors). Previous cyber-attacks have focused on the virtual world, such as interference (i.e., preventing access to sites through denial of service attacks) and espionage (Hollis 2011). Stuxnet is the first known actual attack that used a virtual approach to cause physical harm. The goal in this instance was physical harm to a set of machines, causing their subsequent failure, but the cross-over from virtual to physical harm does not have to stop there. This escalation and modality change in the harm coupled with the growing pervasiveness of the computational effectors leads to our primary concern.

The more the computer-driven effectors permeate our environment, the greater the potential risk to the public. As stated earlier, our automobiles are a good example of the potential risk we face. The modern automobile is a collection of networked computers, sensors, and effectors. If a malicious person or a worm/virus attacked the braking system, for example, accidents could be instigated and injury and death could result. As has been shown by Koscher et al. (2010), these systems are currently rather insecure and the types of effects posited above come directly from the effects they managed to invoke in their testing. Again, though, this is an area of concern that has already been identified and mitigation efforts have begun. Other areas are awakening to the risks of physically-targeted cyberwarefare attacks, including on personal medical devices (e.g., pacemakers, insulin pumps) (Halperin et al. 2008) and the avionics systems of commercial airliners (Arthur 2012).

The escalation of the risk from these attacks takes on two different meanings for the designers and users of these systems depending on which side of the exploit the designer and user are on: the aggressor or the defender. As the viruses and worms move out of their traditional anarchical headwaters and into the mainstream as professionally developed weapons of cyberwarefare, one must ask about the responsibility of the engineers designing them and the states deploying them as weapons. Like other weapons, these tools can be targeted at the military and their supporting manufacturing centers (e.g., like Stuxnet, purportedly), or they can be used against the civilian population directly or indirectly to cause collateral damage. One could imagine a weaponized worm or virus used to disable a country's computerized power grid or to disable the safety features on a nuclear power station causing massive damage to nearby civilians and property. These systems would need to be handled as weapons, which is what they are, and they should be developed and utilized following the provisions allotted to other weapons development programs, and be subject to all established rules of war, rules of engagement, and any additional conventions placed on weapons that have the capabilities of mass civilian destruction. The developers of these systems would by necessity need to understand the extent and uses of their systems and be reconciled with doing weapons work even if they do not believe that such activity is likely to be pursued. If weapon-like capacity is designed, such a capacity should be assumed in the moral considerations of the design process.

Of equal interest are the decisions and the dilemmas of the developers responsible for defending these effector systems against attack. As stated in the introduction, the moral issues related to building weapons or tools that might harm people intentionally is fairly well developed (e.g., *jus ad bellum* and *jus in bello*[5] discussions), but the moral obligation of a developer of a system to keep it secure from such exploitation (foreseen and unforeseen) is a more difficult case to make. Much is made in engineering ethics of holding the safety of the public paramount, but that is primarily in terms of preventing accidents or intentional damage done by side effects of the engineers' own systems and their usage. Only a few areas

---

[5]These are concepts in just war theory: *jus ad bellum* concerns the right to wage a war and *jus in bello* concerns acceptable behavior in waging war.

in engineering (e.g., military systems design and software engineering) routinely incorporate defenses against malicious use of systems. In these situations, the level of care and responsibility taken by the engineer is usually the level requested by each client or user and verified by third party auditors. But, in order for this approach to work, the clients and the designers/engineers need to be aware of the risks inherent in these sorts of systems. As shown with the automobile example, the systems in an automobile were originally designed in a non-networked world or in a world where there was a tightly controlled network amongst the systems of the automobile without external interface points outside of the diagnostic ports inside the car. But with the advent of wireless technologies used to communicate tire pressures from the tires to the onboard computer and dashboard displays, and systems like OnStar which provide active controls to authorized systems over a wireless network, the internal network of the automobile is more exposed than ever and thus new levels of responsibility for security and safety need to be considered.

This shifting of the priorities related to security and safety was exactly what the designers of Stuxnet exploited. The industrial control systems targeted were traditionally not networked together with external access points, so the necessity of providing a secure barrier around the systems was not present during their initial design and development. This made these systems open for exploitation once they began being networked to personal computers inside their facilities. These are the exact types of control systems that are finding their way into all sorts of devices as "smart" technology is deployed to our vehicles, homes, offices, and critical infrastructure systems. As these systems become more pervasive and carry the possibility of having greater impact on our lives through their interactions with us, it becomes incumbent upon the designers of the systems to build in the necessary safeguards to secure the systems directing these effectors and to limit the amount of damage that can be done with them. The users of these systems play a role here as well: they must educate themselves about the risks inherent in the systems they choose to deploy, and they must deploy them wisely with the proper configurations in place to ensure their safe and secure operation.

2.5 The Flash Crash – System Pervasiveness

2.5.1 The Case[6]

On May 6th, 2010 the American stock markets experienced one of the most unprecedented single-day events in their history. In the early afternoon of what was an unimpressive trading day, one firm's misconfigured trade execution program

---

[6]The timeline of this case study is based on information provided in the CFTC and SEC report issued in September of 2010 (U.S. Commodity Futures Trading Commission [CFTC] and U.S. Securities and Exchange Commission [SEC] 2010). The events were reconstructed using market records in their attempt to trace the events of that afternoon back to its root causes.

precipitated a crisis which rippled across the futures markets and into the stock markets, at one point sending the Dow Jones Industrial Average (DJIA) down almost 1,000 points (10 % of the index's value) in a matter of minutes. Then, just as quickly, the slide reversed itself and the markets recovered most of their value.

The Security and Exchange Commission (SEC) and Commodity Futures Trading Commission (CFTC) have performed an extensive analysis of the events that occurred on May 6th, 2010 during the so-called "Flash Crash" using all available records of the trades made that day across all of the markets that were affected. The timeline that resulted from this analysis is summarized below.

May 6th, 2010 – Morning and Early Afternoon

May 6th started as a fairly negative day for the market. News from the ongoing European debt crisis was driving the market lower and by 2:30 PM the DJIA was down close to 2.5 %. The volatility measurements had spiked up (i.e., VIX was up 22.5 %), the Euro was declining against the Dollar and the Yen, and a specific high-volume type of futures product known as an "E-mini" had dropped in value significantly during the session (down 55 %).

May 6th – 2:32 PM

At 2:32 PM, a large trading firm began the execution of a sell program into the E-mini market. The firm was selling 75,000 futures contracts worth around $4.1 billion in order to hedge a position they had already taken in other equities. The traders at the firm decided to use an automated selling program to handle the transaction due to the large number of contracts that would be traded. The program had been configured to sell the contracts at a rate that was solely dependent on the volume of contracts that were currently trading in the market. This trader had executed trades this large before, but always as a combination of manual and automated programs that had their rates controlled by volume, price, and time. Whereas the previous sell programs had executed over a number of hours, the program used in this instance executed the entire sale in 20 min.

The large sales of contracts by the trading firm was initially absorbed by other automated trading programs known as High-Frequency Traders (HFTs), which execute trades in sub-millisecond time frames. These systems tend to trade amongst themselves at high speeds and volumes without substantially changing their overall positions; attempting to profit from arbitraging across the near-instantaneous price disconnects. Some of these systems were trading in just the E-minis, while others were attempting arbitrage between the exchanges. E-mini futures contracts are fundamentally related to the S&P 500 SPDR exchange-traded fund (CFTC & SEC 2010), so there are opportunities to take positions in the futures and in the exchange-traded fund (ETF) and profit from discrepancies in the pricing between the two markets.

May 6th – 2:41 PM

Starting at 2:41 PM, a large volume of E-mini contracts began to trade back and forth between the HFTs, a process which had been set in motion by the initial sales from the hedging trading firm and its volume-only-paced trading algorithm. The increase in volume thus drove the trading firm algorithm to increase its sales volume into the E-mini market. This positive-feedback loop worked upon itself for the next four minutes, affecting the E-mini market and spilling over into the related SPDR ETF market due to those that were attempting arbitrage between the markets.

In the four minutes between 2:41 PM and 2:45 PM, over 140,000 E-mini contracts were traded back and forth amongst the HFTs in the market (representing 33 % of the trading volume in that market). The E-mini contract price had dropped 3 % in those four minutes, and due to the arbitrage with the SPDR ETF market, so had the price of the ETF.

May 6th – 2:45 PM

In the 14 s after 2:45:13 PM, the HFTs traded an additional 27,000 E-mini contracts (representing 49 % of the market during that time period). This accelerating trading and the commensurate drop in liquidity in the market triggered a 5 s market stop in the E-mini marketplace, halting any further buying in E-mini contracts. When trading resumed after the stop, the E-mini market stabilized and prices on those contracts and the related SPDR ETF began to rise.

May 6th – 2:45 PM–3:00 PM

With the crisis over in the E-mini marketplace, it seemed that disaster had been averted. The market had stabilized, and prices began to rise. But during this recovery in the E-mini contract market, a far broader crisis began; one that had been instigated by the problems that had occurred over the last few minutes. As previously stated, the E-mini contract is a futures contract related to the SPDR ETF which in itself is a product that is derived from the values of stocks in the S&P 500. Traders (human and automated programs) in the markets where the S&P 500 equities are traded took the price signal from the SPDR ETF as a portent of some significant unknown event and they began to react. The equities involved and other ETFs related to them then began to see enormous increases in trading volume as the broader markets responded to the price drops seen in the SPDR ETF. By 3:00 PM, two billion related shares (worth around $56 Billion) would be traded in these equities.

The quickly increasing trading volume caused a number of these equities and ETFs to undergo their own liquidity crises as the available shares evaporated from the market and several of them (e.g., Accenture) began trading on "stub" quotes. "Stub" quotes are quotes that are used as a pulse by trading firms and exchanges to essentially keep quotes on a stock continuously in play in the market. If these quotes are not actively being utilized for trading, the quotes are given trading values well outside the normal price range (e.g., a \$0.01 bid, or a \$100,000 offer). During this time period, some stocks experienced enough of a liquidity crisis to cause the stub quotes to become the only actionable quotes, which caused prices to drop to irrational levels. For example, quotes on Accenture dropped from around \$30 to \$0.01 in 7 s during the height of the volume increase (CFTC & SEC 2010). These quotes continued to be purchased since many of the automated programs were issuing "Sell at Any Price" orders, which normally execute in the rational range around the market price, but in this instance executed on the stub quotes.

As 3:00 PM approached, the market mechanisms (human and automated) began to react to the stabilization in the original futures and ETF market that had instigated the crisis, and the prices quickly reverted to more normal levels. In the same way that the automated execution and feedback mechanisms had driven the markets down like dominoes, they just as quickly drove each other back-up to a stable level.

The DJIA numbers for the day show the effects of this event at a macro level with a swing of around 700 points down and 600 points up happening in the span of 15 min before 3:00 PM. But on a position-by-position basis in the market many trades ended up broken and many traders and programs adjusted their positions unnecessarily (albeit that was unknown to most of the participants in the markets at the time) and incurred costs associated with that trading. Regulators and the exchanges determined that 20,000 of the trades that had occurred during the 2:45 to 3:00 PM time period had occurred at prices deemed irrational (further than 60 % away from their prices at 2:40 PM), and these were subsequently reversed, thus mitigating some of the damage done. What could not be mitigated, though, was the damage done to the perception of the stability of the markets and the new cast of characters (HFTs, automated trading programs) which now inhabit them.

2.5.2 Analysis

In this final analysis, we move past the simplistic linear causal relationships that we have been concerned with related to effectors and sensors, and step into the complicated ecology of pervasive interconnected systems. In this scenario, multiple agents involved with the trading algorithm and its environment – designers, builders, implementers, regulators, users, and consumers – are brought into the discussion of assigning responsibility for its behavior and developing approaches for mitigating the risk of this sort of behavior in the future. The sensor-effector relationships are knit into a causal fabric, and we need to examine and understand each piece in order to fully grasp the emerging (and often unanticipated) synergies. To do so, we'll examine the ethical obligations of the primary players and then integrate them to produce an ethical schematic of the environment surrounding the Flash Crash.

Financial Professionals

The individuals who design and execute the financial instruments and strategies used in contemporary markets spend their lives estimating, quantifying, and mitigating risk. Transactions are based on there being, at least theoretically, a buyer and a seller: depending on which way the market turns (or whether there's a late frost, or whether someone defaults on a mortgage, etc.), someone is going to be monetarily worse off than someone else. However, the argument is made that, at the moment the transaction occurred, the act made both parties think they were better off or it would not have taken place.

This is an example of Adam Smith's famous invisible hand – through individual pursuit of selfish interests, the net welfare of the group increases (Smith 1991). It is the reliance on this familiar assignment of aggregate benefit to individual actors that originally made systemic problems such as externalities a difficult issue to explain through economic theory. For example, a paper mill in a small town during the 1970s would provide jobs for both factory workers and loggers in exchange for the market price for their good; this price would cover wages, raw materials, operating costs, etc. What would probably not have been reflected in this price is the cost of the environmental damage that would occur from the release into the environment of chlorine and other chemical agents used in the processing of paper. This is not a cost that is billed every month, but it is a cumulative negative impact directly attributable to the paper mill. What should be done to the price and quantity produced to reflect this adverse side effect? And what if the externality was something less tangible than chlorine levels, such as impact on native animal habitat, or if the damage was not directly attributable to a single producer, such as smog?

As with industrial pollution, economists have long urged what are called "Coasian" solutions (after 1991 Nobel Prize winner Ronald Coase) for such situations: assign ownership to the problem, and then the market will take care of itself. For example, if one farmer's cattle keep wandering over to a neighboring farm and eating corn, all that is required is for each farmer to accept ownership of their cattle or crop and then negotiate between them whether the cow owner should preemptively pay for any bovine transgression, the corn owner should subsidize the cow owner's extra cattle hand, or they should jointly finance a fence (Coase 1960). The anonymity that comes from the large-scale aggregation of the market can act as an inhibitor to these types of solutions; Coase himself argued that his approach to valuing externalities did not function as well when the number of agents involved became large. Unfortunately, that anonymity is also a lubricant that helps the market function as efficiently as it does – you maximize profit by being a step ahead of the herd, which only happens when the herd isn't watching you closely. Additionally, there are often numerous endemic conflicts of interest, such as commission systems and the internalization of stock and bond orders, which keep the field lean and efficient, but perhaps not ethical (Battalio and Loughran 2008). These adversarial, efficient, and often mutually-rewarding relationships run throughout the incentive framework and culture of finance.

In order to keep these competitive drives harnessed, market professionals are subject to several layers of ethical guidelines, such as fiduciary or suitability standards and professional codes of ethics. At the base level of ethical compliance is the accountability level assigned by law, which for financial advisors is a "fiduciary standard" and for stock brokers is a "suitability standard" (Angel and McCabe 2010). A suitability standard only requires the agent find a satisfactory or acceptable financial instrument; a fiduciary standard, however, requires disclosure and avoidance of any potential conflicts of interest and placing of the client's interests above the financial advisor's (Bell 2010). Currently, there is debate as to whether all client-facing financial professionals should meet the fiduciary requirement, which would strengthen the accountability between professional and client. Stockbrokers argue that not having such exhaustive informational requirements allows them to remain unbiased and at much lower cost; financial advisors claim that such positions are merely sales and are often used to soak up securities that suit the broker's interests (such as an in-house offering), rather than offer any cost savings on the client's part (Serchuk 2009). Additionally, the possible arrival and implications of a new standard called "best interest" is now being debated (for a thorough explanation of "best interest," see Fein 2010). Currently, however, there are no professional standards for the individual behind the computer developing the algorithm for statistical arbitrage (this will be discussed in more detail in the next section), which begs the question if we are legislating a solution to a problem, but not the problem we thought we were solving.

Many corporations, such as Charles Schwab and the Seattle Northwest Securities Corporation, and many professional organizations, such as the National Association of Personal Finance Advisors (NAPFA) and Certified Financial Planner Board of Standards (CFP), have documented codes of ethics. Aside from the legal standards mentioned above, such codes are market signals to potential clients that ethical and professional considerations are openly posted, discussed, and, thus, more likely to be heeded (Adams et al. 2001); this signaling serves as marketing, ironically making even codes of ethics part of the competitive framework. The results of the use of these codes of ethics, including whether they generate more ethical behavior, are mixed, though the relationship falls between positive and neutral (Schwartz 2001). Further it can be argued (and very often is) that the self-regulating nature of the market would punish those considered unethical; however, the necessary assumptions of perfect information and no transaction costs may be too stringent to reflect reality. In an industry designed to push the limits of risk and profit on the margins, how do we ensure that the structure given by a sense of professional ethics is not approached in the same fashion?

Software Engineer

The algorithms designed by the financial professionals are actualized as software systems by the software engineers. The systems in the financial marketplace are increasingly expected to react to changes in prices and conditions that are on the millisecond scale. At this speed, the decisions being made through the algorithm are not manageable in real-time by a human user. If a misjudgment is being made by the algorithm's implementation, then potentially thousands of them will occur before anyone will notice and be able to correct or terminate the behavior. Thus, due to the speed of their action and the resultant lack of oversight, these algorithm implementations would have to be autonomous by default. They are provided goals by the user, but then they proceed to execute them per their algorithm, whether pre-programmed or a self-learning variant, in which the algorithm operating at any given moment is not known by the managing user.

The possibility of thousands of unseen failures and the severe monetary consequences that would be engendered leads to these algorithms being extensively tested. But most of this testing is in environments that are pale imitations of the entire interconnected financial systems into which they will eventually be deployed. The failure mode that occurred during the Flash Crash was one that emerged only when the full range of connections and systems encountered in the "real world" were present. Even testing within the first ring of systems the algorithm is connected to will not provide an environment in which this failure mode can be found. Connecting to multiple systems in a test environment does not capture the mode either, due to the fact that unless those systems are connected together through other realistic nodes, it becomes impossible to replicate the complex dynamics of actual interconnected set of systems and algorithms.

These types of failures across interconnected systems of systems are especially pernicious. First, they are dangerous because they are not obviously in a failure mode when considering the constituent systems on their own. There is no method to use to test an individual system and find these kinds of failures. Second, the inclusion of so many systems into the eventual failure mode rapidly leads to the 'problem of many hands' and the difficulty in determining who is responsible for fixing the problem once it is found. In the financial markets, the interconnected systems belong to multitudes of organizations from countries around the world. These organizations are in competition with each other, so the propensity to work together is already low. It becomes too easy to point a finger at your competitors and their "secret" algorithms, and all too easy for them to point back at you.

The other players in the market that can create stability are the interconnection points known as exchanges (e.g., NASDAQ, NYSE) that have the duty to keep their systems up and running for their connected clients, but they can only dictate behavior on the systems' actions that are executed on their exchange. As was seen in the Flash Crash, the failure mode involved systems connected to multiple markets and sending buy and sell signals between the markets. These systems that were attached to multiple markets were seeking arbitrage opportunities (i.e., momentary discrepancies in prices between two markets); they became a critical coupling point between the systems and, though subject to the interface contracts and conditions for each exchange, the signals transmitted through them and their actions in the different markets were a primary cause of the breadth of the failure. Additionally, the circuit-breakers present in each market only exacerbated the problems by creating mixed signals and confusion for those systems that were interconnecting them; this confusion lead to improper orders being executed across all of the systems.

To mitigate the risk exposed by the Flash Crash, the designers of these algorithm implementations and the exchanges they connect to need to be able to test and certify these systems in a large-scale testing environment that can properly simulate the behavior of the full marketplace. This opinion was expressed both by the authors of this paper (Searing 2011) and additionally in a paper published by the government of the United Kingdom (Cliff and Northrop 2011) related to the understanding of the Flash Crash as an emergent condition resulting from the structure of the financial markets as an ultra-large-scale system of systems.

It is this through these new understandings of these large-scale systems of systems and their emergent failure modes that software engineers should be striving to find a way to predict and prevent such catastrophic events, but while this model gives a window into the understanding of the problem and its general cause, it does not provide motivation for the developers of these systems to accept the responsibilities that their autonomous systems may be even partially at fault. What is needed are new moral guidelines, as mentioned earlier and detailed in later chapters of this book, that address the issues related to the 'problem of many hands' in these systems and the propensity of people to ascribe blame to their autonomous creations rather than themselves. The rules discussed in a later chapter of this book and described by one of these authors as a Creator's Ethics (Searing 2012) are the first attempts at laying the groundwork for these new responsibilities for designers of these pervasive and autonomous systems.

Market Participant

For those of us not comfortable with our ability to solve simultaneous equation models or run Monte Carlo simulations, the world of finance may seem beyond our reach and understanding. Just as we let the auto mechanic work on our car and the plumber fix the leaky faucet, we rely on our retained financial experts to increase our net worth and are happy to delegate this task. However, does this absolve us of any ethical transgressions on the part of our professionals? If we take pride in our ability to pick professionals based on how much money they make on our behalf, should we not be ashamed if we pick ones who violate ethical standards? If your broker made you a lot of money by violating insider trading laws, would you rather he or she not have conducted the violation, or that you simply had not known how they did it?

As the purchaser of financial services, market participants have two dominant obligations. The first is to become and remain an informed consumer. We may never be able to conduct complex mathematics or design an algorithm; however, we are capable of assembling a great deal of information on both the tools and the agents who would use them on our behalf. Objecting to something insidiously called a "dark pool" by casual news coverage is easy, but understanding that it exists in order to circumvent a 30-ms advantage given to high-frequency traders before the market gains knowledge of the trade may cast additional (and sympathetic) light on the subject. Further, the effectiveness of any regulations put in place to prevent situations such as the Flash Crash from happening again will vary depending on the course of information – you need to know enough about what happened in order to know which sources of information are giving you unbiased analysis. Ignorance may be bliss, but it is not conducive to ethical behavior.

The second obligation is to take the knowledge you have gained and reveal your preference. In the most straightforward sense, this means to spend your money in a way that reflects your judgment. If you are willing to restrict your potential profit-making in order to provide capital for "green" companies, there is a boutique industry which allows you to do so; if you put more emphasis on the behavior of the end recipients of the money, you may pay more for a company whose published code of ethics (and record of service in line with that code) meets your criteria. If market participants fail to signal with their money that such things are important, the industry will adapt accordingly.

An example of this mechanism is dolphin-safe tuna labeling. Few people would call themselves advocates of wanton dolphin suffocation – it was simply a by-product of the most efficient way of netting tuna for commercial sale. It is not unreasonable to assume that most people, given a choice between two brands of tuna totally alike in all ways but this one, would in fact prefer tuna that did not involve killing dolphins. However, the pursuit of a dolphin-safe method of fishing means higher costs for the fisherman. How was this externality of dolphin safety handled?

In this case, it was a combination of industry self-regulation, government intervention, and product labeling so that the informed consumer could choose to pay more per can if they wanted tuna considered "dolphin safe." Now, all tuna sold at retail in the U.S. needs to meet particular standards of dolphin safety, and consumers have the option of choosing fishing method (which is often proudly displayed on the can; see, e.g., American Tuna) if this is important to them. Since the gathering and posting of information is costly, consumers of both tuna and financial services have an obligation to inform themselves to ensure that the methods of obtaining their services are ethical and then communicate that preference to the market.[7]

Emergent Behaviors and Systemic Responsibilities

We have now discussed the ethical obligations owed between agents, but what is owed to the market itself? An ecosystem populated with complex autonomous

---

[7]The World Trade Organization ruled against the use of "dolphin-safe" tuna labeling by the U.S., siding with Mexico that such information was limiting Mexico's access to the U.S. tuna industry (WTO 2011a); a similar ruling was made recently regarding labeling foods in the U.S. with their country of origin (WTO 2011b). The authors encourage the reader to follow these developments in consumers' rights to information as they unfold.

agents of both natural and manufactured origins begins to show emergent behaviors of its own, such as stability trends, interaction effects, and unforeseen elements. How do you disaggregate in a Coasian fashion an emergent property of the aggregate?

What this case suggests is that, beyond ethical obligations to clients, consumers, and professional standards, participants in the financial industry have an obligation to the market itself to own their share of potential externality. Unlike professional error in the hard sciences, such as an engineer's fallen bridge or a doctor's collapsed patient, the sins of the social scientist or economist can often be quietly aggregated into the very matter of study. This dispersion weakens the feedback loop used to monitor and enforce ethical codes; however, it does not alter the requirement of stability within certain bands to exist for the market (or other subject) to function at all. It is crucial to remember that, despite the recovery of the market in the Flash Crash, this was not an example of market self-regulation and recovery, but rather the delayed and fortunate intervention of both human and human-designed elements which, in their original conception, should have kicked in significantly sooner with significantly greater effect across the markets.

There is legal precedent for this particular approach to market responsibilities. In 2010, two Norwegian traders were found guilty of "market manipulation" crimes for trades made from Oslo in 2007–2008; they discovered that a machine working for an American trading platform would react in a particular way to a particular trade pattern, so they conducted trades that made the machine drive up the share price and give them the profits (Ward 2010). In financial circles, this has caused considerable discussion since the convicted traders were not breaking laws per se by exploiting a discovered weakness in the algorithm. So what was the crime, especially since, in the words of an individual whose firm designs such algorithms: "[i]t's not always easy to guess what an algo[rithm] is doing otherwise a lot of people would be doing it" (Ward and Grant 2010).[8]

The crime, as the Norway court stated, is against the market itself. Regardless of whether any trading regulations were broken or any person endured financial harms, the violation of the system is considered criminal. There is a point of complexity where the causal cloth cannot be separated into strands without losing some of the sensor-effector relationships which have emerged. When this occurs, systemic properties incur systemic ethical obligations. This is not as unfamiliar as you may think: Citizens of the United States both pledge allegiance to and can be executed for treason against the United States as a collective entity (US Constitution, Article 3, Section 3). In addition to protecting the agency of another consumer or the professional standards of your industry group, there is an ethical obligation to the

---

[8] As of this writing, the Norwegian day traders won their appeal (3–2) and had their sentences suspended. The ruling was based on their actions being public and in line with traditional industry behavior ("Norwegian court acquits day traders in algo cracking case." 2012). Unfortunately, industry-specific ethical relativism may not be the path which offers the most stability or long-term benefit for all market participants.

healthy functioning of the ecosystem which contains the financial markets akin to the obligations engineers have to the sustainability of the actual ecosystem. Even if no one suffers financial calamity, the release of an untrained or misunderstood autonomous system undermines the foundations on which the financial markets rest; even though the most damaging of the trades made during the Flash Crash were reversed, this does not eradicate the ethical transgressions made by the agents of various roles active in the market that day. Whether we're eradicating the rats on Guam by introducing snakes or making ourselves millionaires by letting computers execute our algorithms, the ecosystem will endure changes for which those involved will bear responsibility.

2.6 Conclusion

The three cases and associated analyses presented above are meant to give the reader a broad understanding of the types of risks and issues that can occur in these new worlds where sensors, effectors, and systems constructed out of communications and computational resources grow more and more pervasive and autonomous throughout our environment.

Pervasive sensors have invaded our virtual and real worlds, opening up new vistas for those who want to track our every move and click. Data-mining algorithms scan these vast streams of data, assembling profiles of our behavior that can be used without our consent to shape the information that we receive on a daily basis (e.g., your search results and the ads you see across the web). Currently, it is advertising that is being targeted at us, but there is nothing preventing news and other information from being similarly filtered and packaged for your specific consumption. The designers and utilizers of these technologies have a responsibility to the public to gather their data with proper consent for the types of information gathered as well as for the ways in which it is utilized. These responsibilities of the builders and fielders of this technology do not absolve we as users from our responsibilities to be aware of the systems our data flows in or the surveillance we are constantly under; we should demand the rightful ownership of our information and insist that its purveyors use it responsibly and guard it zealously against others who may try to steal it or use against us.

Pervasive effectors simplify our lives and have the capability of making our lives safer and more comfortable, but they also magnify the risks we face as we hand over more and more control of the physical world to these systems. A future where computer viruses do more than destroy your data on your computer is already here. Viruses like Stuxnet and its progeny are the first forays into what will likely prove to be a computational arms race between nation states, corporations, and individuals (e.g., the "hacktivist" group Anonymous), where the stakes transcend the virtual world and the harms caused include damage to persons and property. The dangers here lie also in the inadvertent exposure of the workings of these systems to other malefactors as well. The designers and implementers of these systems must not only worry that their systems can do intentional harm but that even the most benign system may be used by hackers or cyber-terrorists to cause mayhem in unanticipated ways; as these systems become more complex, these potentially harmful paths increase exponentially in number.

Pervasive autonomous systems bring yet another level of risk and ethical concern to the designers, implementers, and users of those systems. Their autonomous nature coupled with their computational speed make these kinds of systems capable of doing enormous damage before human users or managers can even notice something is going wrong. The ethical rules and reasoning in these systems will need to be built into their command modules in order for any moral consideration to be taken before the decisions are executed. Implementing this form of artificial moral agency is not a trivial task (nor a non-controversial one) and is a field that is in its infancy. Without these necessary safeguards and constraints on the designers (or at minimum a strict testing regimen in simulated real-world environments), the risks of a system failure orders of magnitude greater than the Flash Crash are great. When you combine these types of automated systems with effectors that can affect the real-world, the damage will be far more than just a few hundred points on a stock market index.

These new technologies are not just changing our world – they are also changing us. The changes in our behaviors that come about as we accept and use these systems can offer new opportunities for intentional and unintentional harm. The responsibilities for the changes in behavior, from becoming too reliant on the technology to not understanding the limitations of the systems we use, fall upon designer and user alike. It is a brave new world, in which these designers and users need to rethink some fundamental assumptions that have served us well in the use of our technical systems in the past. The worlds we inhabit and we ourselves are changing, and it is not surprising that new rules and new roles will have to be developed and understood for all those involved: designers, builders, and users.

References

2009. 11-year-old boy dies after mom says GPS left them stranded in Death Valley. Associated Press. August 8, 2009. http://www.foxnews.com/story/0,2933,538323,00.html. Accessed online 13 Apr 2012.

Adams, J., A. Tashchian, and T. Shore. 2001. Codes of ethics as signals for ethical behavior. *Journal of Business Ethics* 29(3): 199–211. http://www.jstor.org/stable/25074455.

Angel, J., and D. McCabe. 2010. Ethical standards for stockbrokers: Fiduciary or suitability? September 30, 2010. http://ssrn.com/abstract=1686756. Accessed online 13 Oct 2011.

Arthur, C. 2012. Cyber-attack concerns raised over Boeing 787 chip's 'back door'. *The Guardian*, May 29, 2012. http://www.guardian.co.uk/technology/2012/may/29/cyber-attack-concerns-boeing-chip. Accessed online 29 May 2012.

Bamford, J. 2012. The NSA is building the country's biggest spy center (Watch what you say). *Wired Magazine*. http://www.wired.com/threatlevel/2012/03/ff_nsadatacenter/all/1. Accessed online 13 Apr 2012.

Battalio, R., and T. Loughran. 2008. Does payment for order flow to your broker help or hurt you? *Journal of Business Ethics* 80(1): 37–44. doi:10.1007/s10551-007-9445-x.

Bell, A. 2010. FINRA sticks with securities in suitability proposal. *National Underwriter*, August 19, 2010. http://www.lifeandhealthinsurancenews.com/News/2010/8/Pages/FINRA-Sticks-With-Securities-in-Suitability-Proposal.aspx?page=1. Accessed online 13 Oct 2011.

Brennan, T. 2010. Emergency beacons can be beneficial, but can cause problems for rescuers. *KBTX*, September 16, 2010. http://www.ktvb.com/home/Locating-beacons-provide-benefits-to-users-headaches-for-others-103099444.html. Accessed online 25 May 2012.

Brenner, B. 2012. Analyst: Duqu is all a bunch of hype. *CSO*, December 2011/January 2012, 13.

Clark, K. 2011. *The GPS: A fatally misleading travel companion*, July 26, 2011. http://www.npr.org/2011/07/26/137646147/the-gps-a-fatally-misleading-travel-companion. Accessed online 15 Apr 2012.

Cliff, D. and L. Northrop. 2011. *The global financial markets: An ultra-large-scale systems perspective*, December 23, 2011. http://www.bis.gov.uk/assets/foresight/docs/computer-trading/11-1223-dr4-global-financial-markets-systems-perspective. Accessed online on 1 May 2012.

Coase, R.H. 1960. The problem of social cost. *Journal of Law and Economics* 3: 1–44. http://www.jstor.org/stable/724810.

Denning, T., C. Matuszek, K. Koscher, J. Smith, and T. Kohno. 2009. *A spotlight on security and privacy risks with future household robots: Attacks and lessons*. Ubicomp '09- Proceedings of the 11th international conference on ubiquitous computing, 105–114. Orlando, FL, USA.

Farwell, J., and R. Rohozinski. 2011. Stuxnet and the future of cyber war. *Survival: Global Politics and Strategy* 53(1): 23–40.

Fein, M. 2010. *Brokers and investment advisers standards of conduct: Suitability vs. fiduciary duty*, August 31, 2010. http://ssrn.com/abstract=1682089

Gross, M. 2011. A declaration of cyber-war. *Vanity Fair*. http://www.vanityfair.com/culture/features/2011/04/stuxnet-201104. Accessed online 13 Apr 2012.

Halperin, D., T. Kohno, T. Heydt-Benjamin, K. Fu, and W. Maisel. 2008. Security and privacy for implantable medical devices. *IEEE Pervasive Computing* 7: 30–39.

Herbert, G. 2012. Microsoft 'avoid ghetto' app for smartphones' GPS navigation stirs controversy. *The Post Standard*, January 11, 2012. Syracuse. http://www.syracuse.com/news/index.ssf/2012/01/microsoft_avoid_ghetto_app_windows_phone.html. Accessed online 18 Apr 2012.

Hollis, D. 2011. Cyberwar case study: Georgia 2008. *Small Wars Journal*, January 6, 2011. http://smallwarsjournal.com/blog/journal/docs-temp/639-hollis.pdf. Accessed online on 28 May 2012.

IAEA Board of Governors. 2009. *Implementation of the NPT safeguards agreement and relevant provisions of security council resolutions 1737 (2006), 1747 (2007),1803 (2008) and 1835 (2008) in the Islamic Republic of Iran*, February 19, 2009. http://www.iaea.org/Publications/Documents/Board/2009/gov2009-8.pdf. Accessed online 13 Apr 2012.

Koscher, K., A. Czeskis, F. Roessner, S. Patel, T. Kohno, S. Checkoway, et al. 2010. *Experimental security analysis of a modern automobile*. Paper presented at the Security and Privacy (SP), 2010 IEEE symposium on security and privacy.

Koscher, K., A. Czeskis, F. Roessner, S. Patel, and T. Kohno. 2012. *Experimental security analysis of a modern automobile*. Paper presented at the 2010 IEEE symposium on security and privacy, Oakland, 16–19 May 2012.

Norwegian court acquits day traders in algo cracking case. 2012. *Finextra Research*, May 2, 2012. http://www.finextra.com/news/fullstory.aspx?newsitemid=23677. Accessed online 01 June 2012.

Sanger, D.E. 2012. Obama order sped up wave of cyberattacks against Iran. 2012. *NY Times*, June 1, 2012. http://www.nytimes.com/2012/06/01/world/middleeast/obama-ordered-wave-of-cyberattacks-against-iran.html. Accessed online 21 June 2012.

Schwartz, M. 2001. The nature of the relationship between corporate codes of ethics and behaviour. *Journal of Business Ethics* 32(3): 247–262. doi:10.1023/A:1010787607771.

Searing, D. 2012. *A creator's ethics- beyond engineering ethics- a first step*. Paper presented at the twenty-first annual meeting of the association for practical and professional ethics, Cincinnati, 1–3 Mar 2012.

Searing, D. and E. Searing. 2011. *Playing the market good or well?: The ethical implications of the 'flash crash'*. Case study presented at the 12th annual meeting of the association for practical and professional ethics, Cincinnati, 3–15 Mar 2011.

Serchuk, D. 2009. Suitability: Where brokers fail. *Forbes.com.*, June 24, 2009. http://www.forbes.com/2009/06/23/suitability-standards-fiduciary-intelligent-investing-brokers.html. Accessed online 13 Oct 2001.

Smith, A. 1991. *The wealth of nations*. New York: Alfred A. Knopf.

Tremlett, G. 2010. GPS directs driver to death in Spain's largest reservoir. *The Guardian*, October 4, 2010. http://www.guardian.co.uk/world/2010/oct/04/gps-driver-death-spanish-reservoir. Accessed online 15 Apr 2012.

U.S. Commodity Futures Trading Commission (CFTC) and U.S. Securities & Exchange Commission (SEC). 2010. *Findings regarding the market events of May 6, 2010: Report of the staffs of the CFTC And SEC to the joint advisory committee on emerging regulatory issues*, 30 Sept 2010. http://www.sec.gov/news/studies/2010/marketevents-report.pdf. Accessed online 13 Oct 2010.

US Const., Art. 3, sec. 3. http://memory.loc.gov/cgi-bin/query/r?ammem/bdsdcc:@field%28DOCID+@lit%28bdsdccc0801%29%29. Accessed 14 Apr 2012.

Ward, A. 2010. Norwegians convicted for outwitting trading system. *Financial Times*, October 13, 2010, 7:17 pm. http://www.ft.com/intl/cms/s/0/f9d1a74a-d6f3-11df-aaab-00144feabdc0.html#axzz1sAPjPv00. Accessed 14 Apr 2012.

Ward, A. and J. Grant. 2010. A tale of man versus algo in Norway. *Financial Times*, October 14, 2010, 10:27 pm. http://www.ft.com/intl/cms/s/0/9a4aa5b8-d7bd-11df-b478-00144feabdc0.html#axzz1sAPjPv00. Accessed 14 Apr 2012.

World Trade Organization. 2011a. United States – Measures Concerning The Importation, Marketing and Sale of Tuna and Tuna Products: Report of the Panel." Case Number 11-4239. http://www.wto.org/english/tratop_e/dispu_e/381r_e.pdf. Accessed on 14 Apr 2012.

World Trade Organization. 2011b. United States – Certain Country of Origin Labelling (Cool) Requirements: Reports of the Panel. Case Number 11-5865. http://www.wto.org/english/tratop_e/dispu_e/384_386r_e.pdf. Accessed on 14 Apr 2012.

Chapter 3
Health Information in the Background: Justifying Public Health Surveillance Without Patient Consent

Lisa M. Lee

He who conceals his disease cannot expect to be cured

– Ethiopian proverb

3.1 Introduction

Surreptitious data collection and use is a fact of life for all of us in the global village, whether we are surfing the Internet in a bustling city in the most developed country or texting our kin from a remote village in sub-Saharan Africa. Data capture without our knowledge or consent has become pervasive, leaving people across the planet concerned and in some cases even outraged. Calls abound for laws prohibiting collection and storage of data without consent and for firm punishments for violations. In the United States ethical and legal arguments are made by privacy advocates to limit the collection and use of personally identifiable information. These arguments are backed by this country's foundational liberal political approach to government, its belief that self-determination far exceeds anything other- or government-determined, and its extreme favor of autonomy.

In spite of the individual-centric stance of the United States, the fact remains that we all – even Americans – live in a society with others; our behavior often affects others, known and unknown; and we relinquish some degree of privacy on a daily basis for the sake of the social good. For example, we tolerate the invasion of privacy that accompanies the use of closed circuit video systems used to reduce the collective costs (in the form of higher prices) of the crime of shoplifting. We provide

L.M. Lee, Ph.D., M.S. (✉)
Office of Surveillance, Epidemiology, and Laboratory Services, Centers for Disease Control and Prevention, Atlanta, GA, USA
e-mail: Lisa.Lee@hhs.gov

K.D. Pimple (ed.), *Emerging Pervasive Information and Communication Technologies (PICT)*, Law, Governance and Technology Series 11, DOI 10.1007/978-94-007-6833-8_3,
© Springer Science+Business Media Dordrecht (outside the USA) 2014

our social security numbers, dates of birth, and mothers' maiden names to our credit card companies to reduce the collective cost of theft of credit card information and unauthorized charging.

Often people are sensitive about their privacy with regard to intimate details of their lives, details that many of us would prefer were known only to a very small, select group of close friends and family. For most of us, this particularly sensitive sphere of knowledge encompasses our sex lives, our income, and our health – or, perhaps more accurately, problems with our health.

In the United States, as in many other places, personal health is highly valued and the health of others, including complete strangers, is valued only somewhat less. The value we place on privacy and on health are often in tension. The key question of this chapter is this: How much are we willing to share about our personal health to better the collective health of our communities?[1]

This chapter is presented in three parts. The first is largely descriptive, giving an overview of the historical and contemporary role of surveillance in public health and legal responsibility for public health. The second part takes a more normative turn, briefly exploring the competing values of privacy and public health. The third section provides ethical justification for public health surveillance without consent, including suggested policies and safeguards necessary to protect both privacy and public health.

3.2   Population Health Surveillance

This section describes two forms of population health surveillance – public health and syndromic surveillance – and the legal responsibility for public health oversight and action in the United States.

3.2.1   Public Health Surveillance

Public health surveillance has been used for hundreds of years to monitor and improve community health at the local, national, and international levels. Recognizable elements of public health surveillance were seen first in the United States in 1741 when the colony of Rhode Island required reports to health officials from tavern keepers about persons with "contagious diseases," as indicated by coughing, sneezing, and fever (Thacker 2010). Tavern keepers were required to report instead of health care providers, as persons were more often seen by the former than the latter. By 1874 Massachusetts became the first state to enact voluntary weekly

---

[1] While the chapter focuses on the United States, most modern public health systems conduct similar surveillance and confront issues related to reconciling privacy and public health.

Fig. 3.1 Ongoing, systematic steps of public health surveillance

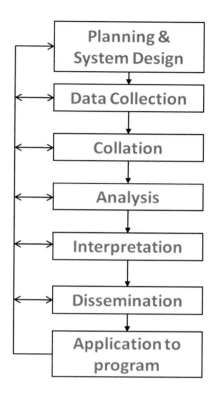

Planning & System Design

Data Collection

Collation

Analysis

Interpretation

Dissemination

Application to program

reporting of infectious conditions using postcards (Bowditch et al. 1915) – a method that was used by states for over 100 years, replaced by telephone reporting in the late 1980s and digital reporting in the 2000s. It was after two severe epidemics in the early twentieth century – poliomyelitis and influenza – that all states began participating in national morbidity reporting (National Office of Vital Statistics 1953). Public health surveillance is defined as the ongoing, systematic collection, analysis, and interpretation of health-related data with the *a priori* purpose of preventing or controlling disease or injury, or identifying unusual events of public health importance, followed by the dissemination and use of information for public health action (Lee and Thacker 2011).

Public health surveillance depends on an ongoing, dynamic seven-step process that provides continuous feedback to ensure each step is informing the previous and next (Fig. 3.1).

Designing the system requires knowledge and precise definition of the condition or behavior to be reported and acted upon. The public health professional, usually an epidemiologist, must understand the source(s) of data – to whom and where the "cases" are likely to present, when during the course of the condition an individual will seek care, or where the behavior might be exhibited, disclosed, or recorded. The epidemiologist must consider the plan for how data will be obtained, whether they will be reported to the health department via notification forms or whether staff will perform active surveillance where cases are sought on a regular basis via phone call, visits, or electronic data exchange.

In addition, the epidemiologist must consider carefully what data elements are necessary to achieve the public health purpose of the system. It is an important ethical principle for the system to contain only the data necessary to achieve its public health purpose. Careful planning ensures that the system does not contain superfluous data that could bring privacy or confidentiality risk to persons about whom data are collected. While deciding what data elements to collect, the epidemiologist also must consider what types of analyses will be necessary to examine the public health question at hand to ensure the needed data are collected about each case. Knowing what an analyst will do with the data is critical to planning, as it serves no one if key data are missing once analyses are started.

Importantly, planning and design also requires engagement of affected communities – both those affected by the condition to promote clear understanding and expectations of the system as well as by those affected by the requirements of the reporting system, usually health care providers. It is often during this stage of system planning and development where public trust is gained or lost. If affected communities are taken by surprise, are unaware of how a new system might impact their privacy and confidentiality and how those risks might be reconciled with the benefits gained by the resulting public health action, there is likely to be little cooperation regardless of any law or policy mandating participation.

The next steps – collecting, collating, analyzing, and interpreting data – are undertaken by experts familiar with the disease, condition, or behavior under surveillance; the case definition; the characteristics of the data and how they are to be collected; and the population from which the data are collected. Knowledge of these important aspects of the system allow the analyst to determine appropriate analytic methods, identify unlikely findings (such as unexpected associations between risk factors and diseases, diseases in atypical places or populations, and false positives), test for data accuracy, and avoid over– or under-interpreting findings.

The final steps in a public health surveillance system require dissemination and communication of findings for public health action. Use of data and findings to affect change for health is considered a key step defining public health surveillance. Collection of data without directed public health action is not public health surveillance, but another form of inquiry, such as research or health surveys. In order to provide the best course of action, findings from the public health surveillance system must be disseminated and communicated to those able to implement change and responsible for ensuring results.

Modern public health surveillance is a cooperative effort that includes health care providers, laboratories, and health facilities, all of which have the legal responsibility to report conditions as indicated by state legislation (see Sect. 3.2.3). Most states adopt a subset of conditions deemed reportable by the Council of State and Territorial Epidemiologists (CSTE), a group constituted by state epidemiologists from each state, in collaboration with the Centers for Disease Control and Prevention (CDC). As of August 2011, CSTE recommended that states require 8 conditions be reported as extremely urgent (within 4 h), including anthrax, botulism, plague, paralytic poliomyelitis, SARS-associated coronavirus, smallpox, tularemia, and viral hemorrhagic fevers. In addition, they recommended 11 urgent conditions to be reported within 24 h and 61 standard conditions to be reported electronically within 7 days (www.cste.org). The list of conditions that are reportable by health care providers to the state health department varies somewhat by state, but a core set of conditions is reported by all jurisdictions. Once collated at the state health department, reports are then deidentified and forwarded to CDC for national-level public health action.

3.2.2 Syndromic Surveillance

Surveillance of early health indicators is called syndromic surveillance and has been defined as "the ongoing, systematic collection, analysis, interpretation, and application of real-time (or near-real time) indicators for diseases and outbreaks that allow for their detection before public health authorities would otherwise note them" (Sosin 2003).

Syndromic surveillance was added to the public health arsenal in the 1990s to facilitate the quickest possible response to urgent health threats. Instead of waiting until a specific condition is diagnosed, public health officials can combine information from signs and symptoms, exposures to infectious agents or environmental conditions, and health-related behaviors to identify unusual patterns in groups or communities that might indicate an impending concern for which planning and decision making can begin before cases are diagnosed. Depending on how closely related these pre-disease indicators are to the development of an actual case of the condition of concern, there will be some proportion of false-positives (persons with the pre-disease indicator who do not develop the condition). The further an indicator is from the development of the condition, the higher the proportion of false-positives.

The concept of collecting information about novel public health events, or events that were not linked to identifiable diagnoses, has been a function of public health surveillance for many years. Numerous 'syndromes' have been identified by astute clinicians reporting unusual symptoms to their state epidemiologists and to CDC through their public health surveillance systems (Goodman et al. 2012). In recent history, public health professionals identified a number of important and new conditions using syndromic surveillance including Reye's syndrome in 1936, Legionnaires' disease in 1976, Lyme disease in 1977, toxic shock syndrome in 1978, HIV/AIDS in 1981, and SARS in 2003 (Goodman et al. 2012). The definition of public health surveillance and many state statutes specify a requirement to report unusual events of public health importance in addition to the list of conditions a health care provider must report. This allows for the early recognition of unknown syndromes or identification of associated risk factors and etiology that can then be used to initiate public health actions for prevention and control.

3.2.3   Legal Responsibility for Public Health

U.S. Constitutional Law restricts the jurisdiction of the federal government to matters specifically enumerated in the U.S. Constitution; the remaining legal matters are left up to the states. As the Constitution is silent on matters of public health (with the exception of matters falling under the commerce clause and licensing and regulation of drugs, biologics, and devices in some public health situations), matters of controlling the public's health fall within the police powers of the states (Nesland et al. 2010).

Mandatory reporting of diseases and other health indicators in the United States is established through state legislative action whereby states require, via law, regulation, or rule, certain diseases, conditions, or health indicators, along with personal identifiers, to be reported by certain professionals (such as health care providers, teachers, and pharmacists) or certain entities (such as laboratories, schools, or clinics) (Roush et al. 1999). Which specific diseases and conditions are subject to reporting is decided through an annual consensus process involving state epidemiologist-members of CSTE and subject matter experts at CDC. CSTE maintains the list of recommended reportable conditions and states decide whether to adopt the reporting requirement. Ultimately individual state input determines what conditions make their list and most states have a provision for unusual or unknown conditions of concern. States update their list of reportable conditions in different ways, depending on whether it is law, regulation, or rule that determines reportability. More states are adopting a flexible model that allows easier additions to and subtractions from the list of reportable conditions, by, for example, using a rule change instead of the creation and passage of an entirely new law.

The state-level legislative process required to add reportable conditions acts as a form of checks-and-balances for the boundary between "necessary to know" and "intrusive data collection." A democratic process allows for public deliberation – through ballot initiatives or election of certain officials – to determine the extent to which collecting information might be considered a 'greater good' for the population. While reasonable people might disagree on what constitutes a greater good, deliberating transparently encourages favorable participation even if persons disagree on the final result.

This process is predicated on public trust in public health professionals and their ability to maintain the confidentiality and security of reported data. Public health largely has been successful in gaining and maintaining that public trust.

3.3   Privacy and Health

3.3.1   Privacy

Philosophers and ethicists have argued whether privacy is a normative value itself or is subsumed in the more fundamental value of autonomy and respect for persons.

Privacy is recognized as an integral part of the human need for protection of one's intimate self; control over disclosure of one's beliefs, desire, and personal history; protection of one's physical self; and assurance that important and sensitive decisions that affect personal and family life are made, and subsequent disclosure regulated, without interference (DeCew 2012; Allen 2004).

Conceptually, privacy can be subsumed in respect for persons insofar as respect entails honoring a person's autonomy; by respecting a person's private decisions and actions, which are assumed to be based on personal and individual judgments of that which is valued in a good life, we respect her self-directed existence. Whether privacy is viewed as an aspect of autonomy or as its own normative value is less important than the broad acknowledgment by most philosophers that privacy is necessary for human dignity.

Privacy has been discussed in the philosophical literature since Aristotle, when he first observed the *polis* (public or politics) and the *oikos* (household or family) as separate spheres in our lives. Concerns about technology and privacy are not new. In the late nineteenth century, Samuel Warren and Louis Brandeis ignited public discussion about how new technologies were invading privacy by disseminating details about the private lives of individuals without their knowledge or permission, which ran counter to the population's expectation of a protected private life. These new technologies – photography and the mass printing and distribution of daily newspapers – led to major changes in how people learned private details about each other's lives (DeCew 2012). In 1890, Warren and Brandeis promoted a "right to one's own personality" and asserted that "the existing law affords a principle from which may be invoked to protect the privacy of the individual from invasion" (Warren and Brandeis 1890). Later, as an Associate Justice of the U.S. Supreme Court, Brandies declared in his dissent to *Olmstead versus United States* (1928) that "the right to be let alone [is] the most comprehensive of rights and the right most valued by civilized men (sic)."

A comprehensive definition of privacy has been elusive. Privacy encompasses many aspects of modern life:

- Physical privacy, as represented in bodily integrity.
- Decisional privacy, or freedom from interference with autonomous life choices.
- Proprietary privacy, including maintaining ownership of one's identity.
- Informational, such as maintaining confidentiality of medical information (Allen 2004).

Warren and Brandeis's pithy description of the "right to be let alone" (Warren and Brandeis 1890) has been used to describe several types of privacy, but scholars disagree about whether privacy is in itself a right or merely a specification of liberty. Either way, the important aspect of privacy with respect to public health surveillance – or surveillance of any kind – is the fact that it involves *being observed*, generally without the knowledge or consent of the observed, who also knows nothing about how or under what circumstances the observations will be used. How can this type of imposition on autonomy, this invasion of privacy, this violation of liberty, be justified ethically?

3.3.2   Health Data Collection for the Public Good

Scientific justification of data collection for the public good is well documented (Brown 2000; Carrel and Rennie 2008; Tu et al. 2004; Verity and Nicoll 2002). Data are needed for scientific and medical research, such as development of chemotherapies or methods of infection control, as well as biobehavioral research that informs behavioral influences on health. Data are also needed to support a learning health system (Friedman et al. 2010) – a health system that improves by learning from itself by establishing a system of quality improvement that combines health services research and comparative effectiveness analyses of routinely collected clinical data. The aim of the learning health system is to improve both quality and efficiency of health care for all patients. In addition to improving clinical medicine for individuals, medical data are needed to drive recognition of public health threats, implement appropriate interventions, and evaluate effectiveness of action for communities and populations.

Public health surveillance data are the foundation of all public health action. The public expects public health officials to act swiftly to reduce morbidity and mortality as much as possible. To do so, officials must ensure the unbiased, complete, representative, and timely collection of information from the populations they serve. The legal justification for public health data collection has a long history and is clear. Often it occurs in the 'background' of the health system with reportable disease notifications sent to local or state health officials by health care providers without individual patient consent per state laws (see Sect. 3.2.3).

3.4   Ethical Justification for Public Health Surveillance Without Consent

3.4.1   Public Health Ethics

Public health ethics developed as a distinct field in the late 1990s as it became clear that the prevailing bioethical approaches were unable to accommodate the increasing complexities of public health responsibilities. Clinical practice differs from public health practice in at least three important ways that create a poor fit of bioethics to public health (Lee 2012).

1. Medicine focuses on the individual as patient, whereas public health focuses on community or population as patient: The health of the individual matters in clinical practice and the health of the community matters in public health practice. By definition, then, clinicians see patients they know (or can come to know), whereas public health practitioners provide interventions for persons most of whom they never see or meet and who remain largely unknown to them.

2. Medicine historically is concerned with curative interventions, either chemotherapeutic or procedural, whereas public health is primarily concerned with prediction, anticipation, and prevention. Public health's tools are not prescriptions or surgeries, but policy and law, behavioral-change strategies, sanitation, and adjustments to the built environment.
3. Clinical medicine relies on a small number of similar disciplines with similar training to carry out its tasks. In contrast, public health relies on a breadth of professional disciplines with varied training and backgrounds to achieve its mission.

These contrasting characteristics bring different ethical challenges to the forefront of medicine and public health, the most obvious of which is the tension between individual autonomy and public benefit. A fundamental question for many public health activities, including public health surveillance, is how far can public health impinge on an individual's liberty for the sake of the health of the community?

3.4.2 Mill's "Harm Principle"

It is nearly universally, albeit naively, held that John Stuart Mill's "harm principle" serves as the normative justification for any state intervention over individual action – and that such intervention is ethically acceptable only when it prevents harm to others. The use of Mill's harm principle to support autonomy as the supreme value stems largely from the field of bioethics and its narrow misinterpretation of Mill's thoughts on liberty (Dawson and Verweij 2008). Mill indeed stated that, "the only purpose for which power can be rightfully exercised over any member of a civilized community, against his will, is to prevent harm to others" (Mill 1859, p. 14). But to stop there is akin to misquoting, as Mill goes on to state:

> His own good, either physical or moral, is not sufficient warrant. He cannot rightfully be compelled to do or forbear because it will be better for him to do so, because it will make him happier, because, in the opinions of others, to do so would be wise, or even right. These are good reasons for remonstrating with him, or reasoning with him, or persuading him, or entreating him, but not for compelling him, or visiting him with any evil in case he do otherwise. To justify that, the conduct from which it is desired to deter him, must be calculated to produce evil to someone else. The only part of the conduct of anyone, for which he is amenable to society, is that which concerns others. In the part which merely concerns himself, his independence is, of right, absolute. Over himself, over his own body and mind, the individual is sovereign. (Mill 1859, p. 14)

Persons opposed to public health interventions often claim that Mill's "harm principle" (as truncated above) requires us to not be paternalistic in any way. This passage clearly shows that Mill acknowledged that we do have good reasons to "reason with" and "persuade" people to "do otherwise," which is what public health often does. Furthermore, actions that society can rightfully censure are limited to those that are "calculated to produce evil to someone else." These all clearly are

L.M. Lee

supportive of public health interventions, not in opposition as suggested by the truncated and misleading version of the passage concerning the "harm principle."

Mill calls attention not only to the liberty a state owes individuals, but also clearly asserts that individuals owe their community:

> Those interests, I contend, authorize the subjection of individual spontaneity to external control, only in respect to those actions of each, which concern the interest of other people. If any one does an act harmful to others, there is a prima facie case for punishing him, by law, or, where legal penalties are not safely applicable, by general disapprobation. There are also many positive acts for the benefit of others, which he may rightfully be compelled to perform; such as, to give evidence in a court of justice; to bear his fair share in the common defence, or in any other joint work necessary to the interest of the society of which he enjoys the protection; and to perform certain acts of individual beneficence, such as saving a fellow creature's life, or interposing to protect the defenceless against ill-usage, things which whenever it is obviously a man's duty to do, he may rightfully be made responsible for not doing. A person may cause evil to others not only by his actions but by his inaction, and in either case he is justly accountable to them for the injury. (Mill 1859, p. 15)

Mill was not writing about public health or propriety of the state's prohibition of super-sized portions of fast food. His essay makes it clear from the opening pages that he was deeply concerned with the importance of liberty with respect to the tyranny of the majority. The complexity and nuance of his thoughts on liberty are done a grave disservice by the simplification that occurs when these ideas are reduced to the "harm principle" and by the dismissal of the remainder of the essay, which describes the responsibilities we have to each other.

There is a long history of those in opposition to public health interventions holding up the "harm principle" as the reason to reject any public health action other than those that prevent direct harm to another. Many ethicists and scholars who believe in the primacy of autonomy hold Mill's abbreviated principle high as proof of great thinkers supporting an entirely autonomous life.

However, the seminal case, which remains key in defending public health interventions today, is the 1905 case of *Jacobson versus Massachusetts* in which Henning Jacobson refused the required smallpox vaccination and was ordered to pay a $5 fine or face imprisonment. The U.S. Supreme Court held that when there is "great danger" the state has compelling interest in using its police powers to enforce the "social compact" it has with its citizens to protect the common good and to do so even when it at times intrudes on the free will of any one man (*Jacobson v Commonwealth of Massachusetts* 1905). The text of the Court's proceedings articulate the delicate balance of personal liberty and societal best interests on both the ethical and legal fronts.

Today scholars are calling for a closer look at Mill to reconsider his notions in the context of public health ethics, where the focus is not on the health of individuals, rather on the health of the population (Jennings 2009). They are asking for a thorough and nuanced look into Mill's writings to better understand the role of liberty vis-à-vis societal interests in a democratic state (Powers et al. 2012).

Early scholars such as Dan Beauchamp (1980) began outlining the tensions between public health and personal liberty in the 1980s, but it was not until alternative frameworks for ethical problem solving in public health were proffered in the 2000s that the field began to separate itself from medical and bioethics. These alternative frameworks have sorted themselves into two broad categories (Lee 2012) – those that come from a very practical perspective focused on the observed needs of public health professionals struggling with ethical questions in their daily practice; and those that come from a theoretical perspective, a specific ethical school of thought aimed at maintaining philosophical rigor regardless of its applicability.

While over a dozen distinct public health ethics frameworks have been offered by various authors over the past couple of decades, all of them, whether they come from a practical or theoretical perspective, specify the need to balance personal liberty with the obligation to protect the community's health (Lee 2012). Reconciling autonomy with the greater good requires a move from the highly liberal ethical stance where autonomy is considered not a *prima facie* value, but the supreme value that trumps all others, toward a more collective perspective where our obligations to each other are demanded by principles such as justice, equity, and transparency, each of which may moderate autonomy.

3.4.3   Justifying Public Health Surveillance Without Consent

It is in the center of this dilemma – when can the state override individual liberty for the sake of improving health – that the ethics of public health surveillance is argued.

In the case of public health surveillance, competing ethical priorities include the *prima facie* values of autonomy in the sense of personal informational privacy, and beneficence in a broad sense, encompassing governmental responsibility in the form of the public health enterprise's obligation to improve population health. This mismatch between bioethics, with its primacy of autonomy, and public health ethics, with its obligation to both benefit the population and not harm the individual, demands resolution.

In the context of popular belief in the primacy of autonomy, much has been written about the need to use health data generally to support the claim that governments and other health care providing institutions are morally obligated to provide the most effective and efficient care to the greatest number of citizens possible. This collection and use of data requires that the public participate, and public participation requires public trust. Gostin proposed national-level policy changes that support collecting health data under uniform rules that protect individual privacy to reconcile the "equally compelling public and private claims from the ethical and constitutional perspectives" (Gostin 2001, p. 332). Scientists and clinicians cannot maximize public health or clinical care benefits without access to public health data, and access to those data depends on the public's trust that they are protected from both rogue access and inappropriate use. The secure space for private information to be used for public good is provided by policies that constrain the use of data to those purposes for which they were intended and protect data from unauthorized access.

Gostin and I have proposed a framework for national privacy protection of public health data collected for any legitimate public health use – including public health surveillance – at all levels of government (Lee and Gostin 2009). These policy protections should be attached to and travel with the data, regardless of where and by whom they are stored or used, for the life of the public health data. The policy protections should be predicated on values of interdependence, ethical oversight, and scientific evidence and include guidance such as mandates to

- collect the minimum amount of data necessary to achieve the public health objective, including leaving off personal identifiers when possible,
- engage affected communities when developing data collection and data dissemination plans, especially when data release might add burdens to an already stigmatized group, and
- ensure that public health professionals who have contact with data are active and responsible stewards ultimately accountable for the protection of data and information (Lee and Gostin 2009, p. 83).

We recommend that such a policy be operationalized with ten basic requirements (Lee and Gostin 2009).

The first two requirements entail ensuring that data are collected only for legitimate public health purposes and that only the minimum necessary data are collected. Quite the opposite of a researcher who can collect whatever data a consenting participant agrees to share, public health officials must collect data judiciously and include only those data that support the public health purpose for which it is needed. Agencies should not hold data they will not need or use. Since nothing of use will come from these data, only two outcomes are possible: nothing or a breach. This type of risk cannot be ethically justified. This principle of *data parsimony* also dictates the destruction of data that have ceased to be useful for a public health purpose as well as any data that are inadvertently or incorrectly collected, such as those false-positive reports collected in syndromic surveillance systems.

The third requirement is to implement strong policies and practices for data security to ensure privacy of personally identifiable information. These policies must include procedures for swift corrective action and appropriate sanctions for violators. The creation and enforcement of such constraints engender public trust.

The fourth requirement includes careful consideration of the rights of individuals and communities. Policies should reflect respect for individuals as well as communities, both in terms of data collection and data release.

Fifth, data collected must be of high enough quality to meet the public health goals of the activity. They should yield accurate evidence that can be applied justly.

Sixth, data must be disseminated to relevant stakeholders for action. Public health officials should share with stakeholders information about how data are collected, how they will be used, and the findings they make possible.

Seventh, if data are to be used for other public health purposes consistent with the intent of their collection, clear data use agreements should be signed by all parties, specifying intent, scope, and disposition of data.

The next two requirements involve data security: Data, paper or electronic, must be held securely at all times, while in use and at rest. Security should be reviewed annually and the latest security measures put in place to secure the information from possible intrusions. In order to minimize risk, only those persons with a need to know should have access to identifiable data, and this should be the smallest number possible.

Finally, all persons involved with the collection, storage, and use of public health data must be active, responsible stewards of the data to which they have access. Authorized persons must be aware of their personal responsibility to protect the data and the need to protect the privacy of the individuals whose data are entered into the system (Lee and Gostin 2009).

Guidelines for protecting public health data are helpful only if they are adopted. Adopting and implementing consistent policies, however, has proven challenging given the legal structure under which public health is practiced in the United States, but this fragmentation only increases the need for such consistent approaches.

In an attempt to reconcile the common good and individual rights, Fairchild and Johns consider it time to "[embrace] a new approach for research in public interest domains" (Fairchild and Johns 2012, p. 1449), including public health. It behooves us to recognize that there are issues that different ethical paradigms will resolve in different ways; it is essential that we apply the right paradigm, then, in the right circumstances.

With more than a dozen public health ethics frameworks, how does one ensure application of the right paradigm in the circumstance of public health surveillance? My colleagues and I examined the question of whether public health surveillance without patient consent is supported by the principles of public health ethics (Lee et al. 2012). We posited that public health surveillance would be ethically justified if its practices "[met] the affirmative and refrain[ed] from violating negative operating principles" of the existing public health ethics frameworks (Lee et al. 2012, p. 41). Although based on different theoretical underpinnings, several common operating principles emerged from the 13 public health ethics frameworks we reviewed. The common ethical principles included community, justice, interdependence, duty, human rights, autonomy, imposing minimal interference, ensuring intervention is necessary and effective, providing evidence that benefits outweigh infringement, reducing inequities, transparency, and inclusiveness. We then evaluated the best practices for the seven steps of public health surveillance and concluded that "a well-designed public health surveillance system that engages affected communities, collects the minimum data necessary, stores data securely, and uses data for public health action (Lee et al. 2012, p. 43)" is supported by contemporary public health ethics frameworks even when conducted without explicit patient consent.

Rubel, finding no adequate guide to the conflicts between privacy and public health surveillance, takes a "basic interests" approach to justifying the collection of public health data without patient consent (Rubel 2012). The foundation for this approach is Rawls's view that persons living in a pluralistic society have basic interests regardless of their conception of a good life and that therefore supersede personal interests based solely on their conception of a good life (Rawls 2001).

Health, maximized in large part through public health, is one of these interests, and unless another person's basic interests are at stake, activities that promote society's basic interests are generally justifiable, perhaps obligatory. Rubel offers several conditions that temper the permissibility of public health interventions that promote health as a basic interest, and calls this the "unreasonable exercise argument" (Rubel 2012, p. 12). This argument allows for conditions where persons could justify a privacy claim over a public health good, specifically where there are important personal interests the exercise of which would not unreasonably burden the basic health interest. Using this approach, Rubel argues that public health interventions – including public health surveillance – that are necessary to further the basic interest of health are justified when implementation does not impose on another person's basic interests.

3.5 Conclusion

Collecting and using data without one's knowledge or consent does not always constitute an ethical affront. In the context of health – considered a human right by some, a basic interest by others – pursuing the best possible outcomes is not possible on an individual level; population health is critical for individual health and the role of public health surveillance in population health is indispensable. The role of a government in protecting and enhancing the health of its people, thus meeting a basic interest of its population, is clear when the activities necessary are those that individuals cannot implement themselves. In a pluralistic society there will be disparate views on how much information the government ought to collect and store about its citizens, but there is no argument that it is possible to collect, store, and use public health surveillance data under ethical circumstances to better the health of a nation.

Acknowledgments The author would like to acknowledge Dr. Frances McCarty for her thoughtful comments on the chapter.
The findings and conclusions in this report are those of the author and do not necessarily represent the official position of CDC.

References

Allen, A. 2004. Privacy in healthcare. In *Encyclopedia of bioethics*, 3rd ed, ed. S.G. Post, 2120–2130. New York: Macmillan Reference USA.

Beauchamp, D.E. 1980. Public health and individual liberty. *Annual Review of Public Health* 1: 121–136.

Bowditch, H.I., D.L. Webster, J.C. Hoadley, et al. 1915. Letter from the Massachusetts State Board of Health to physicians. *Public Health Reports* 12(Suppl): 31.

Brown, P. 2000. Cancer registries fear imminent collapse. *BMJ* 321(7265): 849.

Carrel, M., and S. Rennie. 2008. Demographic and health surveillance: Longitudinal ethical considerations. *Bulletin of the World Health Organization* 86(8): 577–656.

Dawson, A., and M. Verweij. 2008. The steward of the Millian state. *Public Health Ethics* 1(3): 193–195.

DeCew, J. 2012. Privacy. *The Stanford Encyclopedia of Philosophy* (Fall 2012 Edition), Edward N. Zalta (ed.), Available at http://plato.stanford.edu/archives/fall2012/entries/privacy/.

Fairchild, A.L., and D.M. Johns. 2012. Beyond bioethics: Reckoning with the public health paradigm. *American Journal of Public Health* 102(8): 1447–1450.

Friedman, C.P., A.K. Wong, and D. Blumenthal. 2010. Achieving a nationwide learning health system. *Science Translational Medicine* 2(57): 1–3.

Goodman, R.A., J.M. Posid, and T. Popovic. 2012. Investigation of selected historically important syndromic outbreaks: Impact and lessons learned for public health preparedness and response. *American Journal of Public Health* 102(6): 1079–1090.

Gostin, L.O. 2001. Health information: Reconciling personal privacy with the public good of human health. *Health Care Analysis* 9: 321–335.

U.S. Supreme Court. 1905. Jacobson v Commonwealth of Massachusetts, 197 U.S. 11.

Jennings, B. 2009. Public health and liberty: Beyond the Millian paradigm. *Public Health Ethics* 2(2): 123–134.

Lee, L.M., and L.O. Gostin. 2009. Ethical collection, storage, and use of public health data: A proposal for a national privacy protection. *Journal of the American Medical Association* 302(1): 82–84.

Lee, L.M., and S.B. Thacker. 2011. Public health surveillance and knowing about health in the context of growing sources of health data. *American Journal of Preventive Medicine* 41(6): 636–640.

Lee, L.M. 2012. Public health ethics theory: Review and path to convergence. *The Journal of Law, Medicine & Ethics* 40(1): 85–98.

Lee, L.M., C.M. Heilig, and A. White. 2012. Ethical justification for conducting public health surveillance without patient consent. *American Journal of Public Health* 102(1): 38–44.

Mill, J.S. 2008 [1859]. On liberty. In *John Stuart Mill: On liberty and other essays*, ed. J. Gray, 5–128. London: Oxford University Press.

National Office of Vital Statistics. 1953. Reported incidence of selected notifiable diseases: United States, each division and state, 1920–1950. *Vital Statistics Special Report* 37: 1180–1181. Washington, DC: US Department of Health, Education and Welfare

Nesland, V.S., R.A. Goodman, J.G. Hodge, and J.P. Middaugh. 2010. Legal considerations in public health surveillance in the United States. In *Principles and practice of public health surveillance*, 3rd ed, ed. L.M. Lee, S.M. Teutsch, S.B. Thacker, and M.E. St Louis, 217–235. New York: Oxford University Press.

Powers, M., R. Faden, and Y. Saghai. 2012. Liberty, Mill and the framework of public health ethics. *Public Health Ethics* 5(1): 6–15.

Rawls, J. 2001. *Justice as fairness*. Cambridge: Harvard University Press.

Roush, S., G.S. Birkhead, D. Koo, A. Cobb, and D. Fleming. 1999. Mandatory reporting of diseases and conditions by health care professionals and laboratorians. *Journal of the American Medical Association* 282(2): 164–170.

Rubel, A. 2012. Justifying public health surveillance: Basic interests, unreasonable exercise, and privacy. *Kennedy Institute of Ethics Journal* 22(1): 1–33.

Sosin, D.M. 2003. Syndromic surveillance: The case for skillful investment. *Biosecurity and Bioterrorism: Biodefense Strategy, Practice, and Science* 1(4): 247–253.

Thacker, S.B. 2010. Historical development. In *Principles and practice of public health surveillance*, 3rd ed, ed. L.M. Lee, S.M. Teutsch, S.B. Thacker, and M.E. St Louis, 1–17. New York: Oxford University Press.

Tu, J.V., D.J. Willison, F.L. Silver, et al. 2004. Impracticability of informed consent in the Registry of the Canadian Stroke Network. *The New England Journal of Medicine* 350(14): 1414–1421.

Verity, C., and A. Nicoll. 2002. Consent, confidentiality, and the threat to public health surveillance. *BMJ* 324: 1210–1213.

Warren, S., and L. Brandeis L. 1890. The right to privacy. *Harvard Law Review* 4: 193–220.

Chapter 4
Surveillance in the Big Data Era

Mark Andrejevic

4.1 Introduction

In 2012, the British government proposed a change in policing surveillance strategies that reflected emerging regimes of surveillance and monitoring in the digital
era.[1] The proposal represented a shift from what might be described as "targeted"
surveillance – in which police need a warrant to track a particular suspect – to
generalized surveillance, in which everyone can be monitored all the time. Under
the new policy the authorities would be allowed to track everyone's communication
behavior at any time, including details about when, where, and with whom
communication interactions took place, how long they lasted, and what medium
(mobile phone, email, etc.) was used (Mulholland and Booth 2012). To assuage
privacy concerns, the government assured members of the public that the proposed
measures would, "not include the content of any phone call or e-mail" (Mulholland
and Booth 2012). The police were interested not in content but in pattern – at least
initially. In practical terms there is a certain logic to this preference – not simply
to avoid the public relations problem associated with the revelation that police are
reading everyone's email and listening in on their phone calls – but to admit that it
simply is not possible to make sense out of that much content. Much more effective
than attempting to eavesdrop on everyone would be to allow computers to detect
anomalies or other patterns that correlate with suspicious activity. The lesson of

---

[1] As of this writing, the proposed Communications Data Bill in the UK was still generating
controversy, although it looked likely to be passed into law. The published version of the proposed
law would not only allow data to be collected, but to be mined – sifted and sorted for emerging
patterns of behavior (Burton 2012).

M. Andrejevic, Ph.D. (✉)
Centre for Critical and Cultural Studies, University of Queensland, St. Lucia,
Brisbane, QLD, Australia
e-mail: m.andrejevic@uq.edu.au

K.D. Pimple (ed.), *Emerging Pervasive Information and Communication Technologies
(PICT)*, Law, Governance and Technology Series 11, DOI 10.1007/978-94-007-6833-8_4,
© Springer Science+Business Media Dordrecht 2014

this example is, among other things, that content – or referential meaning – tends to fall by the wayside where "big data" surveillance is concerned. The second lesson is that, in the era of "big data" surveillance, the imperative is to monitor the population as a whole: otherwise it is harder to consistently and reliably discern useful patterns. This logic is generalizable beyond the realm of police surveillance proper, to those of marketing, epidemiology, climatology, and so on – to all of those forms of monitoring or surveillance that rely upon increasingly ubiquitous and comprehensive forms of data collection. The approach is inductive: collect as much information as possible and see what patterns emerge. Once you start down this path, the goal is to amass as much data about as many targets as possible.

From a policing perspective this does not mean that everyone is a suspect, but it does mean that for the suspects to emerge, everyone must be subject to surveillance. In an inductive approach, nothing is ruled out of the data set a priori. Embarking on the path of big data surveillance necessitates the policing approach outlined in the UK proposal: the preferred strategy, then, is to replace comprehension with comprehensiveness – to replace detection with collection and let the algorithm do the work. The shift from targeted to "populational" monitoring is facilitated by the advent of interactive, networked forms of digital communication that generate easily collectible and storable meta-data. But the logic is self-stimulating and recursive: once the switch to an inductive, data-driven form of monitoring takes place, the incentive exists to develop the technology to collect more and more information: to expand the monitoring surface of the interface to cover its entirety – and to simultaneously expand the interface to "cover" as much of everyday life as possible.

This goal of total coverage marks a moment of convergence between emerging regimes of monitoring and so-called ubiquitous computing in realms ranging from policing to marketing to political campaigning. From the perspective of the digitally enhanced police force or that of the online marketer, the only way to get complete information is to implement total coverage. Indeed, the proposed policing policy in the UK simply follows the lead of marketers, who have been developing increasingly comprehensive databases of consumer behavior for the purposes of anticipating and influencing future activities (see, for example, Turow 2006). Perhaps the difference is that in the realm of policing and security, data mining tends to be used for the purposes of preventing and deterring undesirable behavior, whilst in marketing the goal is to stimulate and induce desired activities (at least from the perspective of marketers). The development of ubiquitous computing technology has recently taken a commercial route that relies on the logic of "big data surveillance": the use of information gathered about people as a means of supporting the commercial infrastructure for the wired world. This chapter sets out to explore the logic of big data surveillance by considering first the shape that ubiquitous computing is taking in the wireless world of Web 2.0. It then outlines some of the defining aspects of the forms of monitoring and surveillance that rely upon ubiquitous forms of interactivity. Finally, it addresses some of the ethical issues posed by the emerging regimes of population-level monitoring, arguing that classical liberal conceptions that underwrite recent privacy-protection initiatives fall short of addressing the challenge to democracy posed by big data surveillance.

4.2 Rethinking Ubiquity

Early versions of ubiquitous computing envisioned the migration of computer chips into the walls and environs (Wieser 1991) – the material creation of an interactive overlay upon the physical world around us: Rooms that recognize us and adjust the surrounding environment accordingly; doors that open automatically for those authorized to use them; billboards that recognize their viewer and automatically cater to their preferences; and so on. Some of these technologies have been developed or remain in development, but they have not become as widespread as wireless interactivity. The dominant shape ubiquitous computing is taking, at least for the near future, is that of the wireless digital enclosure: not surfaces and places that recognize and respond to us, but portable devices that make our surroundings interactive.

This chapter argues for what might be described as an expanded version of ubiquitous computing wherein networked interactivity pervades the very atmosphere through which we move.[2] Thanks to the proliferation of wireless networked devices, the spaces we are in can, in a sense, respond to us, via portable interactive technology. A smartphone, for example, can "know" where its user is and direct her toward relevant stores or locations. The immediate environment is made "smart" thanks to the intervention of the smartphone. Google is developing interactive glasses that will allow users to custom tag their environments – or share their tags with others (Bilton 2012). The physical environment does not (yet) respond to the presence of users in the world envisioned by Google's goggles, but its data double does. The electromagnetic overlay houses the interactivity via portable, personalized, "addressable" devices such as Google's glasses (devices that can be traced back to individual users). The space does not "know" who is inhabiting it, but the interactive device knows where the user is and can respond in customized ways, incorporating data about location, past behavior, personal preferences, and so on.

There is a certain efficiency to this version of ubiquity, insofar as it does not rely upon equipping the entire physical infrastructure with an interactive capability, but rather enveloping it in an interactive wireless enclosure. Such a solution also allows for more centralized forms of data collection – rather than each space having its own data storage center, those who control the electromagnetic enclosure are able to capture, store, and aggregate data about users who rely on their services. In this regard, the growth of so-called "cloud computing" goes hand-in-hand with

---

[2]The jargon of "ubiquity" seems to have fallen by the wayside, and perhaps the more accurate term is "pervasive computing," to describe the forms of anywhere, anytime access made possible by portable, networked devices. If there is a difference between the two terms, it is that ubiquitous computing envisioned a multi-chip world in which memory and interactivity were embedded in the physical infrastructure. Pervasive computing, by contrast, allows users to access remote computing resources wherever they go – and, down the road, to add an interactive overlay upon the physical world (through forms of geographic tagging) without necessarily embedding chips throughout that world (see Chap. 5 for more on PICT and geographical information and Chap. 8 for more on potential unintended consequences of pervasive augmented reality).

the version of ubiquitous computing described here. The "cloud" (actually large server farms) stores the data captured by interactive electromagnetic enclosures. In this context ubiquity refers not simply to spatial coverage – the ability to gain access to interactive information and communication resources wherever one goes – but also to the growing range of interactive functionality tailored to a widening array of interests and preferences. These two dimensions of ubiquity contribute to the increasing comprehensiveness of the database, which is not limited to telephone, email, and Web-based interactions, but also encompasses where we go, with whom, when, how long we linger *there* and *with them* – in short, an indefinitely expanding range of interests and behaviors captured by interactive devices. The logical extension of the UK policing proposal, for example, will be the ability to capture statistics generated by all of these various interactive applications – an ability already exploited by target marketers and commercial data miners. The world of ubiquitous computing will be characterized by a flood of data – leading to the recently popularized moniker "big data." The forms of surveillance enabled by big data raise a host of concerns somewhat different from those associated with other types of monitoring and surveillance.

4.3   Big Data Surveillance

In the world of big data, different types of monitoring converge, and data gathered for one function – record-keeping, policing, marketing, political campaigning – can be repurposed for another, in part because of the range of data collected and in part because of the shifting role of the surveillance function. If, once upon a time, surveillance functioned as a strategy for catching someone in the act or for gathering evidence that could be used against a prime suspect, big data surveillance switches the order around. Rather than starting with a suspect and then monitoring him or her, the goal is to start with generalized surveillance and then generate suspects. Building on the work of Jean Baudrillard (1994), William Bogard (1996) has described this form of monitoring as "the simulation of surveillance" – not just monitoring as deterrent (the placement of a surveillance camera in a notorious crime spot, for example) but as a strategy for intervening in the future by modeling it. As Bogard puts it, "The goal of information and communication management technologies is simply to control as perfectly and seamlessly as possible all conceivable outcomes in advance. This is the logic behind data mining, profiling . . . and the like" (2006, p. 60). Take the example of predictive policing – the use of statistics about everything from past patterns of criminal behavior to the weather to predict when and where crimes are going to take place before they happen. In an apt turn of phrase, one police consultant observed, "Preventive policing, that's where the future is" (Hamilton 2011, p. 25).

Modeling the future in order to prevent or favor particular outcomes requires comprehensive monitoring: ubiquitous surveillance. It is the data-driven high-tech strategy envisioned by the Pentagon's notorious office of Total Information Awareness (now allegedly defunct), which sought to create and mine a comprehensive database created by aggregating all available databases, combined with information culled from a variety of new, high-tech monitoring devices (*Associated Press* 2003). This plan served as the model for the fictional TV series, *Person of Interest*, in which a renegade computer programmer taps into the government's data-mining apparatus (which he created) in order to predict when and where life-threatening crimes will occur. The show's premise is that automated surveillance has become both ubiquitous and multi-faceted – all spaces and practices are monitored via technologies ranging from cameras equipped with facial recognition technology to telephones with voice-stress analyzers. The show represents the monitoring process by portraying the perspective of an array of automated sensors and monitoring devices through quick intercut shots of people viewed in grainy surveillance video overlaid with terms meant to suggest the various forms of monitoring at work: "voice capture stress percentage;" "GPS: active, tracking location;" "searching: all known databases;" etc. In this world, the environment itself has been redoubled as both setting and spectator. No one in particular is watching, but everyone is watched all the time. The result is what Bogard (1996) describes as "the impersonal domination of the hypersurveillance assemblage" (p. 134).

With each new revelation about the broadening reach of interactive technology and its attendant exploitation by marketers and government agencies, the world portrayed in *Person of Interest* comes to feel less like a paranoid fantasy and more like the future envisioned for us by the developers of the interactive infrastructure that is colonizing our personal and professional lives. From the point of view of marketers the deterrence effect is somewhat different. The marketers' goal is not to prevent a particular action but to pre-empt its alternatives. Even so, the logic remains the same: model the future and then modulate the present to intervene in it. As this chapter argues, the modeling process relies on a very different logic of information collection from that associated with targeted surveillance and the regimes of privacy rights meant to limit it. This is perhaps one of the reasons why conventional privacy rights regimes have had a difficult time keeping up with and adjusting to the shifting forms of surveillance associated with the digital, interactive era.

In the era of big data, monitoring and surveillance have the following six key characteristics, described in the next sections:

1. Tracking is "populational"
2. Correlation and predictability are trump
3. Monitoring is pre-emptive
4. Tracking is interventionist
5. All information is relevant
6. Privacy is irrelevant

4.3.1 Tracking Is "Populational"

Big data makes tracking "populational" rather than targeted. Much of the chapter so far has focused on this aspect of new forms of surveillance: they rely on an inductive logic which requires tracking the entire population. This means that content is less important than pattern, and that individual data contributions gain in value to the extent that they can be aggregated, stored, sorted, and mined. In other words, data has a very different value to those with access to the computing and storage infrastructure than to those without. We might describe this as the big data version of the digital divide: Those who have access to the database, and to data-generating platforms, can make sense of the data deluge and enlist it for purposes of their own devising; those without access and control are unable to make use of the data that they help generate. If targeted surveillance or monitoring was, in a sense, exceptional (only conducted on particular individuals who had been singled out for special treatment), "populational" surveillance, by contrast, only works if it is normalized and ubiquitous.

4.3.2   Correlation and Predictability Are Trump

A further corollary of the shift to "populational" surveillance is the privileging of correlation over causation, predictability over referentiality. The goal of popu-lational surveillance, despite its ubiquity, is not so much to generate an accurate "map of the territory" as it is to generate useful, reliable correlations. This aspect gets to the question of content and comprehension. Perhaps the best description of this shift is provided by Chris Anderson's diagnosis of the fate of theory in the so-called "petabyte" era: "Out with every theory of human behavior, from linguistics to sociology. Forget taxonomy, ontology, and psychology. Who knows why people do what they do? The point is they do it, and we can track and measure it with unprecedented fidelity. With enough data, the numbers speak for themselves" (Anderson 2008). We might push this formula even further: forget about trying to describe a world (and the various impasses this poses) and focus on predicting it.

Data, in this context, becomes detached from what might be described as "refer-entiality" – describing not the world beyond it so much as the data's own patterns of inter-relationships. There is a logic not dissimilar to that of the derivative or other 'postmodern' reflexive financial instruments that, in a sense, liberate themselves from any determinate attachment to underlying economic realities (at least for a while). Here's how Chris Anderson puts it, using the model of Google for guidance: "Google's founding philosophy is that we don't know why this page is better than that one: If the statistics of incoming links say it is, that's good enough. No semantic or causal analysis is required. That's why . . . it can match ads to content without any knowledge or assumptions about the ads or its content" (2008).

In the realm of market research this approach was anticipated by Paco Underhill, famous for developing the so-called 'science of shopping' based on his large database of films that document what people do when they shop. Underhill looks for predictable patterns, measuring how long it takes people to slow down and start browsing once they enter a store, or which direction they typically take when they enter a store (a tendency Underhill dubbed the "Invariant Right" after the habit of shoppers in the U.S.), and the correlation between the route they take through the store and sales. Like data miners (which is what Underhill is, in a pre-digital sense), he searches for robust patterns with predictive power and uses them to generate natural "laws" about shopping (hence, "the science of shopping"). But, as one profile points out, Underhill makes no attempt to explain or interpret the "laws" he discovers: "Uncovering the fundamentals of 'why' is clearly not a pursuit that engages him much. He is not a theoretician but an empiricist, and for him the important thing is that in amassing his huge library of in-store time-lapse photography he has gained enough hard evidence to know how often and under what circumstances the Invariant Right is expressed and how to take advantage of it" (Gladwell 1996). In this regard, Underhill was a man ahead of his time: the goal of big data mining is not to understand the world but to predict it. If someone is more likely to vote Republican, or purchase a product, or commit property theft if they drive a particular model of car in a particular neighborhood, predictive analysts are not particularly interested in determining why – merely in calculating the probabilities.

4.3.3   Monitoring Is Pre-emptive

When the emphasis of monitoring shifts from description to prediction, its goal becomes pre-emptive. As Bogard notes in his analysis of the simulation of surveillance, the goal of predictive analytics is not simply predicting outcomes, but devising ways of altering them. In policing terms, the goal of predicting the likelihood of criminal behavior is to deter it. In marketing or campaigning terms it is to deter alternatives to the desired outcome. Transposed into business jargon, as one digital marketing executive put it, "In the early days of digital marketing, analytics emerged to tell us what happened and, as analytics got better, why it happened. Then solutions emerged to make it easier to act on data and optimize results" (Business Wire 2012). The more data that can be processed faster, the better for turning "big data into a big opportunity" (Business Wire 2012). The promise of predictive analytics is to incorporate the future as a set of anticipated data points into the decision making process: "Historically all Web analytics have reflected data from the past which has been to a certain extent like driving a car using only the rear view mirror … for the first time we can be marketers using data in a manner that allows us to drive while facing the road ahead" (Business Wire 2012). It is a vision of the future in which the structure outlined by predictions is subject to modification along certain pivot points. If, for example, a credit card company can predict a scenario that might lead to losses, it can intervene in advance to attempt to minimize these, as in one example described by the New York Times: "credit-card companies keep an eye on whether you are making purchases of that kind [indicating marital problems], because divorce is expensive and they are paranoid that you might stop paying your credit-card bill. For example, if you use your card to pay for a marriage counselor, they might decrease your credit line" (Nolan 2012). Similarly, in his book *Super Crunchers*, Ian Ayres describes how the credit card company CapOne uses data mining to predict the smallest possible reduction in interest rate that can be used to retain customers. When someone calls in with a complaint about a card's high interest rates, a computer uses detailed information about the consumer combined with information about how similar customers have behaved in the past to rapidly generate a range of rates likely to deflect the consumer's cancellation request: "Because of Super Crunching, CapOne knows that a lot of people will be satisfied with this reduction (even when they say they've been offered a lower rate from another card)" (Ayers 2007, p. 48).

4.3.4 *Tracking Is Interventionist*

Big data surveillance does not rely simply on observation but also on forms of experimentation that generate even more data. The logic of modulation provides a second link between ubiquitous computing and predictive analytics: the ability to transform user environments in targeted and customized ways in accordance with predictions based on the ability to process big data in real time. Thus, the goal of marketers, for example is to customize the available information environment – the messages to which we are exposed, the contexts in which these appear, and so on – in ways most likely to influence consumers in accordance with the marketers' imperatives. This means an ongoing process of experimentation to discover which ads should be placed in which contexts, what types of ads work best in conjunction with which combination of search results, and so on (for more on this, see Ayres 2007 and Pariser 2011). We might describe the commercial use of predictive analytics as having several steps: First, the detection of robust patterns that can be used to identify particular categories of consumer; second, the use of controlled experiments to determine how best to influence this category of consumer; and third, the modulation of consumers' information environment in accordance with these findings.

For an indication of how predictive analytics operates in the context of retail marketing, consider the example of its use by retail giant Target to determine which of its customers might recently have become pregnant. Market research indicates that the birth of a child is a life-changing event that disrupts consumer habits and allows for interventions that might reshape them (Duhigg 2012). So Target searched through its giant consumer database to determine what patterns of purchasing correlate with the eventual appearance of female consumers on its baby registry (abrupt changes in purchase behavior that include large amounts of unscented lotion, dietary supplements, scent-free soap, etc.). Then it determines what patterns of advertising generate the most sales amongst these consumers, conducting controlled experiments on its target population by creating different combinations of advertising appeals (Duhigg 2012). Thanks to its proficiency in data mining, Target is able to determine personal information indirectly about consumers and use this to attempt to influence their behavior. The potentially intrusive character of this type of research was indicated by an anecdote reported to the *New York Times* about a man who complained to Target after his teenage daughter started receiving advertising for baby products: it turned out that the store knew before he did that his daughter was pregnant (Duhigg 2012).

In the future we can expect that predictive analytics will become more sophisticated and will be deployed across a broad range of social life to shape and sort consumer behavior and opportunities. The example of Target's marketing to pregnant women remains perhaps just a tiny foretaste of things to come: detecting details of psychological and physiological changes that render consumers more susceptible to particular types of stimuli, and using this knowledge to deliver these stimuli in the most effective contexts, times, and places. One of the more suggestive details revealed in the coverage of Target's database marketing efforts was the effort the company made to disguise the detailed knowledge it had of consumers by embedding baby-related advertising appeals amongst other non-related ads (Duhigg 2012). The marketing goal was to turn the details of consumers' own behavior back upon them in order to change their behavior, but to do so in ways that were opaque – in part to preserve the predictive power of the data (once people detect the strategies of influence being directed toward them, the power of the influence is affected). The ability of Target to know more about the bodily state of a consumer than her own family is a harbinger of things to come. As marketers like to put it, "Advanced analytics helps retailers know what their customers want to buy before the customers do" (ENP Newswire 2012).

4.3.5   All Information Is Relevant

Because predictive analytics is, as it were, model-agnostic, it does not rule out in advance the relevance of any kind of information. The result is that monitoring in the era of big data ranges across the complete spectrum of available information about the activities of humans and their environment. The proliferation of interactive applications and services doubles as a means of expanding the available range of data collection. When a company like Google, for example, offers a new range of online services, it is also creating a new category of data collection. When it stores your documents, it also learns about the ways in which you use them; when it provides email, it also learns about the details of the content of your messages and your communication patterns; when it provides you with online videos, it learns about your viewing habits and preferences, and on and on. All aspects of life that can be captured within interactive environments enter into the database – with their potential relevance to be determined by their contribution to robust patterns of correlation. The appetite of the database is, for the foreseeable future, insatiable, and there are no logical limits to the expansion of data collection for purposes ranging from marketing to health care to policing and security.

4.3.6 Privacy Is Irrelevant

Any attempt to build a protective bulwark against big data surveillance on the foundation of privacy must confront the fact that much of the tracking is anonymous. Data miners are not interested in the details of particular individuals so much as in the way these individuals fit into patterns of correlation. In some cases data patterns are linked to particular individuals even if these people are not identified. Determining, for example whether past behavior of some kind correlates with a subsequent event – going on a trip to France or becoming pregnant – requires the ability to track an individual over time. However, determining whether a pattern of online comments correlates with, say, the electoral success of a particular party or a fluctuation in the stock market need not require identifying who made the comments. Some forms of monitoring require that a particular individual be tracked in ways that can easily lead to identification, but others need only rely on "scraping" anonymous data off the internet. At the same time, much of the data that is personally identifiable is not generally considered particularly sensitive, in part because we are not yet cognizant of how it can be used. That is to say, its collection may not feel like the kind of intrusion that we associate with an invasion of privacy. For example, we may not think of our patterns of consumption or our movements throughout the day as intimate affairs to be protected by a veil of privacy. After all, they are often publicly visible, but they can nevertheless be used to influence us in unanticipated and unobtrusive ways. The invocation of traditional conceptions of privacy misses its mark in such cases.

Furthermore, just as database monitoring focuses on the population and not on targeted individuals, the results it yields are probabilistic. That is to say, mining big data does not provide any definite answers about what particular individuals will do or how they will react. Rather, it provides probabilities about what someone in a particular category is likely to do. As one data miner put it, "I can't tell you what one shopper is going to do, but I can tell you with 90 % accuracy what one shopper is going to do if he or she looks exactly like one million other shoppers" (Nolan 2012). Such strategies allow for aggregate rather than individualized prediction. Decision making based on these strategies, then, lumps together particular individuals into probability categories: someone who is not ever going to miss a credit card payment might be denied credit because 90 % of those who share similar characteristics are considered to be high-risk consumers. The goal of data mining is to gain enough information to increase the probability of a correct prediction, but the endpoint of perfect predictability is simply not obtainable in a probabilistic approach.

Consider the example of the Heritage Health Prize, a crowd-sourcing competition offering a grand prize of $3 million to whoever can develop an algorithm to most accurately predict whether and how long people will be hospitalized within a year based on their medical histories. Hosted by Kaggle, a company that specializes in crowd sourcing predictive modeling (their motto is "We make data science a sport"), the contest supplies contestants with anonymized data from past patients (Geron 2011). The winning algorithm is intended to be used as a means of deterring costly medical treatment by intervening early – but it has other potential applications as well, especially for a private health care provider interested in screening health insurance applicants to avoid costly payouts. It is possible, then, that someone might find themselves subjected to medical intervention – or, perhaps, denied coverage – based on anonymous data about other people. As Bogard (1996) puts it, "Oftentimes to be effective, these technologies do not have to be intrusive at all (even though in many cases they justify or enable intrusion, and on a massive scale)" (p. 132). At some point, data about particular individuals must be linked to such correlations, but the correlations themselves can be generated without offending traditional conceptions of privacy.

4.4   Ethics of Big Data Surveillance

Any attempt to address the social issues raised by the monitoring and tracking associated with increasingly ubiquitous forms of interactivity needs to come to terms with the ways in which big data changes the surveillance landscape and allows service providers to modulate the information environment to which users are exposed. In particular big data surveillance pushes in the direction of population-level modeling. As the shift is made to correlation and prediction, the goal, inevitably, will be to gather broad-spectrum data at the population level: as much information about as many people as possible. The ability to monitor, in itself, does not necessarily provide those who gather data with power over those from whom it is collected. But to the extent that this information can be used to manipulate or sort individuals and to shape the information that is available to them, data becomes a form of power. In this context we might identify two areas of potential ethical concern: level of influence and social sorting. The latter tends to get a bit more attention than the former (see, in particular Lyon 2002; Gandy 1993), but the two are closely inter-related. Sorting is what happens when, for example, credit card companies cut lending limits because clients enter a category of perceived risk, or when applications for private health insurance are turned down because of information collected online about someone's sudden and urgent interest in a costly ailment. Thanks to the opacity of the algorithm, the reasons for particular types of sorting are rarely made clear to those who are subjected to it – and in some cases they may not be entirely clear to those who do the algorithm's bidding.

Data mining as a form of influence or manipulation takes place when information is used to modulate someone's information environment in order to channel their behavior in accordance with imperatives that are not their own. It is somewhat misleading to narrow this category down to the standard example of targeted or customized advertising: We are entering a world in which the searches we perform online, the information we are shown about our friends, family, and acquaintances, and the world we see around us will be designed in increasingly sophisticated ways to influence our behavior and responses. In his book, *The Filter Bubble* (2011), Eli Pariser describes a world in which the information made available to consumers by powerful new information and communication technologies will be filtered so as to promote consumerism (as opposed to, say, citizenship). Rather than exposing us to the wide range of viewpoints that characterize a vibrant democratic culture our information filters will increasingly show us the information that is most likely (according to market research) to create a positive association with accompanying advertising and to keep users coming back for more. As we increasingly rely on interactive digital platforms to conduct our social, political, family, and professional lives, we will find these imperatives baked into the very media we use for communicating with one another and informing ourselves – not always in clearly identifiable ways. When we browse through results for search terms we do not see what the algorithm has decided to exclude from our results – nor do we know why these have been ranked as they have. The information environment is a constructed one, but the rationale for this construction remains inaccessible to users. Much is taking place behind the interface that influences what we will see and hear, what we will know, and how we communicate.

Commercial interests have long played a role in the way our information landscape is shaped – but as our interactions and communications migrate into the realm of interactive media, this role becomes increasingly comprehensive and pervasive. At the same time, the asymmetry between what we know about the technologies that surround us and what they know about us increases dramatically. In this context, it is not clear that privacy either disappears (there is something deeply, inscrutably private about the content of the database and the machinations of the algorithm) or provides a useful basis for resistance.

When we talk about practices of sorting and influence, we are talking about the workings of power and the need to set limits on its operation. These limits would come in response to the threat posed by database power to democratic life, to personal autonomy, and to social justice. The comprehensive warping of the information environment in accordance with commercial imperatives threatens the promise of the Internet to serve as the most effective tool in history for creating an informed populace. The use of controlled experimentation and data mining to determine how best to influence the behavior of consumers poses a threat to autonomy.

Such forms of influence go far beyond the associational image-based advertising of the twentieth century by trading upon detailed information about consumers' social, personal, and professional lives, about their psychological and emotional states, and even, eventually, about their genetic makeup. Finally, the use of predictive analytics to exclude some and include others (for loans, health insurance, jobs, housing, educational opportunities, and so on) based on probabilistic outcomes poses a threat to conceptions of social justice. Various forms of redlining have long been used to discriminate against potential customers and job applicants based on demographic data, but the development of ever more detailed forms of data collection and mining renders the sorting mechanisms both more sophisticated and more opaque. In the future, it will likely be very difficult to determine what combination of demographic, psychographic, behavioral, genetic, or sociographic data has been used to discriminate against someone seeking a job, an apartment, or a loan.

Just as, over time, societies have developed legal structures for limiting the role played by power in economic and political relationships, it is time to update the regulatory infrastructure to account for power relations in the era of big data and ubiquitous interactivity (see, for example, Marchant et al. 2011). Just as it is illegal to use brute force to influence people in most non-criminal contexts, it is worth considering the limits that we want to set on the use of large quantities of data and covert ongoing controlled experimentation to manipulate and sort them. The market is unlikely to provide solutions to these issues absent regulatory incentive because data mining lies at the heart of the commercial model for the digital era and because much of the activity that takes place behind the interface is non-transparent to users.

To recap, we are entering an era in which ubiquitous access to information resources goes hand-in-hand with increasingly broad and deep – that is, pervasive – forms of monitoring, data-collection, and surveillance. New forms of data collection and management promise powerful benefits in a range of realms from security to commerce, urban planning, and health care.[3] But these benefits come with some potential costs, including the creation of vast, omnivorous, and costly databases concentrated in the hands of large institutional actors, both public and private. Such databases usher in the era of "big data" surveillance, the shift from targeted to population-level monitoring, and the displacement of explanation and comprehension by correlation and prediction. Thus, the ubiquity of computing goes hand-in-hand with that of monitoring and surveillance, and the task we face is that of developing a vocabulary of concepts adequate to the changing information landscape and the issues that emerge against its background. Never in the history of human society have we faced the prospect of having all of our actions, movements, and communications not simply monitored, but also recorded, stored, and sorted by systems whose abilities to process large amounts of data far surpass that of any individual or group of individuals. The technology is moving much faster than the social norms that might regulate and shape its use.

Whether or not it will be possible to catch up and implement meaningful regulation that keeps pace with developing technological capacities and the practices they support remains an open question. For the time being, however, it is worth considering underlying principles that might guide such regulation. Based on preliminary research I have conducted in Australia on public attitudes toward the collection and use of personal information I propose the following principles as potential starting points:

1. Addressing asymmetries in information collection: Commercial entities should be required to engage in full disclosure regarding the amount and type of data collected about users. All users should be able to receive a copy of all data stored about them. Law enforcement should be held to the same standards, with a time-lag to protect ongoing investigations.

---

[3] For more on health care and PICT, see Chaps. 2, 6, and 7 in this book.

2. Limits on "function creep," including the repurposing of transactionally generated data for new forms of data mining and targeting: One of the practices to which people object most strenuously is the re-use of their personal data for a range of purposes other than those for which it was originally collected. Restrictions on function creep would likely entail the deletion of certain types of tracking and transactional data at regular intervals. All forms of data not needed for archival and record-keeping purposes might be provided with a built-in expiration date.
3. The ability to opt out of tracking: All commercial interactive services and platforms should provide a no-track option – including an option that covers third-party ad servers and data collectors.
4. Accountability-in-sorting provisions: When decisions are made about access to goods and services based on data mining and predictive analytics, consumers should have the right to have those decisions explained and the relevant data verified.

Such provisions fail to get at the larger issue, which has to do with the commercial model that structures the online economy and the forms of information provision and communication it supports. This issue might be addressed through the promotion of non-commercial, independent, and publicly supported alternatives to existing online utilities and services (blogging, email, social networking, mapping, and so on). Public, non-profit alternatives would make it possible to provide access points to the digital information world structured by priorities other than marketing and consumption. Search engines and social networking utilities could be developed to structure the information environment to promote civic knowledge and foster democratic deliberation and participation. The fact that these proposals sound somewhat far-fetched bears testimony to the limitations that have already been imposed on the potential of networked digital communication technologies by their wholesale commercialization. It is nevertheless tempting to imagine that the capabilities of digital media far outstrip the commercial models that attempt to contain and control them – that we might shape the technologies in accordance with democratic goals rather than relinquishing them to the not-so-tender mercies of commerce.

References

Anderson, C. 2008. The end of theory: The data deluge makes the scientific method obsolete. *Wired Magazine* 16:07, 23 June: http://www.wired.com/science/discoveries/magazine/16-07/pb_theory. Accessed 12 Mar 2012.

Associated Press. 2003. Bets off on terror futures index, July 29. http://www.wired.com/news/politics/0,1283,59813,00.html. Accessed 28 Dec 2005.

Ayres, Ian. 2007. *Super crunchers: How anything can be predicted*. London: John Murray.

Baudrillard, J. 1994. *Simulacra and simulation*. Ann Arbor: University of Michigan Press.

Bilton, N. 2012. A rose-colored view may come standard. *The New York Times*, April 4. http://www.nytimes.com/2012/04/05/technology/google-offers-look-at-internet-connected-glasses.html. Accessed online 10 Apr 2012.

Bogard, W. 1996. *The simulation of surveillance: Hypercontrol in telematic societies.* Cambridge: Cambridge University Press.

Bogard, W. 2006. Welcome to the society of control. In *The new politics of surveillance and visibility*, ed. R. Ericson, 57–68. Toronto: University of Toronto Press.

Burton, G. 2012. Draft communications data bill "more far-reaching than first thought." Computing.co.uk, July 20. http://www.computing.co.uk/ctg/news/2193180/draft-communications-data-bill-more-farreaching-than-first-thought.

Business Wire. 2012. Adobe digital marketing suite tackles big data with predictive marketing. Press Release, March 21.

Duhigg, C. 2012. How companies learn your secrets. *The New York Times*, February 16. http://www.nytimes.com/2012/02/19/magazine/shopping-habits.html. Accessed 12 Apr 2012.

ENP Newswire (2012). Scala introduces advanced analytics. *Press Release*, March 7.

Gandy, G. 1993. *The panoptic sort: A political economy of personal information.* Boulder: Westview.

Geron, T. 2011. Kaggle's predictive data contest aims to fix health care. *Forbes*, April 4. http://www.forbes.com/sites/tomiogeron/2011/04/04/kaggles-predictive-data-contest-aims-to-fix-health-care/. Accessed 12 Apr 2012.

Gladwell, M. 1996. The science of shopping. *The New Yorker*, November 4. http://www.gladwell.com/1996/1996_11_04_a_shopping.htm. Accessed online 12 Apr 2012.

Hamilton, B. 2011. Misfortune telling – Can the NYPD predict a crime before it happens? A tech guru thinks so. *New York Post*, April 17, 25.

Lyon, D. (ed.). 2002. *Surveillance as social sorting: Privacy, risk and automated discrimination.* New York: Routledge.

Marchant, G.E., R. Braden Allenby, and Joseph R. Herkert (eds.). 2011. *The growing gap between emerging technologies and legal-ethical framework: The pacing problem.* Dordrecht/New York: Springer.

Mulholland, H. and R. Booth. 2012. Plans for greater email and web monitoring powers spark privacy fears. *The Guardian* (London), April 2. http://www.guardian.co.uk/world/2012/apr/02/email-web-monitoring-powers-privacy. Accessed online Apr 10.

Nolan, R. 2012. Behind the cover story: How much does target know? *The New York Times*, February 21. http://6thfloor.blogs.nytimes.com/2012/02/21/behind-the-cover-story-how-much-does-target-know/. Accessed 12 Apr 2012.

Pariser, E. 2011. *The filter bubble: What the internet is hiding from you.* New York: Penguin.

Turow, Joseph. 2006. *Niche envy: Marketing discrimination in the digital age.* Cambridge: The MIT Press.

Wieser, M. 1991. The computer for the 21st century. *Scientific American* 265(3): 94–104.

Chapter 5
We Know Where You Are. And We're More and More Sure What That Means

Francis Harvey

5.1 Introduction

A recent article in *The New York Times* (Duhigg 2012) provides an insightful analysis into the potential of online data collection, data collected in stores, location data, and analytically-determined information about individuals. The article describes how women making online and store purchases from a list of items associated with the onset of a pregnancy were identified and targeted with advertisements for pregnancy and infant products. The targeted advertisements could even arrive before others knew about the pregnancy. For example, a father wrote the company involved complaining about the insult to his teenage daughter who had received these advertisements, but then had to retract when his daughter acknowledged her pregnancy. While there are many privacy and surveillance issues associated with this and similar examples of the collection of personal information (Acohido 2011; Bell 2011; Burmeister 2009; Elwood and Leszczynski 2011; Pogue 2011; Shilton 2009), this chapter considers geographical questions related to determining where an individual is, what can be done with information recorded at different locations, and how this information can be related to individual activities and behaviors. Wide-scale tracking of individual activities and long-term data storage are key parts of an infrastructure that make the pregnancy example possible: Without them, analysis of the relationships between activities, such as purchasing certain items in particular time frame, and locations cannot be used to connect otherwise disparate pieces of information.

Pervasive information technology is crucial to this type of consumer surveillance. This chapter considers the important geographical dimensions of constant data collection, particularly how ubiquitous tracking and long-term data storage of location

F. Harvey, Ph.D. (✉)
Department of Geography, University of Minnesota, Minneapolis, MN, USA
e-mail: fharvey@umn.edu

K.D. Pimple (ed.), *Emerging Pervasive Information and Communication Technologies*
(PICT), Law, Governance and Technology Series 11, DOI 10.1007/978-94-007-6833-8_5,
© Springer Science+Business Media Dordrecht 2014

data reveal penetrating information about individual activities and behaviors. But first to a possible rejoinder: If, in the information age, distance is dead (Cairncross 2001), why is geography relevant? Regardless of the ease with which we now send materials around the world in seconds, or converse with family or colleagues residing in multiple countries, the location and the relations among activities, things, and people associated with a location still matter.

In spite of common school-age preconceptions and popular geography games based on rote memorization of states, countries, and their capitals, geography now emphasizes understanding relationships and interactions (Massey 2005; Sheppard and McMaster 2004; Smith 2004; Sui 2004). Although knowing where things are remains an aspect of geography, the main intellectual emphasis of the discipline today has shifted to a consideration of spatial relationships.

The recent "spatial turn" of a broad range of fields in the sciences and humanities, including fields as diverse as cognitive science and history, may seem novel, but the analysis and study of locations and relations has always been, in fact, a central component of the discipline. Briefly, classical western geography, from Ptolemy and Varenius on, has connected the locations of countries, cities, rivers, lakes, and other political and natural features through their relationships (Livingstone 1992), e.g., "Athens is on the peninsula of Attica in the Mediterranean Sea between Mount Aegaleo and Mount Hymettus". The description of relationships and locations remains a key emphasis in the geography of exploration. In the seventeenth century, Berhnard Varenius described the coast of Eastern Africa and the Arabian peninsula in terms of connections from one geographic feature to another – much like a sailor following the coasts would make use of such features – but following scientific principles of the time and offering a comparative geographical analysis that was the inspiration for Alexander von Humboldt and other geographers. Later, influenced by colonization and German idealism, including contributions from Kant, von Humboldt and others developed geographical enquiry to support the nascent nation states and projects of conquest and subjugation while moving between cosmological and practical geographical questions.

Reflecting these disciplinary developments, most geographical topics taught in elementary and secondary schools in the U.S. continue to emphasize geography's contribution to learning about where things are in the world and how they relate to learn their organization: rogue nations and allies, homeland and foreign, western allies and eastern bloc. During the last 200 years, colonization and imperialism influenced the inclusion of certain subjects and exclusion of others in the educational systems of modern states, leading to a constrained role for geography supporting the state and the commerce of its industry and businesses. Although the role of geography for state's purposes continues to be strong, in the late twentieth century geography began to return to scientific and comparative approaches to understand disparate social and economic developments (Massey 2005; Sheppard and McMaster 2004). Geography, and the related field of cartography, have a long history of studying geographical relationships.

Physical relationships still define issues in the movement of physical items, but understanding a key dimension in the development of the information society – the apparent transcendence of physical distance in most human communication (Castells 2000; McLuhan and Powers 1989) – requires considering how virtual relations increasingly mediate our interactions. These relations leave a trail of data, and while physical distance barely matters in the topological network of the Internet, physical distance continues to have considerable impact. Indeed, location remains a crucial factor in most human communication. However, with pervasive computing technology, data can be collected on any and every interaction.

Geographical information technologies provide enhanced surveillance capabilities for recording and analyzing activities. Smartphones are constantly tracked for assuring technical service, but this data can be requested by government authorities or aggregated and later disaggregated. They connect activities, things, and people in a web of relations that can be readily analyzed to reveal highly specific details of our activities and behavior, such as a pregnancy.

Location-based services offer ways to open up new possibilities and augment existing capabilities. The number of these services and technologies is increasing rapidly, with the smartphone becoming the hardware platform of choice. People can use these capabilities in countless ways, including, in the course of one evening: finding a hotel, choosing a restaurant, getting directions to dinner, programming background music to sooth sleep, and, before retiring, check on the family dog back at home. It is the often the unfettered collection of location data that comes with these uses that leads to hitherto unimaginable capability to track individuals and objects 24/7, collect location data, store this data for long periods of time, combine this data with other data sources, and analyze location data. The possibilities are endless and raise concerns.

Isolated data may offer valuable insights, but it is limited to a portion of activities –merely a part of a complex of relations connected to only limited location information. Tracking allows this data to be placed in relation to other activities, things, and locations. Combining data based on location can easily produce a full picture of relations. For example, the analysis by L. Sweeney demonstrated that only ZIP Code (postcode), birth date, and gender were required to uniquely identify 87 % of the US population (Sweeney 2000). This analysis shows that one locational attribute can be combined with one temporal and another physical attribute to yield the very powerful identification of the vast majority of people in the US. Consider what this means: Otherwise unrelated datasets – say databases of Google searches, Netflix viewing, Amazon purchases, and Facebook "likes" – include these three pieces of data, and they can be combined to reveal intimate details and proclivities of millions of identifiable individuals. Large amounts of relatively detailed location information fundamentally change what we can know about each other and the world.

While this capability has been available since the 1970s, it has been limited by the cost and complexities of data collection. It also has been a niche study in the sciences and engineering, although evidence of geospatial statistical analysis has been present for quite some time. Of course, the potential originates with geospatial statistics and the computational support of complex statistical analysis. For instance, in World War II statisticians were able to determine from serial numbers of captured or destroyed German tanks almost the exact volume of production of German

Fig. 5.1 Portion of John Snow's map. The *number of bars* indicate the number of cholera cases associated with an address. Snow determined that the water pump at the corner of Broad and Cambridge was the source of the outbreak (From http://www.csiss.org/classics/content/8)

armor – a number verified after the war. Interestingly, the actual volume turned out to be only 1/5 of the Allied wartime intelligence estimates of production (Davies 2006). Geospatial statistics begins with these techniques, but extends them to take into account principles of geographical relationships. Ninety years before World War II, John Snow, in perhaps the first geospatial analysis, used spatial statistical techniques to analyze the diffusion of a cholera epidemic in 1854 and establish the source of the outbreak (Fig. 5.1).

With huge amounts of data now routinely collected by smartphones, mobile devices, and fixed sensors, the capabilities and surveillance necessary to collect this data has become widely available. The amount and accuracy of location data now collected by digital devices far outstrips the small data sets used 150 and 60 years ago, as well as the less powerful information processing capacities of just 20 years ago. Sweeney's analysis becomes possible due to the digital storage of much larger data sets and the development of automated and semi-automated geospatial analysis techniques. Snow's analysis techniques now enable the identification of disease vectors and the shopping habits of individuals. Beyond studies of economic and cultural relationships, the analysis of geographic relationships is key to understanding the revolution that ubiquitous computing offers for surveillance in the information age. The result is an unparalleled level of private surveillance, providing the detail and breadth of information that make it more and more possible to generate predictive models of behavior and relationships.

5.2   Location Privacy

Location privacy issues connected to PICT are widespread. These concerns are associated with uses of GIS in epidemiology, health care research, and other areas of social science that use demographic data. Data privacy has been an important concern in these areas, and it is helpful to consider distinct phases in working with geographic information (collection, processing and analysis, presentation) and the impacts among these phases. PICT involves these phases, even if they have been largely automated, and, even dealing with streams involving terabytes of data/day, occur instantaneously, for all intents and purposes.

5.2.1   Data Collection

The starting point for all data is, of course, information collection. Sampling bias remains an important concern with sponsored or authoritative data collection, as well as with crowd-sourced data. Sampling bias in research shows up in attribute errors, positional errors, logical inconsistencies, attribute bias, or positional bias. In some cases, the errors are due to calibration errors, or the loss of accuracy. As anyone using a barometer to measure elevation change can testify, a drop in air pressure as a low pressure weather front moves through an area can lead to surprising increases in elevation, even if one is standing still. These errors can occur without notice to most GPS users. More complex error or bias can come through internal sensor failures, or erroneous referencing. Logical consistencies are often related to each other, but frequently come through misuse of measuring devices or misunderstandings. Further complexities and challenges arise through the interpolation of data. Most data is only collected at selected locations and then interpolated for an area. Beyond attribute and positional accuracy issues that can influence interpolation, the results of interpolation are usually not quality-controlled without a cross check against observed values or experts. These problems also apply to aggregations of population data (Rushton et al. 2006).

5.2.2   Data Processing and Analysis

The processing and analysis of data also is open to errors that can lead to incorrect results. The use of inappropriate or invalid techniques can lead to results that seem reasonable, but again, without cross-checking or quality control, are actually wrong. Through news stories, we are familiar with incidents involving entering wrong data. Map makers regularly would produce small errors in out-of-the-way places to allow them to identify copyright violations (Monmonier 1991). Similar issues arise in the processing and analysis of location data, except that the errors originate in misguided analysis. An especially pernicious problem is the reduction in statistical variance and inflated significance that arises when comparing data aggregated for a large area and then applied to smaller areas (Getis 1999; Unwin 1981). Called spatial autocorrelation, this nuanced problem can lead to wildly incorrect conclusions, even though the statistical functions offer support. Bias in data due to aggregation effects and the choice of statistical techniques require cross-checks and verification runs.

5.2.3   Data Presentation

The presentation of location data is especially prone to explicit and implicit errors and errors in judgment that greatly impact the reliability of data. A classical problem is choosing the appropriate projection for a map or image. All projections distort, but it is possible to control the type and amount of distortion in terms of either area or shape. Scale, selection of features, and generalization are common challenges that can seriously impact what is seen. Equally important in thematic maps that show ranges of values are symbolization choices, especially in the selection of class intervals.

A challenge for all publication of personal data remains the possibility of reverse engineering the characteristics of individuals or small groups. Database relational joins can associate data from separate data sets, making it possible to generate associations or use statistical functions to determine probabilities. Map overlays can help develop more specific attribute information by associating the location of attributes from different data sources. Finally, reverse geocoding allows for addresses to be created from geographic locations. In many areas, accurate geographic locations can be readily converted to street address locations for other purposes.

Even though Mark Monmonier warned that "All maps lie" (Monmonier 1991), it is easy to lose sight of the complexities and contingencies associated with location data. Location privacy is tied up with privacy issues in general, and a movement is afoot to recast fundamental themes and attitudes. Recent work that reassesses the evolving concepts of privacy shows a way forward (Duquenoy 2007; Solove 2008; Weiss 2008; Sullivan 2009; Watson et al. 2009; Burmeister 2009; Fischer-Hübner et al. 2011). The underlying challenge for pervasive computing and location information is understanding how to balance opportunities and risks. To understand the potential, geographical concepts in cultural and information geography can be distinguished following Helen Nissenbaum's analysis of privacy in context.

In her work, especially her recent book *Privacy in Context* (2010), Nissenbaum develops a theoretical framework based on a pluralistic concept of privacy. *Privacy in Context* provides an in-depth analysis of privacy that avoids the pitfalls of attempting to create an inclusive and purified concept of privacy. The central idea she advances is that instances of privacy are grounded in contextual integrity. Contextual integrity reflects individually-calibrated systems of social norms, or rules, that "define and sustain essential activities and key relationships and interests, protect people and groups against harm, and balance the distribution of power. Responsive to historical, cultural, and even geographic contingencies, informational norms evolve over time in distinct patterns from society to society" (Nissenbaum 2010, 3). Information technologies that violate contextual integrity lead to privacy anxieties. Computer scientists have adopted this approach to identify variables and their values that in particular contexts would violate a situation's contextual integrity (The Economist 2007).

This pluralistic concept of privacy speaks to the importance of location. Many of Nissenbaum's examples are geographical in nature. For example: Should Google's Street View data include images with identifiable individuals without their permission? Physical location still matters, but many activities are no longer bound to hierarchical scales of institutions, cultures, and norms. We can get step-by-step directions to a museum in Sao Paolo while speaking in real time with a person in London; we can find out precisely where our children are at any time; it makes less and less difference if the person we are calling is on the other side of the globe or city. We can access Street View images from any place in the world no matter where we are. Increasingly pervasive information and communication technologies are in the process of merging physical and virtual interactions in our daily lives.

Following on Nissenbaum's theoretical framework, location privacy has to explicitly consider the role of physical and virtual interactions in different contexts. Contextual location privacy posits a flexible and selectively permeable membrane people maintain to balance private and public spheres of activities. Following the main ideas of contextual privacy, location privacy may become the way people modify the permeability of this figurative membrane between their physical and virtual location based on their desire for sharing information about their whereabouts and locations of activities.

5.3 Much More Than Knowing Where

This section considers the development and important principles of location-based analysis of data associated with pervasive information technology, particularly online and mobile device location data. These are key technologies of ubiquitous surveillance in the information age. Over-arching issues of pervasive information technology surveillance are addressed in Chap. 1 of this book. Consideration of the potentials and challenges of location data and pervasive IT involves engaging recent geographical research and its context. Since World War II, a growing segment of geography research has focused on information technology development and use. Emphasizing quantitative approaches, often simply because they are more amenable to computational representation analysis, but including qualitative aspects, geographical research in this area has advanced ways of understanding location and relationships. In the same time period, researchers in cultural geography have developed qualitative analysis, building on social theoretical frameworks from the twentieth century.

5.3.1 Quantitative Approaches

Reaching back to work by John Snow in the nineteenth century, quantitative approaches have contributed mathematical methods and related theories to study location and relationships. Cartography has played a central role in providing reliable representations for these techniques and supporting government, private, and military adoption. The advent and wide-scale use of computers has allowed spatial analysis to develop in leaps and bounds beyond these roots.

One important reason for these developments is the availability of data. Whereas 200 years ago John Snow had to visit the neighborhood of the cholera outbreak and, through queries, establish its source, with the ascendency of statistics as a key instrument of state control (Kitchin and Dodge 2011; Hannah 2009; Ettlinger 2011; Elden 2010), this information is widely available digitally, in some cases even mapped. To protect privacy, most of this data is now aggregated, which is simply the process of reducing the information content by assigning the information values to a new geographical unit. In the US, census data on households can be aggregated to census blocks and census tracts with around 4,000 people, the lowest census geographic unit. Census tracts are the most common unit for reporting detailed census data because specific information to identify households is indistinguishable from the average tract value. Even then, some data may be withheld to protect privacy. Census tracts only coincidentally share boundaries with zip codes.

Aggregation is not only a technique for increasing anonymity, but a widely-used technique for reducing the values of information to make simpler and more legible representations. It is used for many kinds of demographic data. However, its use can lead to problems if important distinctions in the original data have been abstracted and conclusions are made from the analysis of the aggregated data. Furthermore, employing additional data and advanced statistical techniques, it is possible to reverse-aggregate (or disaggregate). For example, data from a pet store's customer data base could be used to identify pet food shoppers in a particular income range, thereby possibly defeating the anonymization coming through aggregation. The reliability of disaggregation results depends on the additional data and level of aggregation.

Geocoding can be used in conjunction with aggregated data to positively identify individuals (Mazumdar et al. 2008; Rushton et al. 2006). Geocoding is the term used to refer to the transformation of location information, generally street addresses, but zip codes and other enumeration units as well, to geographical coordinates, usually latitude and longitude coordinates. Transforming addresses to geographic location coordinates allows the data to be combined with other data, using operations that combine the data based on location. In this process, it is also possible to use random numbers or reduce the precision of the coordinates to obscure the exact location of geocoded data.

Reverse geocoding, as the name suggests, is the process for transforming coordinate location to readable addresses or place names (Armstrong and Ruggles 2005). It is an important component of the 911-system responses to cell phone emergency calls, allowing abstract location coordinates to be shared and shown as readable addresses or places. The computation of reverse geocoding can be involved, but is widely available. For example a GeoNames web service (http://www.geonames.org/) provides 37 specialized services to determine the location of geographic coordinates by city, nearby streets, postal codes, etc. In the context of surveillance, reverse geocoding is often used with aggregated data to iteratively narrow down the possible spatial range where an individual can be located. A modern-day John Snow may have ready access to aggregations of demographic data, but reverse geocoding can be used to help determine more precise locations.

Spatial analysis provides a cornucopia of transformations and functions for the analysis of geographic information, including aggregation, geocoding, and reverse geocoding. However, determining location remains a research challenge. People often associate places (my office) with locations (its address) and then relate them to other places (my favorite restaurant) and their locations (one block south and two blocks west) with ease, but this is exceedingly difficult to compute reliably with small amounts of data. Other challenges remain and are often the source of significant errors. In particular, the association of the value of aggregated attribute data to all individuals in the area, known as the ecological fallacy (O'Sullivan and Unwin 2003; Longley et al. 1998; Fotheringham et al. 1994), is particularly relevant and pernicious. A deceptive bias can arise when analysts aggregate data to a different enumeration unit and then use this data for statistical analysis (O'Sullivan and Unwin 2003). A common error is to report aggregated data from several neighborhoods as the average for the cumulative error, often ignoring racial or income related differences. Among other challenges are the role of scale in measuring the physical length of objects (Mandelbrot 1983).[1] Almost 50 years ago,

---

[1]Imagine you are trying to measure the length of a coastline using a one-mile-long ruler. Any feature of the coast smaller than a mile is likely to disappear. If you use a one-inch ruler, almost every squiggle of the coast will be included. Say the one-mile ruler yielded a length of 5.2 miles of coastline; the one-inch ruler might well yield something like 1,035,036 in., or 16.33 miles. All of those squiggles add up to make a much longer coastline.

Julian Perkal challenged the widespread view of map measurements as accurate. His MICMOG paper on stream lengths (1956) shows the scale dependency of length measurements. This an issue we can also consider when we work with demographic data using boundaries that follow natural features and when we use aggregated data about individuals.

5.3.2 *Qualitative Approaches*

The roots of qualitative approaches to spatial analysis go back to the philosophical idealism of the late eighteenth and nineteenth centuries. Oversimplified, qualitative approaches break from Aristotelian scholasticist-influenced, hypothetico-deductive approaches. They take up elements of the Marxist corpus, Frankfurt School, and Pragmatism. The very complex, and at times contradictory, approaches of qualitative spatial analysis fit in neatly with Critical Theory's focus on studying the conditions and processes of the emergence of objects of knowledge. In other words, a persistent skepticism about the possibility of knowing reality associated with idealism leads to enquiries into the constitutive elements at particular locations and the relationships that give location meaning. Work by feminist scholars in geography and philosophy has strongly influenced the recent development of these approaches.

Commonly used is an interpretative analysis that focuses on individuals through ethnographic techniques and inductive analysis of individual situations. The work of Mei-Po Kwan and Marianna Pavlovskaya exemplifies this approach to spatial analysis. In her work on gendered space-time activities and transportation (Kwan 1999, 2007), Kwan uses travel diaries to determine the activities of women during the day, analyzing them using quantitative tools to establish patterns and relationships. Interviews guide the interpretation and provide much additional insight supporting the analytical process that identifies spaces of safety and spaces of concern, or even threats. Pavlovskaya uses the interpretative analysis of activities to analyze survival strategies in post-socialist Moscow and spatially analyze how households in a neighborhood meet the challenges (Pavlovskaya 2004).

Qualitative approaches have very frequently been used in conjunction with quantitative approaches. In many cases, qualitative data is transformed into formats suitable for mapping and the resulting visualizations used to show relations. In a growing number of research studies, data collected using qualitative approaches is combined and then analyzed using quantitative techniques. Usually these techniques rely more on network analysis than an analysis of aggregated statistical data, but they can indeed be combined. Knigge and Cope (2006) provide a rich example of the possibilities of using grounded theory to guide the analytical visualization of community interactions. Another example of this approach can be found in work that analyzes residential dynamics (Omer et al. 2010). Other researchers have turned to qualitative approaches to understand how maps are used and made (Suchan and Brewer 2000). Meghan Cope and Sarah Elwood have published an edited volume (Cope and Elwood 2009) that provides a succinct introduction and a diverse range of examples of qualitative approaches, especially the development of mixed methods.

5.3.3 Hybrids of Approaches; Hybrids of Surveillance

These hybrids are particularly significant to consider when using information and communication technologies that are hidden, invisible, or often unnoticed. The benefits of pervasive information and communication technology (PICT) for behavioral research and other fields is very evident. The next section offers some examples from published research and explores potential use of location data collected from PICT. The potential for abuse has been noted by researchers and is the focus of the following section of this chapter. As PICT seems to involve no systematic quality control, chances are that errors abound as frequently as with crowd-sourced data.

5.4 The Hybrids of Surveillance

The data collected under statutory requirement or administrative procedure is a critical component of state programs (Liptak 2011; National Research Council (US). Panel on Confidentiality Issues Arising from the Integration of Remotely Sensed Self-Identifying Data 2007). For all the critiques of these programs, they have developed reliable principles to protect privacy. Hybrid approaches that rely on PICT, however, go largely without accepted principles to guide the collection, use, and storage of personal data. In considering some examples of hybrid data collection and analysis this section aims to point out the potential uses and abuses. The first two examples come from published academic research and provide evidence of the need for guidelines for protecting human subjects, and consider known applications. The final two examples consider research that articulates the changing meaning of location and the relationships revealed by pervasive information technology.

5.4.1 Behavioral Changes in a Minority Group

In the first example, I consider the abilities of locational data collection to provide unique insight into behavioral changes in a minority group. The researcher, Mei-Po Kwan, uses location technologies to look at the response of Muslim American women to 9/11 and develop a counter-narrative to dominant images of repressive and violent Muslim culture to show the impact of fear on their daily lives (Kwan 2007). The study involved 37 Muslim women in Columbus, Ohio. Oral histories were collected and sketch maps created to show areas the women considered unsafe before and compare them with areas they considered unsafe after 9/11. One Muslim woman's oral history supports the construction of a GIS-based visual narrative. The visual narrative shows the spatial story of how, immediately after 9/11, this woman remained at home almost all the time for several weeks out of fear. As her fear abated and community activities resumed, the range of her daily activities gradually increased. Although pointing to the ability of location technology to expand understanding of minority groups, the example also demonstrates its potential to reveal details about individual behavior through analytically or visually examining specific locations and relationships that otherwise may have remained unknown.

5.4.2   Locational Data and Personal Information

These issues are at the center of a report from the National Research Council (2007). The report points to the challenges that arise when locational information is linked to personal information (see Chaps. 2, 6, and 8 in this volume for additional related discussion). While these capabilities make new types of social science research possible, adding locational information also makes it possible to reverse-engineer identities. This not only violates the assertion of confidence in the protection of anonymity, but opens up the door to associating additional information with the individual. The ethical and legal issues remain slippery, and the report offers cautious guidance and a proposal for further research to determine what levels of location and personal information produce unacceptable risks to the protection of confidentiality.

The Electronic Freedom Foundation and others would readily claim that the train has already left the station, and the unregulated world of personal data collection and re-use has already advanced to a point where many individual behaviors are known and predictable. Location is seen as key information needed for associating behaviors and other factors with individuals. Since the use of computers has become widespread in marketing, commercial entities have steadily been developing data collection techniques to associate location with behavior, especially for consumer-related activities and characteristics. Micro-scale marketing analysis in the 1980s and 1990s enabled ZIP Code (postcode) level identification of consumer types (Goss 1995). Small-scale marketing analysis provides means to describe behaviors of individuals and households. The increase in the geographic resolution of this analysis is mainly due to the enhanced collection of data on individuals. Advances in analytical capabilities play a far lesser role, but are crucial for making sense out of the ever-growing mountains of data.

The types of analysis that are now possible have been covered in a variety of venues. An eye-opening investigative article (Duhigg 2012) provides a great deal of insight into how in-store surveillance is currently used with other data collected in shopping transactions to analyze shoppers' activities, develop models, and then contact individuals directly with marketing materials aimed to increase their purchasing.

5.4.3   RFID Surveillance

That industry has already begun to understand that the possibilities of further enhanced surveillance and data collection have raised the concerns of citizen groups. Katherine Albrecht and Liz McIntyre in their book *Spychips: How Major Corporations and Government Plan to Track Your Every Purchase and Watch Your Every Move* (2006) highlight the potential of widespread use of Radio Frequency ID tags (RFID). Companies praise the tags for improving the ease of managing inventory, while their marketers suggest the tags will improve availability of products, ease consumer negotiation of the complex market place, and remove the onerous check-out till. Albrecht and McIntyre report on many of the less scrupulous industry activities, including: following shoppers to record car license plate numbers, scanning garbage and analyzing rates of product use, and connecting wireless RFID toll road passes with travel behavior, including visits to stores.

5.4.4   Geoslavery

Pervasive information technology is essential to assuring that visions of ubiquitous computing become reality. For many, cell (mobile) phones are the key technology, and certainly the bridge technology until comprehensive sensor and monitor networks can be implemented. Of the many writers who consider the surveillance potential and privacy challenges of mobile devices, Jerome Dobson and Pete Fisher have written the most poignant review of pervasive location monitoring. In an article published in 2003, Dobson and Fisher refer to the real potential that mobile phone tracking can be used to create Geoslavery – persistent monitoring that leads to control (Dobson and Fisher 2003). This is not control in the physical sense, but rather control in the sense of Orwell's *1984*, wherein surveillance plays on an individual's fear of being 'out of place.' Risk and fear make it possible to regulate how and where an individual moves in the real world.

5.5   Conclusion

In summary, I have focused on existing technologies, analysis techniques, and nascent technologies. To complete the consideration and raise an issue that may likely become more relevant in the coming years, I should mention unmanned aerial vehicles (UAVs), which are becoming increasingly common platforms for surveillance. Functional UAVs are available for less than 1000 USD. They are very limited, but quite capable of overflying an event, such as a gathering or party, carrying a small sensor that can record visual images. Larger, more capable UAVs can carry larger and more sensors and stay aloft for longer period of time. While their use is likely to remain limited at first, local governments are gearing up for more wide-scale usage (Electronic Privacy Information Center 2013). For now, regulation of airspace sharply limits their use.

Regardless of the technology, PICT is and will continue to be an ever more widely used means to collect data with location characteristics. Given the breadth the depth of this data collection, regaining control of privacy will remain a very challenging issue (see Chap. 2 for relevant discussion of GPS-related issues). The Electronic Frontier Foundation also provides more practical information on location privacy issues and ways to minimize tracking. Proposals for the implementation of a "Do-Not-Track" opt-in provision can offer a way for individuals to at least minimize further location data collection.

As other authors in this book suggest, information and communication technologies that are hidden, invisible, or often unnoticed are already common and will continue to proliferate. Knowing where individuals are, tracking them, and analyzing relationships associated with location will undoubtedly become more commonplace. The Geoslavery concept points to a central risk of these developments that perhaps may outstrip the benefits. Sensors intended for inventory control, identification, and system monitoring are being released into the 'wild,' where a multitude of unintended consequences awaits. This development signals a new era in which people no longer understand or control the on/off switch, and location awareness moves into uncontrolled forms of 24/7 tracking.

Faced with dystopian perspectives, and perhaps naively, the proponents of mobile technology and commercial surveillance seem to deny the issues raised by GeoSlavery. Or perhaps the communities involved with these technologies will be blissfully unaware that they are lost, just as drivers who unquestioningly follow routes generated by satellite navigation systems. Indeed, perhaps, our concepts of location privacy can develop to a point to allow us to distinguish between problematic re-use of location data (aggregating data on our application use to other data about our preferences) from benefits we immediately have (finding a good restaurant) and possible benefits we stand to enjoy (finding good restaurants we like in the future).

PICT involves constant interfaces among people and ICT – pervasive indications of the growing ubiquity of ICT in our interactions. The concepts of location-based analysis of data associated with pervasive information technology, particularly online and mobile device location data, are key technologies of constant surveillance in the information age. The assembling of data about where things happen and the analysis that helps construct relations into constantly available infrastructures greatly enhances the ability to take information about where we are and have been and assess what that means.

Acknowledgments I would like to acknowledge the help of R. Ruffenach in the preparation of the final chapter text.

References

Acohido, Byron. 2011. Privacy implications of ubiquitous digital sensors. *USA Today*, January 26, 2011, P1B.

Albrecht, Katherine, and Liz McIntyre. 2006. *Spychips: How major corporations and government plan to track your every purchase and watch your every move*. New York City: Plume Books.

Armstrong, M.P., and A.J. Ruggles. 2005. Geographic information technologies and personal privacy. *Cartographica: The International Journal for Geographic Information and Geovisualization* 40(4): 63–73.

Bell, Killian. 2011. *27,000 users sue Apple for $25 million over locationgate*. http://www.cultofmac.com/109211/27000-users-sue-apple-for-25-million-over-locationgate/. Accessed 1 Dec 2011.

Cairncross, F. 2001. *The death of distance: How the communications revolution is changing our lives*. Cambridge: Harvard Business Press.

Castells, Manuel. 2000. *The rise of the network society*, 2nd ed. Oxford/Malden: Blackwell.

Cope, Meghan, and Sarah Elwood. 2009. *Qualitative Gis: A mixed-methods approach*. Los Angeles: Sage.

Davies, Gavyn. 2006. Gavyn Davies does the maths. *The Guardian*, July 19, 2006. http://www.guardian.co.uk/world/2006/jul/20/secondworldwar.tvandradio. Accessed 27 May 2013.

Dobson, Jerome E., and Peter F. Fisher. 2003. Geoslavery. *IEEE Technology and Society Magazine* 22(1): 47–52.

Duhigg, Charles. 2012. How companies learn your secrets. *The New York Times*, February 13. http://www.nytimes.com/2012/02/19/magazine/shopping-habits.html. Accessed 31 May 2013.

Duquenoy, P. 2007. The information society: What next? *The information society: Innovation, legitimacy, ethics and democracy in honor of professor Jacques Berleur sj*, 263–68.

Duquenoy, Penny, and Oliver K. Burmeister. 2009. Ethical issues and pervasive computing. In *Risk assessment and management in pervasive computing*, ed. Penny Duquenoy and Oliver K. Burmeister. Hershey: Information Science Reference.

Elden, Stuart. 2010. Land, terrain, territory. *Progress in Human Geography* 34: 799–98.

Electronic Privacy Information Center. 2013. *Domestic Unmanned Aerial Vehicles (UAVs) and Drones*. http://epic.org/privacy/drones/. Accessed 23 Apr 2012.

Elwood, Sarah, and Agnieszka Leszczynski. 2011. Privacy, reconsidered: New representations, data practices, and the geoweb. *GeoJournal* 42(1): 6–15.

Ettlinger, Nancy. 2011. Governmentality as epistemology. *Annals of the Association of American Geographers* 101(3): 537–560.

Fischer-Hübner, S., P. Duquenoy, and M. Hansen. 2011. *Privacy and identity management for life*. Berlin: Springer.

Fotheringham, Stewart, Peter Rogerson, Donna J. Peuquet, and Duane F. Marble (eds.). 1994. *Spatial analysis and Gis. Technical issues in geographic information systems*. Bristol: Taylor & Francis.

Getis, Art. 1999. Spatial statistics. In *Geographical information systems*, ed. P.A. Longley, M.F. Goodchild, D.J. Maquire, and D.W. Rhind. New York: Wiley.

Goss, Jon. 1995. Marketing the new marketing: The strategic discourse of geodemographic information systems. In *Ground truth: The social implications of geographic information systems*, ed. J. Pickles. New York City: The Guilford Press.

Hannah, Matthew G. 2009. Calculable territory and the west German census boycott movements of the 1980s. *Political Geography* 28: 66–75.

Kitchin, R., and M. Dodge. 2011. *Code/space: Software and everyday life*. Cambridge: MIT Press.

Knigge, L., and M. Cope. 2006. Grounded visualization: Integrating the analysis of qualitative and quantitative data through grounded theory and visualization. *Environment and Planning A*38(11): 2021.

Kwan, Mei-Po. 1999. Gender, the home-work link, and space-time patterns of nonemployment activities. *Economic Geography* 75: 370–394.

Kwan, Mei-Po. 2007. Affecting geospatial technologies: Toward a feminist politics of emotion. *The Professional Geographer* 59(1): 22–34.

Liptak, Adam. 2011. Court case asks if 'Big Brother' is spelled GPS. *The New York Times*, September 8. http://www.nytimes.com/2011/09/11/us/11gps.html. Accessed 31 May 2013.

Livingstone, David N. 1992. *The geographical tradition*. Oxford: Blackwell.

Longley, Paul A., Sue M. Brooks, Rachel McDonnell, and Bill MacMillan (eds.). 1998. *Geocomputation: A primer*. New York: Wiley.

Mandelbrot, B.B. 1983. *The fractal geometry of nature*. New York City: Wh. Freeman.

Massey, Doreen. 2005. *For space*. Thousand Oaks: Sage Press.

Mazumdar, S., G. Rushton, B.J. Smith, D.L. Zimmerman, and K.J. Donham. 2008. Geocoding accuracy and the recovery of relationships between environmental exposures and health. *International Journal of Health Geographics* 7(1): 13.

McLuhan, Marshall, and Bruce R. Powers. 1989. *The global village: Transformations in world life and media in the 21st century*, Communication and society. Oxford: Oxford University Press.

Monmonier, Mark. 1991. *How to lie with maps*. Chicago: University of Chicago Press.

National Research Council (US). Panel on Confidentiality Issues Arising from the Integration of Remotely Sensed Self-Identifying Data. 2007. *Putting people on the map: Protecting confidentiality with linked social-spatial data*. Washington, DC: National Academy Press.

Nissenbaum, Helen. 2010. *Privacy in context: Technology, policy, and the integrity of social life*. Stanford: Stanford University Press.

O'Sullivan, David, and David J. Unwin. 2003. *Geographic information analysis*. New York: Wiley.

Omer, I., P. Bak, and T. Schreck. 2010. Using space–time visual analytic methods for exploring the dynamics of ethnic groups' residential patterns. *International Journal of Geographical Information Science* 24(10): 1481–1496.

Pavlovskaya, M. 2004. Other transitions: Multiple economies of Moscow households in the 1990s. *Annals of the Association of American Geographers* 94(2): 329–351.

Perkal, J. 1956. On epsilon length. *Bulletin de l'Academie Polonaise des Sciences* 4: 399–403.

Pogue, David. 2011. *Wrapping up the apple location Brouhaha*. http://pogue.blogs.nytimes.com/2011/04/28/wrapping-up-the-apple-location-brouhaha/. Accessed 26 Aug 2011.

Rushton, Gerard, Marc P. Armstrong, Josephine Gittler, Barry R. Greene, Claire E. Pavlik, Michele M. West, and Dale L. Zimmerman. 2006. Geocoding in cancer research, a review. *American Journal of Preventive Medicine* 30(25): 516–524.

Sheppard, Eric, and Robert B. McMaster (eds.). 2004. *Scale and geographic inquiry: Nature, society, and methods*. New York: Blackwell.

Shilton, Katie. 2009. Four billion little brothers. Privacy, mobile phones, and ubiquitous data collection. *Communications of the ACM* 52(11): 48–53.

Smith, Neil. 2004. Scale Bending. In *Scale and geographic inquiry: Nature, society, and methods*, ed. Eric Sheppard and Robert B. McMaster. New York: Blackwell.

Solove, D.J. 2008. The end of privacy? *Scientific American* 299(3): 100.

Suchan, Trudi, and Cynthia A. Brewer. 2000. Qualitative methods for research on mapmaking and map use. *Professional Geography* 52(1): 145–154.

Sui, Daniel Z. 2004. GIS, cartography, and the "third culture": Geographic imaginations in the computer age. *The Professional Geographer* 56(1): 62–72.

Sullivan, C. 2009. Digital identity – the legal person? *Computer Law and Security Review* 25(3): 227–236.

Sweeney, Laura. 2000. *Uniqueness of simple demographics in the U.S. population: Laboratory for international data privacy working paper*, LIDAP-WP4. Pittsburgh: Laboratory for International Data Privacy, Carnegie Mellon University.

2007. The logic of privacy. *The Economist*, January 4. http://www.economist.com/node/8486072. Accessed 13 Dec 2011.

Unwin, David. 1981. *Introductory spatial analysis*. London: Methuen.

Watson, P.G., P. Duquenoy, M. Brennan, M. Jones, and J. Walkerdine. 2009. *Towards an ethical interaction design: The issue of including stakeholders in law-enforcement software development*. Paper read at Proceedings of the 21st annual conference of the Australian computer-human interaction special interest group: Design: Open 24/7, Melbourne.

Weiss, S. 2008. The need for a paradigm shift in addressing privacy risks in social networking applications. *The Future of Identity in the Information Society* 262: 161–171.

Chapter 6
Preserving Life, Destroying Privacy: PICT and the Elderly

Cynthia M. Jones

6.1 Introduction

Without doubt, technology has substantially increased both the length and the quality of human life in the last century, but our reliance upon technology is greater than ever and growing by the day. As the Baby Boomers age, a substantial proportion of Americans and Europeans will be increasingly reliant upon technology. As their health declines and their ability to live on their own decreases, they will be prime candidates for assistive technology and pervasive information and communication technologies (PICT) in their residences. The benefits to the elderly deriving from increases in health outcomes, autonomy of place and of movement (i.e., being able to choose to live safely in one's own home longer than would otherwise be possible, given declining health and mobility), and potentially longer lives must be weighed against the costs of decreased privacy, decreased general autonomy, and the potential for harm arising from fear or mistrust of technology and the dehumanizing aspects of pervasive technology.

Other chapters in this volume explore significant moral concerns for PICT, such as the issues surrounding the collection of public health data, the problems involved in the sheer magnitude of information about people that is continuously collected and stored, and the ease of deception arising from applications of PICT. Some of these issues are also particularly troubling when considering the situation of the elderly in the U.S., many of whom are wary or fearful of technology and many of whom may have decreased capacities for fully understanding the consequences of technology in their homes and in their lives.

This chapter will evaluate the relationship between privacy, competency, paternalism, coercion, and PICT in the elderly – a group that will likely be the first

C.M. Jones, Ph.D. (✉)
Pan American Collaboration for Ethics in the Professions (PACE), The University
of Texas – Pan American, Edinburg, TX, USA
e-mail: jonesc@utpa.edu

K.D. Pimple (ed.), *Emerging Pervasive Information and Communication Technologies*   89
(PICT), Law, Governance and Technology Series 11, DOI 10.1007/978-94-007-6833-8_6,
© Springer Science+Business Media Dordrecht 2014

to have pervasive technology invade their residences. In addition, I will discuss certain issues that are in some ways unique to the elderly, such as living wills and vulnerabilities arising from diminishing capacities. The chapter concludes with an examination of the fear and mistrust of technology often experienced by the elderly, the potential for deception and dehumanization in PICT and elderly citizens, and suggestions for best practices for minimizing harm in dealing with PICT and the elderly. The goals for this chapter are thus to weigh the positive aspects of PICT in residences of elderly individuals against the negative aspects, and to suggest ways to avoid or to mitigate as many of these negative aspects as possible.

6.1.1 Key Terms

For the purposes of this chapter, I offer the following definitions.

Privacy refers to the moral and legal right to be left alone in one's own sphere of influence or to control information about oneself.

Competency refers to the ability to make reasonable or rational decisions and can be either situation-specific (an individual can be competent to make decisions about some things but not others) or general (a generally competent individual should be allowed to make life-or-death decisions, for example, even if her physician or family disagree with her decisions).

Autonomy refers to the ability to be self-determining or to make decisions free from external influences or coercion, and it is typically considered to be the moral basis for privacy rights.

Paternalism refers to acting in the perceived best interests of another individual or group of people, with or without their consent. Respecting an individual's autonomy in health care decision making can often be at odds with acting paternalistically towards that individual, as people do not always make decisions that health care providers would deem to be in their best medical interests. In recent decades in the U.S., the health care system has moved away from health care providers acting paternalistically towards patients and making decisions for them, and towards respect for patient autonomy and informed consent and allowing patients to make decisions for themselves, given the relevant information, whether or not those decisions are in their best medical interests.

Advance directives are intended to specify the wishes of an individual when he is no longer able to express them personally, due to diminished capacities or declining health. Advance directives include living wills, do-not-resuscitate (DNR) orders, and giving another person durable power of attorney over health care decision making. Recent trends in advance directives also represent a less paternalistic approach to end-of-life decision making and demonstrate a greater emphasis on individual autonomy.

Aging in place refers to elderly individuals remaining in their own residences rather than moving to a nursing home, an assisted living facility, or a health care facility.

6.2   Privacy, Competency, Autonomy, and Paternalism in Dealing with the Elderly

The potential benefits from integrating assistive technology into homes occupied primarily by elderly individuals are significant. Robotic assistants and computer technologies that offer reminders to take medications, suggest healthful food choices, and call for outside help in case of an emergency are already in place in the homes of some elders. Studies suggest pervasive technology in the homes of elderly individuals can increase health outcomes, increase satisfaction with care, and potentially increase longevity. Aging in place can thus be facilitated, despite decreasing health and physical abilities, by PICT. Given that many individuals prefer to stay in their own residences as they reach the last period of their lives, pervasive technologies in homes of the elderly offer many the opportunity to remain in their homes longer than they could otherwise, likely leading to a substantial increase in happiness and positive self-image. Of course, there are obvious advantages for elders who leave their homes for the easily-accessible health care assistance available in nursing homes and assisted living facilities, but PICT offers elderly individuals the opportunity to maintain autonomy by providing the ability to monitor vital statistics in a reasonably non-invasive manner and instantly call for help when needed. However, the tradeoff for this kind of autonomy seems to be a decrease in other types of autonomy, such as the ability to control personal privacy and the sharing of personal health data.

Consider the following example.

> Linda, an elderly Alzheimer's patient, is living at home with her husband, Chris, who has no signs of dementia although he has had a heart attack and a subsequent angioplasty. Their adult children have installed monitoring devices in Linda and Chris's home so they know if there is a medical emergency. While the couple knows the technology is present, they do not know the extent of the monitoring capability, which allows their children to know when they get up, when they take their medications, and whether their vital signs change significantly. Linda and Chris have maintained a sexual relationship and the first time they are sexually active after the monitoring technology is installed, paramedics rush to their house, at their children's request, as their vital signs changed significantly and they haven't answered the phone. Linda and Chris are both embarrassed and annoyed by the situation. Their children suggest that Linda and Chris notify them first whenever they plan to be sexually active so they don't call the paramedics again.

Given that privacy rights are often construed as the ability to be left alone within one's own sphere of control, the tradeoff for autonomy of place for the elderly with PICT in their residences is decreased control over personal health information, and perhaps other kinds of information, as the above example illustrates. But such concerns may be addressable to some extent. The simplest way to mitigate such concerns over privacy and autonomy for the elderly in their residences would be to fully disclose to the affected individuals what type of data is being collected and for what purposes, as well as the identity of the recipients of such data, and allow the affected individuals (or their family members if competency to consent is an issue) to consent or not. Another worry, however, is that many elderly in these situations will likely face the inherently coercive "choice" between consenting to PICT in their homes or being forced to move to a nursing home or assistive care facility. Unless other viable options are available, the coerciveness of this choice may be unavoidable.

Issues of privacy are undeniably central moral concerns in PICT, as many aspects of individual privacy seem to be unavoidable casualties of the ubiquity of technology in our lives and in our homes. However, the situation is acute for the elderly, for whom privacy tends to decrease along with competency and autonomy. As a result, ethical concerns regarding infringement upon privacy seem less significant in end-of-life situations and in elderly individuals with decreased competency. When privacy is pitted against health, privacy is likely to lose. On the other hand, it may be argued that diminishing capacities make the elderly as a group more vulnerable to coercion and we should thus be more careful to protect their autonomy. What is clear is that decreased autonomy of movement and potentially decreasing mental faculties render many elderly more vulnerable to manipulation and harm. It is far too easy to project incapacity onto elders when the key issue is actually the convenience of caregivers. The consequences of vulnerability will be explored in more detail in the next section, but for now it is important to note that privacy, competency, and autonomy are tied together and can be serious issues for many elderly individuals, given the prevalence and scope of different kinds of senile dementia and the declining physical abilities many elderly experience. In examining the costs and benefits of PICT in homes of the elderly with diminishing mental capacities, the cost/benefit analysis may need to be frequently adjusted to correspond with changes in situation or declining mental or physical health, as designers and monitors of PICT in homes of elderly individuals are surely aware.

As some elderly experience diminished reasoning capacities that threaten their competency to make appropriate decisions for their health, paternalism requires that others make decisions for them, assuming they have left no advance directives for health care. Before turning to a discussion of issues that can arise regarding advance directives and living wills for elderly individuals with pervasive technologies in their residences, it should be mentioned that paternalism may suggest installing technologies without the consent or knowledge of the elderly resident. Obviously, it is preferable to have the fully informed consent of the affected individuals when PICT is concerned, but this may not be possible in many situations. It might be questioned whether PICT applications that are minimally invasive and thus virtually undetectable are morally problematic in general (for all residences) and specifically in homes of elderly individuals who are likely more vulnerable to external abuses if others control the technology in their homes. But such reasoning fails to consider privacy, autonomy, and respect for individuals. Just because data is easy to collect and because such collection is virtually undetectable, it does not follow that data collection without informed consent is morally permissible. This issue is addressed in other chapters in this volume in greater detail, but the significance of privacy and autonomy in considering the application of PICT in residences of elderly individuals requires that the designers and implementers of PICT are conscious of the unique situation present in residences of the elderly, given the potential mental and physical health challenges of the occupants.

The interconnectedness of privacy, competency, autonomy, and acting in the best interests of the elderly should be considered when making decisions regarding installing and monitoring pervasive technologies in residences. In the preliminary stages, a cost/benefit analysis weighing perceived benefits against expected harms would be prudent. Even though the potential benefit from PICT in residences of the elderly seems in general to be greater than the possible harms, minimizing the potential harm is key. It does not seem prudent to place elderly individuals in virtual fishbowls, where they are monitored "for their best interests", even if they are unaware of the monitoring, as the undermining of privacy in general seems problematic on a societal level. Section 6.5 of this chapter will expand on this theme, but the unique challenges arising from end-of-life concerns and vulnerability issues in the elderly require addressing first.

6.3 Autonomy, Competency, Advance Directives, and Vulnerable Populations

Two central moral topics in the sphere of ethics and aging are end-of-life concerns and vulnerability issues. End-of-life concerns include advance directives like living wills whereas vulnerability issues center on the increase in vulnerability and the potential for coercion that often accompany a decrease in competency. These topics are significant enough in ethics and aging that they require consideration in an evaluation of PICT in the homes of elderly individuals.

Given the recent trend in health care of recognizing the rights of patients to make decisions that fit with their life narratives (even if those decisions are not, strictly speaking, in the best interests medically of the patients), it is important to recognize what a person would have wanted, if competent, as many people feel revulsion at the idea that they may end up as a "vegetable" in a PVS (persistent vegetative state) or, perhaps even worse, as a conscious but significantly mentally compromised individual.

The relationship between autonomy, competency, and advance directives is worth discussing here as the desire to avoid a lack of autonomy is often a compelling factor for individuals who enact advance directives. There is a significant psychological component to privacy and autonomy, as embarrassment and the desire to control personal data and private information have much to do with self-image. It may be that a person with compromised psychological competency is less vulnerable to the psychological harm of privacy violations; however, friends and family members may well suffer such harm on the elderly person's behalf, even if the elder herself cannot completely experience embarrassment. And again, such worries often drive people to enact advance directives.

A colleague once relayed a compelling story about a good friend and former mentor who had been a well-known researcher but who was reduced by senile dementia to the equivalent of a 5-year-old playing with a top at the senior center that cared for him. As he told the story of his former mentor, he was visibly shaken as he described the once-brilliant man's embarrassing state and went on to detail all of the important publications and theories for which his friend was responsible. Clearly, the embarrassment he felt for his friend was significant, even though his friend could feel no embarrassment for himself. This is the kind of experience that reminds us of the importance Western culture places on autonomy, as the thought of being in such a state ourselves in the future drives many people to consider specifying what kinds of treatment in certain circumstances they want to avoid. This story also illustrates that the kind of autonomy most of us desperately wish to retain is related to the autonomy we can easily lose as the pervasiveness of technology becomes all-encompassing.

Even though the percentage of people with living wills in the U.S. is still quite low (studies report between 25 and 40 %[1]), there are a growing number of people who wish to specify the types of medical treatment they want employed and the types of medical treatment they want to avoid in certain situations when they are unable to speak for themselves. Again, most people who enact living wills or DNR (Do Not Resuscitate) orders are attempting to avoid being in a compromised situation like existing in a hospital in a PVS while hooked up to machines to stay alive. Several questions might be asked in dealing with elderly individuals who have living wills and who have PICT in their residences. Should the technology be modified such that outside assistance is only summoned under certain circumstances? Consider a hypothetical situation:

> James has a living will stating that no extraordinary measures during or after a health crisis, such as a stroke or heart attack, should be taken to preserve his life if there is a significant chance of brain damage. His health is monitored by a number of devices in his home that are able to detect such events and make a reasonably confident assessment of his condition. James wants the technology in his home to be programmed to not issue a call for help if the probability of resuscitation is low or if the probability of brain damage is high.

Should PICT in homes of elderly individuals be making life and death "decisions" for the occupants? If so, who has the power to change such programming? In situations of diminished decision making capacities with elderly patients, family members typically make decisions if the patient cannot. As a safeguard, should PICT in the residences of elders be required to ask a designated family member or guardian to make the decision before alerting health care providers or calling for assistance?

Fears regarding technologies in our homes making euthanasia decisions for us may seem a bit far-fetched, but considering worst-case scenarios for use and misuse of technologies in the homes of elderly individuals is nonetheless a worthwhile

---

[1] The Pew Research Center for the People & the Press reported in 2006 that 29 % of those surveyed had living wills. http://www.people-press.org/2006/01/05/strong-public-support-for-right-to-die/. (Accessed 8.19.12). Another source reports a range between 25 and 40 %, depending upon the survey. http://www.freelegaladvicehelp.com/trust/wills/Statistics-On-Living-Wills.html. (Accessed 8.19.12)

exercise from a moral standpoint. Understanding how technologies may be misused before they are operational can help avoid future problems. Many further questions can be asked in considering advance directives. For example, can PICT be a category of medical treatment that an individual can decide for or against in designing an advance directive? Perhaps another important safeguard for PICT in the homes of the elderly is to educate those who are enacting advance directives for themselves in the current technology trends so they can understand the costs/benefits of PICT while they are able to understand the implications and consequences.

Turning specifically to vulnerability issues in dealing with the elderly, it is worth noting that vulnerability arising from diminished capacities can and does exist in many elderly individuals and this vulnerability may be further compounded by a fear of or by mistrust of technology. In health care ethics, labeling a group of people as a "vulnerable population" entails recognizing that the group is more likely to be subject to problematic coercion and thus more likely to have their autonomy violated. Even though it seems that the reduced competency of some elderly individuals might allow employing technologies without their consent, designers and implementers of PICT should be wary of categorizing all elderly individuals on this basis. Indeed, the history of health care ethics demonstrates that protecting the autonomy and safety of vulnerable populations is important for respecting autonomy generally. Two infamous examples of violating the autonomy of medical research subjects or their families are the Tuskegee Syphilis Study and the Willowbrook Hepatitis Experiments.[2] Both Tuskegee and Willowbrook are significant for highlighting the moral issues inherent in using vulnerable groups in research, but the lessons learned from these studies are also directly relevant to employing technology on vulnerable populations. Populations such as children, the poor, the imprisoned, and the mentally challenged (including those suffering from senile dementia or diminished reasoning capacities) require extra consideration and consent procedures because their ability to freely and fully consent is questionable or diminished.

---

[2]The Tuskegee Institute in Alabama was the site of a U.S. Public Health Service observational study of a population of poor and mostly illiterate African-American sharecroppers. The study began in the mid-1930s and examined the long-term effects of syphilis, for which there was no standard treatment when the study was initiated. The study's major ethical issues include deception: The subjects were told they were being treated when they were not, and they were not informed that they were part of a study, making it impossible for them to consent to the study. About fifteen years after the study began, penicillin became the standard treatment for syphilis, but subjects were not treated with it. The study was finally terminated in the mid-1970s.

The Willowbrook experiment is significant for applied and biomedical ethics for similar reasons, primarily because it involved using mentally challenged, institutionalized children in non-therapeutic research (research from which they did not stand to directly benefit medically). The children at the Willowbrook State School for the Retarded were intentionally infected with hepatitis (which admittedly was endemic to the institution) for the study and the consent obtained from their families was arguably incomplete and coercive.

Synopses of these and other cases can be found in (Rothman 2003).

6.4 "Forced" Ubiquity, Fear, Deception, and Misunderstanding of Technology

There are well-documented generational differences in adaptation to new technology.[3] Elderly individuals are generally more reluctant to employ and to adapt to new technology and generally are more mistrustful and fearful of technology in their homes. There have, however, been great strides in anthropomorphizing certain kinds of assistive technology, although the jury is still out on the kinds of traits that older individuals find most appealing. For example, it was thought that more "human" qualities in assistive technology would lead to greater acceptance by users, but this has not been the case across the board – more "humanlike" appearances for robots do not necessarily result in greater acceptance of the technology. Some anthropomorphized characteristics may even result in rejection by users.[4] It is clear from the literature on assistive technology in the homes of the elderly that preliminary screening on a case-by-case basis is a good way to match technology with the user. For example, many elderly express preferences for small, female-sounding, non-threatening robots that are perceived as "not too autonomous."[5] And some studies have demonstrated that matching needs of the elderly (such as reminders to take medications or perform daily tasks, help with mobility, help with hearing or vision, etc.) with technology that directly addresses their needs increases acceptance. In other words, it is possible to have some idea in advance of the characteristics of technology to which an individual will respond positively (Broadbent et al. 2009). In integrating PICT into residences of the elderly, the highest rate of acceptance and success requires some individual preliminary evaluation. Alternatively, it might be effective to explain the limitations and abilities of particular technologies and allow potential users to make some choices on appearances and abilities.

Returning to issues of competency and informed consent procedures for PICT in residences of elderly individuals, the coercive and forced aspects often associated with health care and the elderly can be compounded by a mistrust or fear of technology. Given the previous discussion of the relationship between privacy and competency, a serious concern for PICT and the elderly arises from the potential to "force" elderly individuals to accept the presence of pervasive technologies in their

---

[3]For a review of literature on responses to robots and technology in health care settings, including home health care, and differences between older and younger generations, see Broadbent et al. (2009). In addition to documented differences in acceptance of technology arising from age and generational differences, it has been demonstrated that culture, gender, and possibly education all have an impact on technology acceptance and thus should be considered as well when installing PICT in elders' homes.

[4]Masahiro Mori's "Uncanny Valley" hypothesis, and the subsequent research it spawned, is the most obvious example. See (Misselhorn 2009) for a discussion.

[5]A small cat-bot was determined to be more popular with the elderly than with younger individuals (Libin and Libin 2004, cited in Broadbent et al. 2009).

residences. It was suggested earlier that acting in the best perceived interests of some elderly clients could allow installation and use of PICT in their residences without their consent, without their knowledge, or even against their expressed wishes, if the potential benefit is great enough and if the "invisibility" of the technology is high. Such "forced ubiquity" is generally frowned upon in the general population, but some may consider it permissible if the user's competency is compromised, which may be the case in residences of the elderly. It should be recognized, however, that elderly individuals are more likely, as a group, to have health decisions foisted upon them, whether or not they possess the competency to make such choices for themselves. Many elderly who do not experience competency challenges are treated paternalistically merely based on their age, although doing so is a clear infringement on their autonomy and thus detrimental. Again, those who design and employ PICT in residences of the elderly need to be cognizant that many of the users do not suffer from diminished competency, and this should figure into design and implementation.

6.5 "Dehumanizing" Aspects of PICT

Aside from the standard concerns over privacy, autonomy, and deception and their detrimental effects on the elderly, and the specific concerns regarding competency, living wills, and mistrust of technology that are directly relevant to the elderly, the pervasiveness of technology raises moral concerns regarding *dehumanization*, or treating individuals as less than people by treating them in a manner that deprives them of certain characteristics like freedom or empathy that many take to be essential to rational human beings.

Dystopian novels like Yevgeny Zamyatin's *We*, Aldous Huxley's *Brave New World*, and George Orwell's *1984* warn of a future filled with technology that has stripped individuals of central aspects of humanity like autonomous decision making, individuality, and free thinking. *1984* in particular illustrates how pervasive and fully integrated technology can be used by a state to oppress its citizens by stripping away privacy and by aiding in deceiving citizens into believing everything the state tells them. *Brave New World* suggests that the apathy arising from having more information than anyone could process would result in the inability to distinguish useful information from irrelevant information. Although many of the central themes of these dystopian novels are social/political in nature, the implications of pervasive technology for privacy, autonomy, and "humanity" that they portray is relevant to this discussion – pervasive technology has the potential to undermine or minimize significant characteristics of what it means to be a rational human being.

Other chapters in this volume mention two significant moral concerns of PICT: a significant decrease in privacy for those involved and a significant increase in the ability to deceive people. The pervasiveness of technology has the potential to destroy traditionally-conceived privacy rights as well as the potential to deceive its intended subjects, for example, by enabling them to think they are not being monitored and manipulated, when they in fact are constantly monitored and manipulated. Although dystopian novels are works of fiction, they illustrate a clear potential for misuse of technology in people's homes and lives. In dealing with elderly citizens, this situation is exacerbated, given the already dehumanizing aspects present in end-of-life care. Of course autonomy of place and aging in place can go a long way to maintain dignity and self-respect in elderly individuals, and this is a definite benefit of PICT in residences of the elderly, but it is important to be cognizant that we do not trade one kind of dehumanization (condemning the elderly to sterile hospitals or nursing homes with uncaring attendants) for another kind of dehumanization (condemning the elderly to virtually transparent environments where they are monitored and observed without their consent).

In addition to the general "dehumanizing" aspects of technology, PICT in homes of the elderly has the significant potential to decrease the amount of human contact for affected individuals. A recent conversation with the head of a home health care agency, who proudly reported an increase in the agency's "efficiency" rate thanks to the decreasing number of nursing visits to clients' homes, left me with concerns for the clients involved. Recently installed technology that monitors medications and food intake had significantly decreased the need for nursing visits to clients' homes. This increase in technology in clients' homes resulted in cost savings and more "efficient" use of resources, but also resulted in significantly fewer hours of human contact for clients, most of whom are elderly and most of whom are sorely lacking in human contact in general. Although pervasive technology in the homes of elderly individuals has the potential to increase their quality of life in many ways, it also has the potential to isolate them from society by making their homes so efficient that outside human contact is virtually unnecessary until a serious problem arises that requires outside intervention.

6.6   Conclusion

Previous sections in this chapter have suggested that those designing, installing, and monitoring PICT in homes of elderly individuals should be cognizant of the possible harms that the technologies may cause. Even though PICT in homes of elderly individuals seems to offer the potential for greater benefit than harm, recognizing potential harms is an important step in preventing or mitigating these harms. Other chapters in this volume discuss transparency, disclosure, and effective communication as tools for minimizing harm from PICT. These are useful tactics for minimizing potential harm from the combination of PICT and the elderly as well. Educating affected individuals and obtaining informed consent should be added to this list of tactics, to the extent that informed consent can be obtained from the individuals in question or from their families. Even if individuals cannot fully understand the implications and consequences of PICT, respect for human dignity and autonomy requires that they be informed as best as possible, assuming that the discussion itself is not harmful. Another alternative is to inform and obtain consent from family members or medical decision makers, if consent from the individuals affected is not possible. Perhaps the best advice that can be offered at this point is that designers and implementers of PICT in residences of the elderly should be cognizant of the history of abuse in health care and research ethics in dealing with vulnerable populations. Making decisions in the best interests of others is always an endeavor filled with potential landmines, and implementing PICT in residences of the elderly should be approached with equal caution to using vulnerable populations in research, even if it seems to be in their best interests.

References

Broadbent, E., R. Stafford, and B. MacDonald. 2009. Acceptance of healthcare robots for the older population: Review and future directions. *International Journal of Social Robotics* 1: 319–330.

Libin, A.V., and E.V. Libin. 2004. Person-robot interactions from the robopsychologists point of view: The robotic psychology and robotherapy approach. *Proceedings of the IEEE* 92: 1789–1803.

Misselhorn, Catrin. 2009. Empathy with inanimate objects and the uncanny valley. *Minds and Machines: Journal for Artificial Intelligence, Philosophy, and Cognitive Science* 19(3): 345–359.

Rothman, David J. 2003. *Strangers at the bedside: A history of how law and bioethics transformed medical decision making*. Hawthorne: Aldine de Gruyter.

Chapter 7
When Cutting Edge Technology Meets Clinical Practice: Ethical Dimensions of e-Health

Katherine D. Seelman, Linda M. Hartman, and Daihua X. Yu

7.1 Introduction

The purpose of this chapter is to explore the ethical dimensions of *Electronic Health* (eHealth or e-Health) systems in order to identify barriers to value-based clinical conduct. The use of e-Health inspires hope that health care will be more justly distributed around the world. Its use also generates concern about complexity and whether or not ethical responsibility for e-Health system performance can be ascribed to human beings, in particular clinicians (Duquenoy et al. 2008). The chapter identifies problems generated by e-Health in order to examine their impact on clinical conduct and to propose modest ameliorative strategies.

Health care is primarily a moral enterprise in which action means values (Snyder 2012). E-Health is being introduced into a well-developed biomedical ethics framework of patient protection, well-being, and confidentiality of information. The clinician's primary value commitment must always be to the patient's welfare and best interests. A clinician is responsible for her patient. Therefore, the normative basis for changing practice is an important consideration. E-Health introduces new responsibilities for which established bioethical norms may or may not be adequate. This may be particularly true with the introduction of the Internet into health care. While the clinician may have the responsibility for confidentiality, he or she may not have the capacity to protect medical information which moves

K.D. Seelman, Ph.D. (✉)
School of Health and Rehabilitation Science, University of Pittsburgh, Pittsburgh, PA, USA
e-mail: kds31@pitt.edu

L.M. Hartman, M.L.S
School of Health and Rehabilitation Sciences, Health Sciences Library System (HSLS),
University of Pittsburgh, Pittsburgh, PA, USA

D.X. Yu, M.S.
Health & Rehabilitation Informatics Lab, University of Pittsburgh, Pittsburgh, PA, USA

K.D. Pimple (ed.), *Emerging Pervasive Information and Communication Technologies (PICT)*, Law, Governance and Technology Series 11, DOI 10.1007/978-94-007-6833-8_7, © Springer Science+Business Media Dordrecht 2014

over multiple territorial and organizational jurisdictions and borders, often using complex information and communication technology (ICT). For example, the ability to merge multiple databases containing intimate details that patients originally revealed for specific purposes poses a threat to patient autonomy (Layman 2003). Because of the increasing globalization of health care using e-Health, the security, confidentiality, and functionality of health information also involves the certification of health information professionals throughout the world (Kluge 2011).

E-Health is the cutting-edge technology referred to in the chapter title. Society is the "lab" in which e-Health is being introduced. The e-Health system is under ongoing construction and is thus a "moving target" as a focus of analysis. The scope of e-Health is global and may not respect traditional authority such as that reposing in social norms, culture, and national governments. The e-Health system is complex, and a description of it involves unfamiliar technology and terminology. E-Health also involves more familiar social factors such as government policy, hospital and clinical policies, and culture and clinical conduct. Issues emerging from the introduction of health information technology into the clinical environment are relevant to all of us as consumers of health care.

The discussion in Chap. 6 of technology in one's residence touches upon several ethical principles. Autonomy of the individual is at stake when decisions are made about whether or not technology is installed in his or her home. Vulnerability is invoked with the discussion of "forced ubiquity." Grown children may unknowingly coerce parents when giving the choice of technology in the home or moving to a facility. This chapter discusses issues with which clinicians and health care professionals must be concerned when attempting to provide the best care to the most people at the best price.

7.1.1 Description of the E-Health Socio-technical System

The System

The following description will serve as an initial introduction to the e-Health system and to the system model we developed and use in this chapter. A comprehensive introduction of e-health appears in Sect. 7.2 of the chapter.

In an earlier period, health information was recorded on paper by health information personnel. Collection, transfer, and linkage of personal health information were limited by location, copying and transmission techniques, and speed. Now, health information personnel are trained in e-Health and are responsible for the management and maintenance of *Electronic Health Records* (EHR) – essentially software that collects, transfers, and links health-related data (Abdelhak et al. 2012) with an ultimate goal of having *Health Information Exchanges* (HIE) over regions, nations, and the world. Patient medical records are transmitted electronically within and well beyond the boundaries of a hospital or clinic – in fact, anywhere in the world. E-Health includes a broad range of products such as EHRs and patient engagement tools such as personal health records (PHRs) (Institute of Medicine (U.S.), Committee on Patient Safety and Health Information Technology 2012).

E-Health involves the use of computers as well as information and communication technology in health care. The term "electronic" in e-Health refers to transmission of EHRs by telecommunications and related clinical activity such as medical consultations and health interventions at a distance. *Mobile health* (mHealth or m-Health) is an area of e-Health that involves the use of mobile devices such as cell phones and, often, wireless transmission. The point of care may be the bedside or the workplace – in fact anywhere the patient is located. Its adaptability and the relatively low-cost cell phone make it particularly attractive for use in under-resourced areas of the world (Vital Wave Consulting 2009). M-Health is composed of pervasive information and communication technologies (Michalowski et al. 2005) which are integrated into a health care system. At the body level, these components may include wearable and implantable sensors that wirelessly transmit the resulting data, such as blood pressure readings, to external devices such as smartphones, diagnostic systems, and medical data servers. Based on sensor information or directed commands, body area networks can also control medical devices and medication dosages in personal networks (Karulf 2008). Body area networks involve communications technology located in, on, and near the body. A wireless body area network system can use a wireless personal area network as a gateway to reach longer-range networks. The integration of the human system and the e-Health body area network obscures boundaries between humans and machines. Ethical problems emerge about whether decision making reposes in the human or the technology and, if in the technology, about the identity of the morally responsible agent.

Software, Computers, and Telecommunications

Traditionally, the application of computer technology in health care has been divided into three categories (Bhaskar and Somu 2011; Poon et al. 2006). Administrative applications include office management, scheduling, and accounting tasks. Special purpose applications include the use of computers in some aspects of pharmacy. Clinical applications of computers include anything that has to do with direct patient care, such as diagnosis, monitoring, and treatment (Bhaskar and Somu 2011; Poon et al. 2006).

Clinicians feel the high impact of *Health Information Technology* (HIT) when electronic health record vendors, hospitals, and clinics acquire and implement new modules of their main vendor's electronic health record in their inpatient settings. Physicians, nurses, and other clinicians then move from occasional use of HIT to dependency on HIT (Leviss 2010). Personnel trained in *Health Information Management* (HIM), sometimes referred to as *Health Informatics*, an emerging field, are newcomers to the clinical environment. They maintain and care for EHRs. Like clinicians, they are not necessarily schooled in the social impact of e-Health as it is introduced into the clinical environment. Like most innovation, EHR is disruptive. Introduction of new, unfamiliar technology and personnel with expertise different from existing clinical know-how can disrupt workflow patterns and impact traditional roles.

The introduction of *Clinical Decision Support Systems* (CDSSs) software into the clinical environment is an example of EHR innovation. CDSS is the source of considerable controversy and ethical concern because it introduces the possibility of non-human clinical decision making which, in turn, obscures moral responsibility. CDSS forms a significant part of the field of EHR clinical knowledge management technologies. This software can be designed to execute various levels of decision making in medical inpatient and outpatient settings. It has the capacity to support the clinical process and use of knowledge, from diagnosis and investigation through treatment and long-term care. Depending on software design, clinical decision support systems may override an actual practitioner's decision or substitute for it. Therefore, the design of software has important ethical dimensions relating to whether it will support or substitute for human beings. These decision support systems are often cited as a cause of errors, termed *adverse medical events* (Falas et al. 2003; Institute of Medicine (U.S.). Committee on the Public Health Effectiveness of the FDA 510(k) Clearance Process 2011; Leviss 2010). A basic concern for EHR vendors, hospitals, and clinics is managing the risks created by the complex HIT system so that benefits of EHR and e-Health can be maximized (Arnrich et al. 2010; Bergeron 2001, 2003, 2004; Haux 2006; Seelman 2013).

E-Health and Complexity

The e-Health socio-technical system has many unrelated body-level, local, organizational, ICT network, national, and international jurisdictions which confound attempts to determine decision points, system boundaries, accountability, and assignment of moral responsibility. The e-Health system is often compared to an ecosystem. Both are composed of a complex set of relationships which must operate interdependently. The e-Health system is designed to network and interoperate through interfaces adapted from existing systems and data exchanges. While the aim is interdependency, these networks were not necessarily designed to work together to handle the interoperability, security, and privacy challenges posed by the new age of EHR. Issues such as privacy and technical reliability are among the most significant. Clinicians must trust health information technology (HIT) in order to adhere to the values of their profession, values such as fidelity, veracity, and trust.

7.1.2   E-Health Socio-technical System Models

There are a number of models of e-Health. Many include both technical and social elements (Harrison et al. 2007; Sittig and Singh 2011). We have developed a model of the e-Health socio-technical system which is presented in Sect. 7.2. Our model is designed to identify problems created when e-Health is introduced into the clinical environment. The model is composed of four elements: (a) health information technology (HIT), (b) vendors and health care entities such as hospitals and clinics, (c) laws and regulations, and (d) broadband and Internet providers.

The performance of HIT is an important focus of the chapter, but so are the management characteristics of the vendors and health care entities with which the clinician works. Laws and regulations, while external to the e-Health system, are also very important and often lag behind technological innovation. If laws and regulations are developed to address problems that are generated in the performance of e-Health, they can provide guidance about the proper use of the system, put constraints on components of the system, and collect data to guide improved system performance. Laws and regulations, ideally, provide the public and the patient with protection against unsafe and ineffective technology and intrusions into their private medical information. Like laws and regulations, broadband and Internet providers are also components of the model which are external to the e-Health system. They serve the system and must provide reliable and secure service. The performance of each of the four components will be examined in Sect. 7.2 in order to identify problems which impact the conduct of the clinician and to determine ethical dimensions of the problem such as respect for persons and autonomy or justice.

7.1.3 Ethics

Ethics plays an important role in the development and implementation of cutting edge technology such as EHRs. Ethical guidance often precedes and informs the process of developing laws and regulations. E-Health, like so many cutting edge technologies, is subject to lags between the capacity of the technology and the policies, regulations, technical standards, and clinical standards needed for its optimum use. Of course, some cutting edge technology cannot be constrained by existing governance tools either because of the characteristics of the technology or lack of political will (Zhang et al. 2011).

Some ethical dilemmas generated by the introduction of e-Health, such as EHRs in hospitals and clinics, exist at the intersection between the corporate duty to provide financial returns to investors and corporate obligation to ensure that products are safe, effective, and beneficial to patients and those who treat and care for them (Goodman et al. 2010). Others involve pressures exerted by a government which wants its policies implemented. Some problems involve the ethical basis for introducing and managing change in the workplace. Still others involve criteria on which to repose decision-making authority. On the one hand, clinicians may opt to accept, resist, or reject software packages such as CDSS. On the other, software developers and vendors may regard CDSS as necessary to the implementation of e-Health. HIM personnel are trained to manage and maintain the EHR component of the e-Health system.

The Common Morality Approach to the Ethical Dimensions of E-Health

In this chapter, we use a Common Morality bioethics approach (Beauchamp and Childress 2009) to apply ethical principles to e-Health case studies. These principles are: respect for persons and autonomy, beneficence, non-maleficence, and justice. Case studies are introduced to provide examples of activities of each of the components of our socio-technical system model. The case studies for HIT, for example, may identify activities involving problems in safety and effectiveness which would suggest violations of the principle of beneficence because the clinician cannot trust the system, and also the principle of non-maleficence which cautions that we must do no harm.

The Common Morality approach assumes that normatively, moral agents (human beings) can do no more than to specify their considered judgment as coherently as possible. The approach encourages adaptability. If the results from examination of e-Health case studies suggest that existing norms, rules, and guidelines for ethically obligatory clinical behavior are insufficient, then additional guidelines may be proposed. This adaptability is particularly important for clinicians practicing in environments with new technologies such as EHR, because standards of clinical practice and clinical codes of ethics were developed prior to the introduction of e-Health and may provide little or no guidance for clinical competencies and conduct. Problems identified in case studies presented in Sects. 7.2 and 7.3 are re-examined in Sect. 7.4, the Ethics section of this chapter. The adequacy of biomedical ethics is assessed and biomedical, computer, and human–machine ethics are mined for guidance in the development of ameliorative strategies.

While Common Morality assumes that human beings are the sole ethical agents and that human agents and human action are the focus of ethical judgment, some characteristics of e-Health make it difficult to assign moral authority to human beings. Software is driven by algorithms which provide step-by-step problem-solving procedures for decision making in areas such as medication dosage. Software-based decisions may be unmediated by clinicians. There is no widely adopted equivalent to human agency in Biomedical Ethics which can be applied to technology performance. The ethical virtue of trust is a useful bridge between individual human judgment and the performance of technology and organizations. In addition to biomedical ethics, ethical subfields such as computer and machine ethics are examined. A supplementary approach is to educate all health consumers about the trade-offs between the risks and benefits of e-Health. However, the level of expertise necessary to comprehend risk may be a limiting factor in reposing decisions in the consumer. The Common Morality approach is used to consider and posit modest judgments in response to questions about the basis of authority for questions such as:

- What problems generated by components of the socio-technical systems and by the clinical environment have an impact on the performance of ethical clinical conduct?
- What are the ethical dimensions of these problems?

- Who should decide about the design, implementation and proper use of the e-Health system – technologists, industry developers, industry health care providers, clinicians, government, members of the public – using what criteria and processes?
- What strategies can be implemented to ameliorate some of these problems?

7.1.4   The Problem and Its Significance

Telehealth uses telecommunication technologies to distribute medical services. It is envisioned to be the predominant health care delivery system of the future, and its reach is global (Vital Wave Consulting 2009). Therefore, it has significance for all human beings. Clinicians, in particular, must have an ethical and expertise framework that guides them in meeting the challenges of adoption decisions related to e-Health, HIT, system management, and law (Kluge 2007, 2011; Moor et al. 2011). However, the public also should have a framework to guide them in acceptance and adoption decisions and to engage in basic questions about the purpose of e-Health and the protections of vital rights such as privacy of medical information and the design of personal health records.

Clinical and Health Information Personnel and the Management of Risk

The ECRI Institute of Plymouth Meeting, Pennsylvania, an independent nonprofit organization that studies improvements to patient care, names the Top Health Technology Hazards each year. ECRI lists staff misunderstanding as a technical hazard for medical device use (ECRI Institute 2012; Landro 2008). These hazards create risk in the clinical environment. Alarms on medical devices were named #1 on the 2012 ECRI list. Alarms on infusion pumps, ventilators, and dialysis units are designed to warn of potential dangers to patients. But alarms can also contribute to adverse events. One major reason is "alarm fatigue." The staff may become desensitized to the frequency with which alarms are sounded and delay needed action. In general, HIT project failure rates involving introduction of EHR are estimated at about 70 % (Leviss 2010).

As a compensatory strategy for misunderstandings by the clinical staff, a hospital or clinic may assign health information management personnel to clinical or semi-clinical roles that fall outside their core competencies, due in large part to advancement in informatics and applications used at the point of care. In addition to creating risks to patient well-being, clinician-patient-organizational trust can be undermined by this practice. Trust is a valued clinical character trait that applies to both individual behavior and organizational functioning within the health-related entity. Within an organization, trust is a basis for successful implementation of organizational ethics and professional conduct (Hosmer 1995; Watson 2005).

Emergence of the Field of Biomedical and Clinical Informatics

The introduction of e-Health technology such as EHR into the clinical environment raises many issues, including questions about the content of an adequate knowledge base for e-Health and the core competencies for clinical and HIM personnel education and training. Staff competence generates trust, trust in the individual and in organizational competence. The training of clinical professionals and the need for inter-professional training has been addressed in a number of Institute of Medicine (IOM) reports. IOM has identified five domains to which continuing education in the health care professions should be directed, including biomedical and clinical informatics, inter-professional teams, and quality assurance to identify errors and hazards in care (Institute of Medicine (U.S.) Committee on Planning a Continuing Health Care Professional Education Institute 2010). In Sect. 7.4, ethics, standards of clinical practice, and codes of ethics are examined for coverage of these domains.

E-Health Science, Technology, Society, and Ethics Studies

Finally, the concept of a socio-technical system is significant for the development of ethics and e-Health. It is a useful conceptual tool applied throughout this chapter and should undergo continuing development. A socio-technical system involves problems that constitute the essence of the systems engineering approach and problems that contain ethical, social, and political elements. In particular, the concept can be used to probe the fundamental problem of identifying moral responsibility in complex systems (Johnson and Miller 2009). This problem involves vertical conceptual links between the organizational level and the individual level which can further elucidate interactions and impacts. The concept of a socio-technical system is useful in practical ethics as an analytic framework to examine the real experience of practitioners as innovation is introduced into the clinical environment. The socio-technical system concept has a rich history in technology and society studies, and most recently as an example of a theoretical framework in Informatics (DeLone and McLean 2003; Harrison et al. 2007; Jasanoff 1995; Koppel and Kreda 2009; Leviss 2010; Sittig and Singh 2011). Informatics frameworks and related models will receive further attention in Sect. 7.2, the socio-technical system.

7.1.5   Approach and Methods

We have developed an e-Health system model and applied it to activities of the socio-technical system components mainly using case studies. The components are: HIT, health care vendors and entities, Internet and broadband providers, and laws and regulations. Activities are examined at the macro level of the socio-technical system and the micro level of individual conduct. Activities at the macro and micro level have impact on each other. At the micro level, there are many individual actors such as clients and patients, clinicians, HIM personnel, vendors and health system managers, and executives. The unit of analysis at the micro level is the conduct of the clinician and, to a lesser extent, the patient. At the macro level, the units of analysis are activities of the socio-technical model components: performance of HIT technology and the technology of Internet and broadband providers. Units of analysis also include management activities of vendor companies and health-related entity organizations and the governance activities of legal and regulatory agencies. These activities are examined using Common Morality principles introduced earlier. While the principles are content-thin, the case studies are content-rich; the combination of both provides the basis for determining the ethical dimensions of problems generated by e-Health for which clinicians need guidance.

While an extensive literature search has been conducted, a limited number of clinical e-Health case examples have been identified. Clinical concern about liability for e-Health errors and lack of legal requirements for EHR error reportage may be two reasons for the apparent dearth of case studies. Our case studies routinely derive from blogs; Institute of Medicine and governmental agency reports such as those from the Office of National Coordinator for HIT, the Agency for Healthcare Research and Quality (AHRQ), and the Office for Civil Rights, all within the Department of Health and Human Services; the Food and Drug Administration (FDA), an independent regulatory agency; and to a lesser extent from professional organizations such as the American Health Information Association (AHIMA).

7.1.6   Sections of the Chapter

Section 7.2 provides a comprehensive introduction to the socio-technical system and related issues. It also addresses the stages in the development of e-Health technology such as research and development (R&D), manufacturing, regulation, and service delivery. Each stage involves ethical dimensions such as decisions about software algorithms at the research and development stage that determine who makes decisions in a clinical situation. Section 7.2 also introduces a series of case studies illustrating the activities of components of the socio-technical system. These activities include: HIT performance, vendor and health care entity management, law and regulatory governance, and Internet and broadband performance. Section 7.3 explores problems faced by clinicians in the implementation of ethical clinical conduct within the e-Health clinical environment. In Sect. 7.4, Ethics, problems identified in Sects. 7.2 and 7.3 are reexamined. Both biomedical ethics and emerging subfields of ethics such as computer ethics are probed for their appropriateness in providing guidance for clinicians working in e-Health. The emerging and evolving fields of Informatics and Health Information Management are also briefly examined for relevance to the problems posed in this chapter. Finally, this section looks at adverse event data based on software error derived from a U.S. Food and Drug Administration (FDA) database. The ethical dimensions of software development and the use of software in medical devices and as medical devices (EHR) are of particular interest because software can be designed to perform with or without human agency. Software malfunctions generate errors and adverse events which impact on clinical trust. In Sect. 7.5, the focus returns to the original purpose of the chapter: to identify and examine the ethical dimensions of problems in e-Health and the barriers those problems generate for the expression of ethical clinical conduct in pursuit of patient safety and well-being. Ameliorative strategies are considered and seemingly intractable problems are identified.

7.2   Our E-Health Socio-technical System Model and the Socio-technical System

The purpose of this section is to provide an extensive introduction to our e-Health socio-technical model including socio-technical system concepts, terms, and component activities. The system model is introduced by Fig. 7.1 and described in an extensive narrative. Later in the section, a second figure is introduced which illustrates stages in the development of HIT, beginning with research and development and ending with HIT use in clinical service delivery. A series of case studies are then introduced which provide examples of the actual performance of system components. In all cases, questions of moral responsibility in decision making within the ethical dimensions of Common Morality principles are probed.

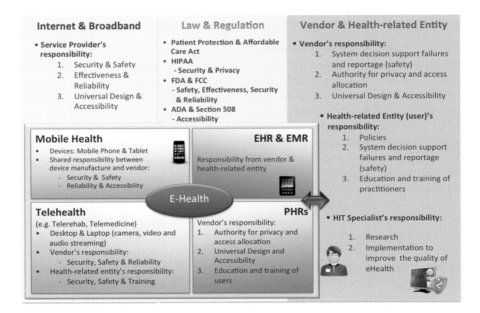

Fig. 7.1 Model of the e-Health socio-technical system illustrating components and relationships

7.2.1 Other Models

Theorists of the e-Health system have developed models, often for the purpose of anticipating errors and eventually being able to predict them. For example, a senior research scientist at the U.S. Agency for Healthcare Research and Quality (AHRQ) engages in model building that can be used to anticipate unforeseen consequences which may require trade-offs (Harrison et al. 2007). Computerization, for example, may enhance reliability, but this must be traded off against safety hazards created when clinical judgment and direct communication are impeded. Models may also help discern genuinely unforeseen consequences as they emerge in HIT implementation (Sittig and Singh 2011). Studies that apply some of the models to the HIT socio-technical system have shown problems in each of its dimensions including hardware and software, workflow, and external rules and pressures (Sittig and Singh 2011).

Models and their analysis may also serve the broader purpose of normative ethics. A registered health information administrator examined the conflicts among the ethical principles of beneficence, autonomy, fidelity or faithfulness, and justice to the patients as they relate to e-Health and the technologies of health informatics (Layman 2003). She then provided a devastating repudiation of e-Health in which she argued that these principles are compromised. For example, beneficence comes at a price, which Layman describes as "often the loss or abridgment of other rights, such as privacy." The ability to merge multiple databases in which people reveal intimate details for specific purposes poses a threat to autonomy. While health leaders list the importance of fidelity as their highest concern regarding the security of medical records, Layman observes that widespread breaches of security justify this concern. She also argues that the technologies are used in ways that conflict with justice. Too much access may be a problem when, in the spirit of accountability, HIT administrators of some publicly funded programs make health data available on the Internet. Justice is threatened when that data originates only from citizens with low incomes or from certain geographic areas.

7.2.2 Introducing Our Model of the E-Health Socio-technical System

Our model of the e-Health socio-technical system is introduced in Fig. 7.1 which illustrates system components and their relationships. The figure is color-coded and arranged to suggest system relationships and responsibilities. An extended narrative follows that introduces the purpose, functioning, and issues of the various components, beginning with HIT electronic health record technology, which is divided into two primary categories, provider-centric systems and consumer-centric systems.

Provider-Centric Systems

Provider-centric systems, such as electronic health records (EHR) and the electronic medical record (EMR) are designed and developed from the care providers' perspective to manage and support providers' services within secure portals. EHR technology is used to provide clinicians with comprehensive health data, clinical decision support, and enhanced communication, and as a tool to reduce medical errors and improve patient safety.

As indicated earlier, the high clinical impact of health information technology occurs when e-Health vendors acquire and implement new modules of their main vendor's electronic health record into inpatient settings, a process that takes physicians and nurses from occasional users of HIT to dependency on HIT (Leviss 2010). Computerized physician/provider order entry (CPOE), such as for medication, is the computer system that allows direct entry of medical orders by the person with the licensure and privileges to do so. Directly entering orders into a computer is justified based on the assumption of benefit from reducing errors by minimizing the ambiguity of hand-written orders. Debate about CPOE is ongoing in a number of issue areas (Oregon Health & Science University 2011) such as:

- Should CPOE be made mandatory and are escape mechanisms for avoiding CPOE necessary?
- Should system designers give clinicians what they want or what designers think they need?
- What part of CPOE should be under local modification and control?
- Who should decide: The software designer? The knowledge company that will create a medical knowledge base for the use of the clinician? The clinician?
- Who is responsible for knowledge updates and software updates?

Bar code medication administration occurs as each drug in the hospital is labeled with a unique bar code. When a patient is prescribed a medication, the prescription is faxed, sent electronically, or hand delivered to the hospital's pharmacy and entered into a computer system by a pharmacist. The pharmacist dispenses the bar coded dose of the drug to the patient's floor. When it is time for the clinician to administer the medication, he uses a hand-held device to scan the bar codes on his identification badge, the patient's wristband, and the drug. If the bar coding prescription system does not match the drug to be given with the order in the system, it alerts the clinician with a visual warning. Warnings can be problematic because of multiple false alarms and clinical "alarm fatigue." The staff may become desensitized and delay needed action. In this case, the clinician may be found responsible because he or she is supposed to respond to alarms.

The health information specialist appears in Fig. 7.1 as the e-Health system implementer. He or she has the responsibility of maintaining and caring for health records in hospitals, health departments, clinics, or in a facility that provides care or maintains records. Issues emerge around the health information specialist and clinical roles and relationships if the health entity has not developed policies to guide roles and workflow. The ethical dimensions also involve questions of whether or not new practices have value for patients.

Consumer-Centric Systems

The second category of the technology component is consumer-centric systems. Consumer-centric systems, such as the personal health record (PHR) (Gearon and California HealthCare Foundation 2007; Institute of Medicine (U.S.). Committee on Patient Safety and Health Information Technology 2012) are designed and developed from the patients' perspectives to store their health-related information and to manage their personal care activities within secure portals or in software services. Patients have the option of using insecure portals or software services, which then puts them at risk for unauthorized incursions on their health information. PHR has the potential to increase patients' self-management of their health by providing them access to their health information (Wagner et al. 2010). Physicians may also benefit from using PHR in their practice and their interactions with patients (John and Mary R. Markle Foundation., Robert Wood Johnson Foundation., & Connecting for Health (Organization) 2004). For instance, health professionals rely on patients to provide information about their medical history in emergency situations (Rybynok et al. 2010). Another key value of PHR is that it can be used by multiple providers when those providers are unable or unwilling to communicate among themselves (Simborg 2009).

Issues around PHR include protecting privacy and avoiding medical identity theft (AHIMA 2012a). Still other issues are at least as basic. For instance, can a caregiver access information about a patient without his or her permission (Gearon and California HealthCare Foundation 2007)? Additionally, PHRs and portals allowing consumers to access their own health information are underdeveloped and largely unavailable (Miller 2012). Information flow and exchange may be problematic because proprietary systems create barriers for sharing data, and interoperability among HIT systems is "under construction." Nonetheless, lack of integration of the consumer into the EHR is a major ethical concern. The U.S. Department of Veterans Affairs (VA) Blue Button technology provides a model for consumer PHRs (U.S. Department of Veterans Affairs 2012). The Blue Button approach is a simple concept in which a patient is provided with a highly visible, clickable button that is used to download his or her medical records in digital form from a secure website offered by their doctors, insurers, pharmacies, or other health-related service. People can log into this secure website to view and have the option to download their health information so they can examine it, check it, and share it with their doctors and others as they see fit.

In conclusion, EHR and especially PHR development and implementation involve many unresolved technical issues, consumer issues, and lags. Electronic records may vary in architecture, format, and features. Development of specific information technology standards would help to resolve system integration and portability issues and facilitate interdependence with other data sources. Consumer issues introduced early in this chapter are basic to health care policy and service delivery. They involve the development of PHRs as a means of empowering consumers and supporting patient-centered care. Current research and government guidelines for Meaningful Use of e-Health are mostly concentrated on the provider's perspective and provider's needs (Institute of Medicine (U.S.). Committee on

Patient Safety and Health Information Technology 2012). Those with chronic conditions and disability, for example, could benefit from e-Health services such as support groups, easier communication with their health care providers, and self-management training and information (Simpson 2010a, b). However, e-Health systems must be accessible and usable.

Telehealth or Mobile Health

Telehealth and mobile health are extended services which are either provider-centric or consumer-centric. Telehealth systems are mainly focused on long-distance medical care that uses desktop or laptop computers at the client's side or point-of-service to relay health information by video and audio streaming to communicate with a clinician from the health provider's office. *Mobile health* (mHealth or m-Health) technical system components are pervasive information and communication technologies with services rendered through the broad scope of wireless communications such as Bluetooth, infrared, General Pocket Radio Service (GPRS), and wireless fidelity (mHealth Regulatory Coalition).

A simple example of m-Health technologies is a tablet computer that includes a software app that integrates data from a blood glucose meter, a weight scale, and a blood pressure cuff. M-Health may be used by patients for self-management and self-care to improve quality of care. Information that patients enter from mobile health may also be valuable for clinicians in decision making about appropriate treatment. Security, safety, and reliability are important responsibilities for both vendors and health-related entities as well as broadband and Internet providers. The particular technical and clinical requirements might be different when patients have different types of conditions such as particular chronic diseases or impairments. Security, safety, and reliability as well as interoperability of HIT are issues in telehealth, perhaps especially for clinicians who work within the bioethics framework of protection of medical information. Biomedical ethics instructs clinicians to attend to the principle of beneficence, which involves "doing good" for the patient. Still another major concern is the increasingly remote patient-clinician relationship, generating the need for greater specificity about under what conditions telehealth practice is justified and when it is not.

Vendors and Health-Related Entities

The ethical dimensions of vendor and health entity activity are within two ethical frameworks, biomedical ethics, such as our Common Morality approach, and business ethics. Business ethics incorporates values of stewardship, trust, honesty, and corporate social responsibility.

System vendors contract with health-related entities such as the U.S. Department of Veterans Affairs and the University of Pittsburgh Medical Center to provide e-Health systems. The vendor and health-related entity relationship is usually contractual. Both parties are involved in agreements about language on intellectual property disclosures and on disclosure of system errors and hold harmless clauses which absolve vendors of responsibility for errors or defects in their software. Depending on the contract language, vendors may or may not be held accountable for the performance of mechanisms that relate to the design and development of an effective and reliable e-Health system. Nonetheless, health-related entity users have a responsibility to manage errors and train personnel. Vendors of these products have the primary responsibility of establishing a systematic approach to entering, storing, and transferring medical and/or health-related information over the Internet to enhance interoperability. *Meaningful use* of health information and logical operational flow of the system are important to support daily personal and clinical uses. As described later in this section, under Laws and Regulations, a *Meaningful Use Program* has been established by the Centers for Medicare and Medicaid Services (CMS) in cooperation with the Office of the National Coordinator of HIT in the U.S. Department of Health and Human Services. Ideally, meaningful use of an electronic health record enables significant and measurable improvements in population health through a transformed health care delivery system (Health IT Policy Committee 2009). Failure of system supports leads to medical errors which can cause significant harm to patients. Establishing an authorized access process and an audit trail of users is essential for an e-Health system to protect patients' privacy and safety.

Health entities, such as hospitals, have management responsibilities for the development and execution of policies and processes to use EHR software interdependently with the workflow processes and in conformance with laws and regulations. Quality management and change management are among the tools available to meet these responsibilities.

Accessibility and the design of the e-Health system are equal access issues. There are existing guidelines and standards that can guide HHS in the development of EHR standards (Simpson 2010b). They include web accessibility guidelines, electronic and information technology standards, and standards in the Communication Act rules about access to telecommunication services. The e-Health system should be compatible with assistive technologies such as screen readers for people who are blind. These system capabilities, which impact users' experiences, are also vendors' responsibilities. Engagement of the clinician before the system is purchased and proper training on all HIT is crucial for success. Some facilities do very minimal training and/or the vendor does not provide proper training on these systems. Health vendors and health entities are typically for-profit organizations that have responsibilities to shareholders as well as to the public. Therefore, the ethical dimensions of their problems involve weighing the interests of both parties based on criteria developed from business ethics, an approach that shares some values with bioethics, such as trust, but does not focus on protecting the patient.

Internet and Broadband

Internet and broadband providers, like health care entities, also function within the framework of business ethics. Unlike vendors, hospitals, and clinics, Internet and broadband providers are components of our socio-technical model which are external to the e-Health system but exert constraints on it. E-Health vendors and health-related entities are served by Internet and broadband providers such as AT&T and Verizon who, in turn, transmit medical information within and beyond hospitals and clinical systems. Internet and broadband providers are constrained by law and regulation. If serving a covered entity, these companies must comply with the *Health Insurance Portability and Accountability Act* (HIPAA) regarding privacy and security. Their activities are also of interest to the Federal Communications Commission which has developed broadband policy. Wireless transmission of patient medical data raises concerns about privacy, integrity, and confidentiality of the data and authentication and authorization of users. For people with chronic illness and disabilities who depend on wireless for emergency services while participating in the community, reliability of service is another major issue.

Laws and Regulations and the Role of the Obama Administration

Health information management personnel, in particular, are sensitive to the Health Insurance Portability and Accountability Act (HIPAA) (U.S. Department of Health & Human Services 2010). The objective of HIPAA is to ensure the safety and security of the health care system. The Department of Health and Human Services (DHHS) is mandated under HIPAA to provide guidance, which it does through rules to protect the basic privacy of the individual's health information, including the exchange of information in a networked environment.

HIPAA regulates the use and disclosure of protected health information held by covered entities. Many issues are unresolved. Who is responsible for tracking use of patient data? May patients view the audit trails of those who have seen their data? The Health Information Technology for Economic and Clinical Health (HITECH) Act made significant changes to HIPAA. The biggest change to HIPAA compliance is the significant toughening of data breach notification laws, which now not only impose larger fines and require more extensive public notifications when data is lost, but also apply to a health care provider's business associates. HIPAA coverage is dynamic and changing so that today it may not cover all PHRs but coverage is increasing. These issues involve questions of who is responsible and often highlight unresolved liability problems (SearchHealthIT.com 2010).

E-Health received a boost from the Obama administration with the passage of the *American Recovery and Reinvestment Act* (ARRA) of 2009. ARRA includes the HITECH Act which initially made available over $20 billion for health care practitioners who become meaningful users of HIT. The HITECH Act established the Office of the National Coordinator for HIT in the federal government. As part of the HITECH Act (See Table 7.1 Health Information Technology for Economic and

Table 7.1 E-Health-related laws and regulatory agencies

U.S. laws and agencies	E-Health purpose
Law: Health Insurance Portability and Accountability Act of 1996 (HIPAA)	Ensures the safety and security of the health care system. Under certain conditions, internet and broadband providers are subject to HIPAA
Law: Patient Protection and Affordable Care Act of 2010 (PPACA)	Contains provisions to make available affordable health care
Law: Section 508 of the Rehabilitation Act of 1973 as amended in 1986 and 1998	Requires electronic and information technology in federal workplace to be accessible
Law: American Recovery and Reinvestment Act of 2009 (ARRA)	Includes the High Tech Act which made available over $20 billion for HIT and established the position of National Coordinator for HIT
Agency: U.S. Office of National Coordinator of HIT created in 2004 and legislatively mandated in Health Information Technology for Economic and Clinical Health Act (HITECH Act) of 2009	Charged with coordination of nationwide efforts to implement and use the most advanced health information technology and the electronic exchange of health information. Created in 2004, and legislatively mandated in the HITECH Act of 2009
Agency: U.S. Centers for Medicare and Medicaid (formerly Health Care Financing Administration established in 1977)	CMS administers Medicare, and works in partnership with the states to administer Medicaid. Implements the insurance reform provisions of the Health Insurance Portability and Accountability Act of 1996 (HIPAA). Provides incentive payments to eligible professionals, eligible hospitals and critical access hospitals (CAHs) as they adopt, implement, upgrade or demonstrate meaningful use of certified EHR technology
Agency: U.S. Food and Drug Administration dates back to 1906 Pure Food and Drugs Act, the milestone that marks the beginning of the modern Food and Drug Administration (FDA)	Regulates medical devices through device manufacturers

Clinical Health Act), a Meaningful Use Incentive program encourages meaningful use of HIT by professionals and hospitals (Moor et al. 2011; U.S. The Office of National Coordinator Health Information Technology 2011). The program outlines a framework for measuring how EHRs are used. It is intended to unfold in three stages with escalating requirements over 5 years. The program, which is administered by CMS, ties financial incentives to the use of EHR certified technology in Medicare and Medicaid. Stage 2 Meaningful Use rules should take effect in 2012. Meaningful Use objectives and criteria are characterized more by technical performance than by criteria informing areas of value for human beings, including clinicians and consumers. Meaningful Use criteria do not address use by patients. However, for the first time, Stage 2 Meaningful Use rules do refer to responsibilities for accessibility (U.S. Department of Health & Human Services 2012).

Providers, clinicians, and patients will carefully watch developments related to other links between e-Health and HIPAA, such as HIPAA standards for e-Health transactions for the International Classification of Disease (Centers for Medicare & Medicaid Services 2012) and the Patient Protection and Affordable Care Act (PPACA). HIPAA privacy rules will be applied to some provisions of PPACA. Besides containing provisions to make affordable health care available, PPACA is also designed to increase collaboration in health care, such as in patient-centered medical homes. In turn, these homes may benefit from the e-Health system which transmits medical information to and from the point of care and the clinical center. There is a huge literature indicating that older adults and people with disabilities prefer to remain in their homes rather than live in a nursing facility. Therefore, medical homes appear to have value for patients.

The framework for accessible telecommunications has been established but its application to e-Health lags. Section 508 of the Rehabilitation Act, for example, requires that Federal agencies' electronic and information technology be accessible to people with disabilities. Accessibility of EHRs for individuals who are blind or have other disabilities is an ethical dimension corresponding to the principle of justice.

Medical devices such as glucose meters are not primarily included as health information technology or e-Health. Nonetheless, vast numbers of HIT systems interface with multiple medical devices. These devices are important to monitor vital signs and/or collect health-related data that might support a clinician's decisions. The U.S. Food and Drug Administration (FDA) regulates medical devices by creating requirements for manufacturers. The FDA is included in our model because of the number of medical devices that interface with e-Health. Regulation of e-Health for safety and effectiveness and reportage of adverse events would contribute to clinician trust in HIT.

Conclusions

This section has introduced each component of our socio-technical system model and emerging issues. On the individual level, clinicians are under pressure to adjust to the introduction of e-Health which could move them from dependence on their own judgment to dependence on the performance of HIT. Thus, clinicians are involved in an ethical dilemma – to resist introduction of e-Health and depend on their own judgment and competencies or to accept a different basis for decisions. Nonetheless, clinicians must provide services in an e-Health clinical environment.

On the socio-technical level, vendors and health care entities operate within at least two ethical frameworks: biomedical, in which the patient is primary, and business, in which the shareholder is primary. If driven solely by the profit motive, vendors and the shareholders from vendor companies, for example, unless constrained by corporate social responsibility policies and law and regulation, would tend to make decisions which provide the largest financial gain to meet their ethical responsibilities to shareholders. Their decisions involve integration and upgrade of

Fig. 7.2 Technology
development in eHealth

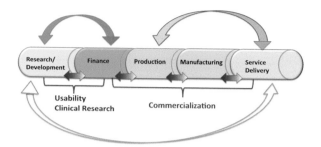

technology, clinical roles, workflows, and risk factors, all of which have safety and effectiveness implications for consumers. Largely unresolved are liability issues related to who is responsible for errors and under what conditions. There is no wrap-around regulatory scheme for e-Health that would provide a point of decisional responsibility and generate more interdependence among the components while also representing the interests of the public. System fragmentation emerges as a major feature of e-Health.

Many factors may play a role in the government's apparent reluctance to develop PHRs to enhance consumer involvement and to require regulation and mandatory reportage of adverse events in protection of the public. Nonetheless, if PHR usability data and adverse event reportage data were readily available, researchers could use it to help determine what works and what does not work. However, the process would probably complicate adoption of e-Health. Applying the Common Morality approach in ethics, government inaction is incompatible with the ethical principles of non-maleficence, because patient well-being is threatened, and beneficence, because the patient is not being empowered by available or potentially available e-Health benefits. Justice involves the equitable distribution of benefits and costs/risks, including accessibility, affordability, availability, and harm.

7.2.3   Technology Development Pipeline

Fragmentation in the socio-technical system becomes more apparent by examining the e-Health HIT development pipeline. E-Health technology, like all technology, is developed in stages, and upgrades routinely occur for each generation of a software product. Each stage has ethical dimensions which can impact clinical conduct. Figure 7.2 presents the technology development pipeline showing stages of technology development of particular relevance to e-Health: Research and development (R&D), manufacturing, and health care service delivery. Laws and regulations introduced in Table 7.1 are infused into each stage. This figure is a dynamic, interactive model. For example, if technology is not commercialized, there will be limited funds for research and development and for service delivery.

Research and Development (R&D)

The ethical dimensions at the research and development (R&D) stage include HIPAA privacy provisions for research subjects, design of software, software evaluation, and usage. Privacy protection corresponds to the principle of autonomy that directs the clinician to respect patients and to protect vulnerable populations.

Ethical dimensions of software design issues include whether or not software will be a support for human decision making or a substitute for it. Software may or may not be designed to create value for designers, developers, health care entities, clinicians, clients, and the public. Software design algorithms may bar, limit, or enable end user control options such as those that can be incorporated into an electric wheelchair, which impacts on the principle of autonomy. The development and use of rigorous software EHR evaluation tools would contribute to the effort toward more technical interdependence and operability in the e-Health socio-technical system, leading to increased privacy protection for medical information and increased adherence to the principle of non-maleficence.

A potential research project involves the University of Pittsburgh's e-Health system, HealthTrak. The system is voluntary and permits the use of a proxy for individuals with disabilities and others. Proxy access allows a UPMC HealthTrak member to access another member's record and perform other functions such as making appointments, refilling prescriptions, conducting eVisits, using an online billable medical evaluation and management service, communicating via UPMC HealthTrak with UPMC's billing office regarding bills, etc. Ethical questions involve under what conditions proxy requests should be granted and patient satisfaction with decision makers, whether they be the patients themselves or designated others. These questions correspond to the ethical principle of autonomy.

Finance and Manufacturing Stage

The finance and manufacturing stage of e-Health development is particularly important. At this stage ideas emerge from the research stage and are transformed into actual products. If financing is found, these products go to market where they may be purchased. While the process for uniform specifications for EHR software continues to evolve, manufacturers and vendors subject existing EHRs to a process of software validation, testing, and certification using guidelines developed by the U.S. Office of the National Coordinator of HIT. These tests are important for the safety, effectiveness, and reliability of HIT. Standards and criteria for PHR which show value for patient use should also be tested and made available.

EHR manufacturers, unlike medical device manufacturers, are not regulated by the U.S. FDA even though many medical devices such as glucose meters interface with e-Health. The ethical framework for EHR lags in identifying a decision maker with responsibilities to identify and create value for end users, and safety and effectiveness protections for the public. Common Morality requires a human agent to which to attribute moral responsibility. Using the FDA model, EHR manufacturers and software developers are the obvious human agents in the responsible design and manufacture of EHRs.

Health Care Delivery

During the health care service delivery stage, vendors and health-related entity organizations have engaged in contractual relationships to deliver, maintain, and upgrade HIT. If the system is unreliable, the clinicians may receive incorrect information or receive medical information about the wrong patient. This erodes clinical trust. As indicated earlier, some contracts between vendors and health entities may involve agreements to hold vendors harmless for e-Health system malfunction and some may not. General consensus about ethical responsibility for these decisions about vendor responsibility is lacking.

The Patient Protection and Affordable Care Act is an important law for the service delivery stage. It provides for affordable and available health care and, along with HIPAA privacy rules, will provide additional protections to health care consumers. The Americans with Disabilities Act and Section of 508 of the Rehabilitation Act are among the laws that address accessibility. Accessibility of e-Health for people with disabilities serves the principles of justice.

Conclusions

Laws and regulation permeate the e-Health pipeline at the state and federal level and, as with the case of liability, are often not in harmony with each other (Miller 2012). If law and regulation move beyond evident lags and become more technologically relevant to e-Health and to the public, justice will be served by equitable distribution of health resources, benefits, and costs/risk. The case studies below further illustrate activities of components of the socio-technical system.

7.2.4   Case Examples of HIT, Health-Related Entities, and Laws and Regulations

The case studies that follow provide examples of the performance and activities of HIT, health care vendors and entities, and governance agencies.

Health Information Technology

Case 1: In 2011 the IOM released a study of the FDA regulatory process. Among its recommendations, the IOM addressed software issues (Institute of Medicine (U.S.). Committee on the Public Health Effectiveness of the FDA 510(k) Clearance Process

2011). Recalls of medical devices in which the problem was caused by software have been climbing for years (Centers for Medicare & Medicaid Services 2012). According to the IOM, software is complex and creates uncertainty, in part because of its multiple usages and also because of the context in which it is used. Software is within a device, is a device (EHRs), and is a tool in producing medical devices. Software also performs within networked systems that can range from body-level networks to global transmissions.

Identifying the cause of a software error is complex because of the difficulty of identifying the location of the problem, which can be situated in the software or the networked system. For example, a patient has a medical device that transmits data to a receiver in his home (Brennan et al. 2011). In turn, the data is sent to a server that eventually places the data on a physician's laptop. The communication may work in two directions. After the physician evaluates the patient data, she may transmit a signal to change the settings in the medical device by, for instance, changing a medication's dose or its frequency.

The IOM recommends that the FDA study questions and concerns about software in medical devices, including how the FDA should evaluate a device with respect to safety, dependability, security, reliability, and privacy. These indicators correspond to the ethical principle of non-maleficence and are responsive to clinical concerns which correspond to beneficence. Case 2 in the Law and Regulation section below shows that in a different IOM study, the IOM panel was very dubious about the FDA's ability to pursue evaluation and was concerned about the negative impact on e-Health innovation and implementation. Decisions about the nature of regulation of EHR seem to have been politicized. Powerful interests, including the Obama Administration and industry, are in strong support of innovation leading to the marketplace but have not expressed strong interest in support of what is commonly regarded as the public interest.

Vendors and Health-Related Entities

Case 1. ECRI Institute staff reported that most hospitals have good policies and procedures for handling alerts and recalls as they come out. However, when it comes to reporting failures and errors, it becomes very difficult to identify a problem as software-related or network-related. Perhaps for this reason, ECRI acknowledged that problems are underreported to the FDA (Centers for Medicare & Medicaid Services 2012). Reportage is an indicator that corresponds to the principle of non-maleficence.

Case 2. According to a hospital manager, many hospitals still have separate clinical engineering and information technology groups. But because the technology is evolving, with more software-related hazards and recalls, these groups are forced to work more closely together and need more cross-training (Pearson 2011). Competence is an indicator on the clinical level that corresponds to the principle of autonomy and on the system level is an indicator of change management and training, which relate to non-maleficence.

Case 3. Another hospital finds that telehealth networking problems account for upwards of 90 % of all problems. These network failures are distinct from failures pointing to software inside devices, but the two modes can be difficult to distinguish from each other so both are considered when preparing to check with the device manufacturer. There are many software-related issues because everyone is in a hurry to compete in the marketplace, so they get the product out sooner than they should (Centers for Medicare & Medicaid Services 2012). Software and network failures are indicators of the safety and reliability of a product, which are the responsibility of the manufacturer and possibly the risk management responsibilities of the health-related entity. Software validation is also an FDA regulatory responsibility. These examples involve the principle of non-maleficence.

Case 4. A hospitalized patient's blood clotting time becomes dangerously elevated. Findings from an investigation show that the patient received double doses of an anticoagulation medication due to an error in how the medication was processed by the pharmacy computer system after being entered by the computerized provider order entry system (Leviss 2010). Again, the failure is one of technical performance and corresponds to non-maleficence.

Case 5. A nurse administered a drug to a patient who was allergic to it. The patient experienced respiratory arrest. When the error occurred, the medication dispensing machine was down and was unable to access the patient's medication record, including his allergies. The nurse selected and administered a similarly spelled medication to that ordered, which triggered the adverse event. While in the past this type of medical information might be shared or available on paper, the nurse had become dependent on the machine and did not check further. The vendor did not report the downtime because a fix was imminent. The failure in technical performance and the vendor's lack of reportage correspond to the indicators of safety and reliability and error and risk management, and to the principle of non-maleficence. The need for change management and training corresponds to the principle of beneficence.

Law and Regulation

Case 1. In 2010, the FDA issued a report on HIT safety issues (U.S. Food and Drug Administration 2010a) that provided a review of medical device reports in the FDA's Manufacturer and User Facility Experience database. The findings indicated that 49 % of the errors were errors of commission, such as accessing the wrong patient's record or overwriting one patient's information with another's. Twenty-seven percent of the errors were errors of omission or transmission such as the loss or corruption of vital patient data. Twenty-two percent of the errors were in data analysis such as medication dosing errors of several orders of magnitude. Two percent were attributable to incompatibility between multiple vendors. A review of events leading to serious injury or death provided limited insight into the clinical impact of the reported events. The FDA speculated that the limitation may result from an absence of mandatory regulations and requirements including manufacturer investigation of the event.

The FDA provided an individual review of death reports using computerized physician order entry and EHRs. Three reports documented errors of commission such as the user entering the wrong patient name in a study image, resulting in the wrong patient receiving therapy. There were two errors of omission such as the user being unaware that an exam had a note attached containing positive clinical findings. There was error in data analysis so that patient chemotherapy was inaccurately prepared.

A number of standards were compromised in areas in which law and regulation may have prevented serious injury or death, but has limited oversight. Errors in HIT software and network performance relate to indicators of reliability, safety and effectiveness, and the principle of non-maleficence. The origins of the problem may be located at the manufacturing and/or service delivery stages. Problems with management of risk and adverse events correspond to non-maleficence, while training and workforce related to change management and the principles of autonomy, and beneficence. Problems with clinical competence correspond to the principle of autonomy and clinical consciousness in system safety to beneficence.

Case 2. As indicated earlier, in 2012 the IOM released a report on HIT and patient safety (Archer et al. 2012). The report advised against FDA regulation of e-Health. The IOM argued that the FDA lacks the funds, investigative capabilities, and human resources to investigate health IT tools, including electronic health records, health information exchanges, and personal health records. The IOM noted that FDA investigations could restrict innovation in the health IT industry. The report states that strict regulations "can negatively impact the development of new technology by limiting implementation choices and restricting manufacturers' flexibility to address complex issues." The IOM calls for the Department of Health and Human Services to create and fund a new, independent watchdog agency to conduct investigations of health IT safety issues and develop recommendations for health care organizations, health IT vendors, and government officials. The proposed agency would not have enforcement power. The report also states that health IT vendors should be required to report adverse events associated with their products. Health care providers could voluntarily report health IT-related safety issues. The report did not provide protection for the public. Equitable distribution of health resources, benefits, and costs/risks is a matter of justice.

Case 3. The passage of the American Recovery and Reinvestment Act (ARRA) of 2009 made available over $20 billion for health care practitioners who become meaningful users of HIT. The Obama Administration is firmly behind implementation of HIT. The U.S. ARRA investment in HIT may be responsive to the need for available and affordable health care and thus correspond to the principle of beneficence. However, lack of standard clinical guidance on Meaningful Use across organizations such as the Joint Commission (The Joint Commission 2012), DHHS, ONC-HIT, AHRQ, and AMIA may lead to harm and thus violate the principle of non-maleficence.

Case 4. The Office of the National Coordinator's HIT Policy Committee conducted a hearing to gather EHR experience from the field (EHR: Experience from the Field 2012). Many speakers commented about electronic health record (EHR) vendors, implementation, and functionality. The impact on productivity was described by one physician as "death by a thousand clicks." Another said that clicking through screens, inputting data, and checking boxes took time away from the patient. One clinician notes, "Vendor solutions are often awkward and time-consuming." They may accomplish the meaningful use task, but are not very usable themselves. Another commented, "EHR implementations fail when they become IT projects instead of clinical projects involving technology." The selection of an EHR should be workflow based; the vendor must have a common sense approach to workflow. One speaker said that EHR vendors are scrambling to keep up with the changing governmental demands for reporting functionality. This frequently results in misrepresentation of the software's current abilities. The report noted that there is deep concern that practices are rushing to install EHR systems to meet meaningful use, only to find out that the EHR does not meet the needs of the practitioners – this will be very costly in the end.

7.2.5 Conclusions

Clearly there are a number of barriers to realization of optimal HIT performance, vendor and health-entity management, and law and regulation. Many of them relate to the principle of non-maleficence. They are compounded by a complex and fragmented system in which time and place variations occur in the development and implementation of the technology and by the lack of shared jurisdictions in which legal and managerial authority might repose. These problems confound attempts to identify morally responsible agents. Many of the barriers to ethical conduct relate to the performance of software and integration of software into complex networks. In the larger picture, lags in developing uniform standards of clinical practice in e-Health are impacting management and policy. Lags in adoption of e-Health regulation are dependent, in part, on regulatory theory and applications appropriate to HIT and to political compromise among contending interests. These technical failures and clinical and governance lags have serious implications for the conduct of clinicians.

7.3 Clinical Practice

The purpose of this section is to identify e-Health problems generated in the clinical workplace and to explore their impact on ethical clinical conduct with special sensitivity to the clinical values of trust, veracity, and fidelity. Clinical practice is the social end of the socio-technical system spectrum involving the clinician and the patient/client. The clinician, often unconsciously, absorbs the impact of problems that originate in the technology at the R&D, manufacturing, or service delivery stages of development and also problems in management and inadequacy of laws, regulations, and professional codes. Nonetheless, the clinician must provide a standard of care for the patient which, traditionally, has been characterized by unmediated communication with patients and colleagues.

An ongoing concern of this chapter has been the ethical basis and process for dealing with change while reaffirming what is fundamental in healthcare. Guided by bioethics, the patient-clinician relationship entails special obligations to serve the patient's interest because of the specialized knowledge and skill the clinician possesses, the confidential nature of the relationship, and the imbalance of power between patient and physician. The clinician's primary commitment must always be to the patient's welfare and best interests. Yet, according to the ECRI Institute, one of the top ten causes of technical hazards for medical devices involves a misunderstanding by the end user.

As the case studies will show, patients, too, are becoming important users of HIT. As the point of care shifts to the home or wherever the patient is located, the patient may receive care services using e-Health or m-Health such as a cell phone or an iPad. A series of case studies are introduced to illustrate problems experienced by patients/consumers. Case studies illustrating clinicians' problems, in particular, show emotional reactions to change introduced by e-Health.

7.3.1   Case Studies

Case 1. A deaf person needs a sign language interpreter available when communicating with a health professional face-to-face or remotely, as in the use of a video telephone relay system or telecommunication devices for the deaf (TDD). However, these health consumer needs must appear on the patient's intake health form. Often this information is either not requested or the form cannot accommodate it. Form design for an e-Health system is executed in an office of health medical records in the medical system. Health information management (HIM) personnel are not familiar with the communication needs of deaf users and do not include alternate modes of communication in the list of necessary items in the design of health intake forms. HIM personnel, either through university education or post-university training, should be made aware of the accessibility needs of people with disabilities. HIM personnel did not make the system accessible, an indicator of problems in training, competence, advocacy, consciousness of the system at the individual level, and accessibility policies at the health entity level. The result is an unfair distribution of benefits corresponding respectively to the principles of autonomy, non-maleficence, and justice.

Case 2. An electric power wheelchair user with quadriplegia participates in many activities in the community using a smartphone for communication, assistance with executing tasks, and emergency support. The wheelchair is equipped with many smart functions, including a robotic arm which permits him to manipulate objects, prepare meals, and perform other activities of daily life. He has worked with designers to develop an interface on his mobile phone to accommodate his usability needs. The wheelchair can be controlled by the user, the caregiver, and a remote controller. Using high-speed broadband, he can press a quick key and dial a remote assistant to work cooperatively with him to perform a task. At one point, the broadband signal dropped out and the task was interrupted. The wheelchair transitioned to a safety-state, and was set to resume operation once the broadband connection was re-established. Reliability, safety, and security problems of Internet and broadband transmission correspond to violations of principles of autonomy and non-maleficence.

Case 3. *E-psychotherapy and counseling* is an Internet-based modality for therapist-client interaction in non-clinical settings (Lee 2010). The therapist must be conscious of a number of issues including the possibility of misunderstanding, maintenance of professional boundaries, the issues of confidentiality, and the interruption of services. Professionals must also be aware of the limitations in the use of e-psychotherapy. Appropriate consciousness of these limitations involves screening out clients with an immediate crisis because of the difficulty of ensuring a safe, accurate assessment without visual cues or the physical proximity of the clients. Self-harm is a concern due to limiting factors within e-therapy. For example, those who offer e-therapy through e-mail communication will find that it is not immediate enough to be an appropriate way to communicate with a suicidal or homicidal client. The therapist may not know the location of the client. Professional organizations should update their guidelines to address ethical concerns in e-therapy and related compliance procedures. The case study uses indicators such as conscientiousness of e-Health system capability and limitations as guidelines for its use. The therapist therefore seeks to avoid harm and exhibits lovingness and kindness which correspond to beneficence. The author/therapist's reference to updating ethical guidelines in the professions corresponds to preventing harm and the principle of non-maleficence.

Case 4. A client is tele-assessed for autism spectrum disorders by a Rehabilitation Counselor using a teleportal within the medical system's HIT. The clinician needs a system that can deliver assessment with the same validity as an assessment delivered face-to-face. Because evaluating eye contact is important in the diagnosis of autism, a teleprompter may be used to simulate direct eye contact. The counselor is also interested in assessing the client's social interactions. Therefore, a tablet is used to display the visual stimuli, usually pictures, so the clinician can evaluate whether or not the client engages the clinician in her responses to the stimuli. The teleprompter and tablet products were identified and integrated into the videoconferencing and documentation system by HIM professionals. The practitioner did extensive education on autism with the HIM personnel in order to sensitize them to the needs of both the client and clinicians. The client needed to have a system design that was streamlined and would not distract her from carrying out the assessment. The clinician needed the ability to see multiple views of the client and to manipulate those views. The scoring forms are integrated into the system because the clinician needed an electronic means of documenting client responses and the ability to reference those notes when completing the scoring form. Health information management (HIM) personnel tried to make the system as usable as possible for clinicians. The counselor and HIM personnel are engaged in inter-professional collaboration after developing competence through training, which corresponds to the principle of autonomy, and have displayed a consciousness of system safety features corresponding to the principle of non-maleficence.

Case 5. A series of vignettes involving critical care nurses' experience with software failure illustrates the impact of that failure on the nurses' self-efficacy. One critical care nurse experienced the failure of an IV pump which delivered an incorrect amount of medication without setting off an alarm (Haghenbeck 2005). Another nurse had to remove a patient from a malfunctioning ventilator and was about to provide oxygen for the patient using a hand-held device called an ambu bag when the bag's pressure flow meter fell off. Both nurses thought they were doing everything right but a faulty piece of equipment "just throws you". These nurses, who are members of a larger sample in a study, began to distrust the reliability of the technology, their own competence, and their own professional image. The nurses felt frustrated, powerless, inadequate, and ignored when they reported the malfunctions. Further, they felt professionally threatened because an incident that could result in patient harm must be reported to the supervisor. The nurses in this study were cautious about reporting malfunctioning technology because the individual clinician is held responsible and accountable even if the errors were system-based. One nurse stated she was upset by the many false alarms as opposed to the small number that reflected actual adverse events or system errors. The critical care nurses were also upset and shocked when alarms did not occur on malfunctioning machines and the malfunctions were only discovered by chance.

Case 6. Physicians have expressed their frustrations with e-Health in the Disease Management Care blog, among other sites, and through newspaper articles (Hsieh et al. 2004; Kelly 2012; Sidorov and Disease Management Care Blog 2011). Vignettes capture their reactions. One doctor mused about how often alarm overrides lead to preventable adverse drug events. He indicated that one system sent out 7,761 alerts of which 6,182 were overridden by physicians. A study showed that all the overrides were clinically justifiable.

Case 7. This case study provides an example of the tensions among industry, professional, and consumer groups generated by the introduction of hearing e-Health. In October, 2011, the largest U.S. insurer by revenue, United Healthcare (UHC), announced that it would provide subscribers and the general public with online hearing testing and allow the purchase of hearing aids via the Internet through its subsidiary HealthInnovations[TM] (HI). Its parent company, United Health Group, introduced its 2012 Medicare Advantage Plans and began marketing to elderly subscribers. These, apparently lower-cost hearing devices are targeted at the 36 million Americans with hearing loss. An estimated 75 % of people who can benefit from hearing devices do not use them, largely due to high cost or stigma. The announcement about online testing and purchasing coincided with United Health Group's announcement that it would provide a $50,000 grant to the National Council on Aging for health care (UnitedHealth Group 2011).

The Hearing Loss Association of America (HLAA), the largest consumer group of people with hearing loss in the U.S., has taken the position of "giving innovation programs such as this one a chance" (Battat 2012). The HLAA position is based on the need to open more doors and lower the hurdles to seeking and receiving hearing health care. HLAA believes that this approach may reduce costs and relieve the stigma associated with hearing loss and the related assessment process. The American Academy of Audiology and the American Academy of Dispensing Audiologists are adamant about the risk for patients inherent in the UHC/HI program (American Academy of Audiology 2012). They are also questioning whether the hearing health benefit will be in conformance with licensure requirements and requirements such as FDA regulations. The Academy petitioned the FDA and the hearing test was removed from the market, at least temporarily.

Industry and consumers have aligned in support of the program. The consumer organization, in particular, represents the needs and values of those with hearing impairments. HLAA was an early supporter of an e-Health hearing assessment and device purchase delivery system. Because of its mission as a consumer organization, HLAA, unlike industry for example, has enhanced responsibility for educating consumers and advocating for guidelines and regulations that support technical safety and effectiveness, as well as medical and clinical competence. As in other examples of e-Health implementation, data from monitoring and reportage, after purchase, would provide evidence for researchers on which to base recommendations to improve safety, quality, and consumer satisfaction. Clinicians are duty-bound to protect the client and therefore should develop clinical guidelines for e-Health hearing services that assure that they are "good" services, i.e., have medical and clinical efficacy. Clinical activity would be representative of the principle of beneficence while HLAA advocacy and education would correspond to the principle of autonomy.

7.3.2 Conclusions

The case studies provide examples of e-Health problems in health care for both clients/patients and clinicians. Software intake forms are not designed to accommodate accessibility needs of deaf persons. Wi-Fi failures, located in the telecommunications component of the system, endanger a person with a significant disability who cannot use his phone to seek assistance. Nurses become dependent on technology which fails, leaving the nurse with considerable psychological trauma and feelings of incompetence and the patient severely harmed. Physicians make their own judgments about response alarms warning of system malfunctions. The problem of trust in the system is a prominent theme that corresponds to all the principles in Common Morality.

7.4   Ethics

Throughout this chapter, the ethical dimensions of problems generated by e-Health have been approached using the Common Morality approach, a classic approach in bioethics. The purpose of this section is to examine the adequacy of ethics to provide guidance for clinical conduct in the e-Health environment, in light of the problems identified in Sects. 7.2 and 7.3. Approaches and theories such as those in biomedical, computer, and machine ethics will be assessed for their value in providing guidance for clinicians. However, socio-technical system components, such as health vendors, for-profit health entities, and Internet and broadband providers may be guided by a different or an additional ethical framework of business ethics. Therefore, business ethics, too, will be examined for its usefulness in understanding the ethical dimensions of problems generated by e-Health.

Biomedical ethics is the traditional basis for normative standards for health care. Bioethics provides guidance in the development of clinical standards of care and codes of ethics and in Health Information Management practices. In turn, this guidance is important in determining clinical education and training. The emerging fields of Medical Informatics and Rehabilitation Informatics provide an important knowledge base for e-Health and for the evolving field of Health Information Management. Health Information Management and clinical practice personnel, acting as a team, are necessary for successful adoption and implementation of e-Health. Therefore, these fields and professions are particularly important in support of ethical clinical conduct. They, too, will be explored in this section.

Problems experienced by clinicians in the e-Health environment often have their origins in the socio-technical system. Some originate at stages of development such as manufacturing where software EHR and PHR design is an important consideration. As illustrated by the case examples, when medical devices malfunction clinicians feel distrustful of themselves and their health-entity organization. They become frustrated and lose confidence in their competence to protect their patients – a sacred trust.

Standards for performance of the socio-technical system are re-visited by focusing on software performance identified in FDA reports. Software and the complex information and communication networks into which it is integrated have been the source of significant risk to the welfare of patients and those who care for them. Software problems are manifested in each of the components of the socio-technical system and for clinicians. As a result, ethical dilemmas have developed for e-Health professionals and for the larger community of those concerned about attribution of moral responsibility in complex health systems and the need for strategies for identifying moral agents.

Table 7.2 Ethical theories and approaches in historical sequence

Theory	Source (examples)	Description
Virtue ethics	Plato (427–347 BCE) Aristotle (384–322 BCE)	Key idea is to find proper end for humans and to seek that end. People seek perfection/excellence and seek to live virtuous lives. What sort of person should I be? Contributes to the understanding of professional ethics and in the training necessary to produce ethical professionals
Deontological theories	Immanuel Kant (1724–1804)	Deon (deontological) means duty in Greek; science of doing our duty. Thus, doing the right thing might not always lead to an increase in the good
Teleology/ consequentialism	Utilitarianism Jeremy Bentham (1748–1834) John Stuart Mill (1806–1873)	Maximize the good of situation; the greatest good to the greatest number; make a decision dependent on consequences of an action
Caring ethics	Feminist ethics (contemporary)	Raises questions about relationships and other factors in the context of doing health care; recognizes the impact of the uneven distribution of power on ability to make autonomous decisions
Common morality approach	Tom L. Beauchamp & James F. Childress (contemporary)	Morality contains some action-guiding norms and specific "privileged norms" that are constitutive of morality itself. These norms are the basis of a universal moral community

7.4.1   Bioethics, Organizational, and Business Ethics

Clinical codes of ethics are based on approaches and theories derived from bioethics. As the prefix bio would suggest, biology is the focus of research and practice and the individual is the level and unit of analysis in bioethics. The most commonly used biomedical ethical theories and principles are presented in Table 7.2. While organizational and business ethics are separate from bioethics, they are also based on the individual as the morally responsible agent. In ethics, organizations are also studied on a group level in order to examine and identify values underlying policies, management practices, and culture.

Biomedical Ethics, Theories, and Approaches

The Common Morality approach, itself, conceives of the task of ethicists as critical reflection on actual and proposed moral norms and practices or, as in this chapter, guidelines needed for clinical conduct in the e-Health environment. At the socio-technical system level concepts that connect the socio-technical level with the individual level are necessary for analysis because, according to Common Morality, only humans are recognized as moral agents. Trust is a particularly useful concept; in this case, clinical trust in the safety and effectiveness of e-Health systems.

At the individual level, virtue ethics emphasizes the role of character and virtuous action such as in whistle blowing in the case of dishonesty in describing an error related to treatment of a patient or medical forms which are not designed to include information on accessibility. However, until liability issues are clarified clinicians may be reluctant to identify errors in the current framework in which clinicians are morally responsible agents in the delivery of patient care while not necessarily the cause of an error.

Other biomedical ethical theory is concerned with the analysis and evaluation of volitional action; with what makes a chosen action right or wrong, good or bad, whether in terms of intentions and obligations as in deontological theory or in terms of outcomes of good for the greatest numbers as in consequentialism. Duty ethics might motivate a clinician to take a course in health information management in order to develop better skills and competency in HIT, especially in system failure response. However, a clinician who has become dependent on software-generated decision-making may face ethical dilemmas about the basis for her judgment and the scope of her responsibility in clinical care. Caring ethics focuses on the relationship between the clinician and the client. A clinician motivated by caring ethics may place greater value on assisting the patient, directly manifesting kindness and trust developed in face-to-face interventions than on mediated delivery of care which they may regard as of less value to the patient. These clinicians may have difficulty with trusting their hospital or clinical organization and e-Health technology if they require technologically mediated relationships with the patient which appears to be unjustified by patient need.

Clinicians, motivated by the need for ethical rules developed to extend to the new demands within complex clinical environments, may seek skills that will create enhanced consciousness of system safety. Extension of traditional character traits to include consciousness of technical systems may then become a norm of virtue ethics and a character trait for clinical adoption. Consciousness of system safety at the individual level may lead to requests for the professional organizations to develop clinically-based guidelines for risk management for e-Health system failure in order to process responsibility for error. Professional collaboration in development of competencies in clinical practice and health information management and clear designation of roles will help to clarify moral responsibility in the e-Health environment. Health entity organizational policy is also important in determination of the roles of professionals within their purview.

Organization and Business Ethics

Principles in organizational and business ethics are relevant and useful to health-related entities, especially as their authority extends to HIT (Singer 1991; Zoubul 2009) in part because new workflow configurations generated by e-Health require innovative management. Business ethics include individual character traits of stewardship, fidelity, trust, honesty, and organizational policies which include corporate social responsibility. Bioethics and business ethics both play an important role in maintaining trust through guidance in organizational policies for management of change and risk. Corporate policy that adopts change management is supportive of developing and training of teams composed of clinical and HIM personnel that may advance the needs of all users. As the clinical case study about the deaf user and medical records suggests, corporate policies and a culture of accessibility affect all individual users, but in particular people with disabilities across the age span.

If consequentialist ethics drives health-related entities that utilize e-Health and EHRs, these entities may advocate for clinical testing and certification of EHR systems and software. Health professional organizations, such as the American Physical Therapy Association and the American Speech-Language-Hearing Association, might educate and lobby for any number of issues such as requirements for vendors and health care entities to report adverse events, additional program accreditation guidelines for inter-professionalism, accessibility, and usability in order to extend beneficial outcomes to the greatest number.

However, a thread running through the chapter is the pressure to innovate, to market, and to implement e-Health. While business ethics can provide constraints within this competitive process, its primary interest is to meet responsibilities to the shareholder, not the patient. Therefore, business ethics has significant limitations in protecting the patient and those who deliver e-Health services.

Computer Ethics

Computer ethics is involved with ethical issues related to human use of computers. Therefore, problems associated with the design, usability, and accessibility of computers are within its purview. Computer and information ethicists share with the field of engineering concern for design, often within the context of obligations of designers (Johnson and Miller 2009; Manders-Huits 2011; Nickel 2011; Stahl 2004). Some computer ethicists have expressed concern about the design of direct computer interfaces (DCI) and decision support systems in which some of the intellectual tasks of the clinician are taken over by the computer. For example, DCIs collect patient data, draw inferences from the data, and respond back to the patient. The knowledge base for computer ethics and biomedical ethics has the potential to be mined to provide guidelines for software development and related networks. The two areas of ethics, if integrated as a subfield, could provide guidance for an ethical e-Health environment, perhaps especially in the clinical design of software and its use.

Health information management professionals (Abdelhak et al. 2012; Harman 2006) work closely with technical fields such as computer science, which provides the theoretical knowledge base for HIT. Information and computer ethicists have introduced a range of relevant ethical issues into the clinical practice mix. Like biomedical ethicists, information and computer ethicists recognize the centrality of issues such as privacy and security of data, but they are also sensitive to societal, structural, and policy dilemmas. They see a need for balancing concern for privacy and security against the desirability of linking disparate sources of information. Clearly, the operationalization of global health care data exchange would serve justice if the number of underserved in health care were diminished. Nonetheless, tradeoffs between privacy, security, and data exchanges pose ethical dilemmas. While there has been continuing progress in the development of standards for delivery of secure accurate health data, privacy, security, and accuracy of data are matters of major concern.

Machine Ethics

The emerging field of machine ethics is concerned with adding ethical dimensions to machines (Allen et al. 2006; Anderson and Anderson 2007; Andersora et al. 2006; Birmingham 2008; Honarvar and Ghasem-Aghaee 2009; Tonkens 2009; Waser 2009; Kraemer et al. 2011). It is concerned with ensuring that the behavior of machines toward human users, and perhaps other machines as well, is ethically acceptable. While some machine ethicists argue that systems deserve no special moral consideration, others argue strongly for machine ethics as an appropriate and effective approach to the problem of errors and failures in complex technology such as e-Health. While one strategy for making machines behave converts the Common Morality into a software program to guide machines in ethical conduct, another might design software specifically based on the characteristics of machines rather than on the characteristics of human beings.

Conclusions

Biomedical and computer ethics provide important guidance to clinicians and HIT personnel. However, serious ethical concerns exist about machine ethics involving the question of whose ethical approaches and values would be designed and programmed into software and how to identify moral responsibility. Nonetheless, computer and machine ethicists are involved with the problem of locating legitimate decision points for attribution of moral responsibility (Iserson 2000). Machine ethics is embroiled in an ongoing controversy about whether or not to imbue machines with ethical agency.

7.4.2   *Clinical Standards and Ethical Codes*

Bioethics has guided the development of ethical codes in HIM and clinical practice. Therefore, there is a common ethical basis for cooperation. However, reform of clinical and HIM academic education and post-university training programs to include interprofessional coordination and support will require considerable negotiation. There are huge barriers because HIM and each clinical practice field have developed as silos. Nonetheless, a number of practice areas are addressing standards for telepractice (Seelman 2013). Clinical standards and codes have been evolving over a decade or more to address telepractice, but not necessarily EHR. In 2000 a proposal for an ethical code in telemedicine was introduced (Iserson 2000). The code was based on virtue ethics. In 2008, the American Telemedicine Association (ATA) released its Core Standards for Telemedicine (American Telemedicine Association 2009). The American Health Information Management Association (AHIMA), the professional organization for health information management professionals, has recognized the need for collaboration with telepractice in its code of ethics (AHIMA 2012b).

A leading physician expert in informatics observed that introducing information systems into clinical care requires changing the way clinicians interact with patients and colleagues (Leviss 2010). It challenges their decision making at the point of care in front of colleagues and patients. This expert notes that to succeed, health systems must use a quality management approach such as interdisciplinary teams (Leviss 2010).

7.4.3 Emergence of Informatics and the Evolution of Health Information Management

As evidenced throughout this chapter, the health care industry is undergoing a fundamental change in the way health care data and information are collected, processed, communicated, and managed. As a result of advances in information and communication technology, the paper-based patient record environment of an earlier period is transitioning into an electronic health record environment. A number of professions have been transformed, including informatics and health information management.

Biomedical Informatics is an interdisciplinary field combining basic informational and computational sciences with application domains including health care, biological research, and education (Johnson and Friedman 2007). Interdisciplinary efforts across biomedical informatics and health applications, science, and clinical practice, have clashed. Nonetheless, some clinical fields have adopted models for training in the e-Health environment. Rehabilitation, for example, has developed a multidisciplinary model "for next generation rehabilitation information" (Schopp et al. 2003). The University of Pittsburgh School of Health and Rehabilitation Science has established a rehabilitation informatics department, the Department of Health Information Management, which is essentially health informatics. HIM personnel are involved along with others in informatics and clinical practice in establishing a health care information infrastructure that aims at supporting quality health care.

In summary, the emergence of informatics and health information management and especially training of clinicians has lagged behind the implementation of e-Health. The Institute of Medicine has recognized the problem and recommended that today's professionals' continuing education include informatics and interprofessionalism (Institute of Medicine (U.S.) Committee on Planning a Continuing Health Care Professional Education Institute 2010). While important, these strategies to develop an appropriate knowledge base, competencies, and standards of practice cannot solve some of the more profound questions generated by the introduction of e-Health into health care. Some of the problems associated with software are examined below within the context of regulation.

7.4.4 Regulation Practice as a Guide to Development of Ethical Guidance

U.S. Food and Drug Administration (FDA) regulatory experience with medical devices may contribute further to our understanding of the ethical dimensions of EHR software. EHR is software and vast amounts of medical devices are integrated into EHR and their networks. Nonetheless, EHR is not regulated by the FDA. As indicated in Sect. 7.2, U.S. government constraints on EHR sit at the intersection of CMS' meaningful use requirements and software certification requirements which are issued in the Office of the National Coordinator of HIT. Depending on use, software certification may or may not be mandatory.

In 2010 testimony before the HIT Policy Committee, Jeffrey Shuren of the FDA presented the agency's perspective on potential approaches to address HIT-related safety concerns (U.S. Food and Drug Administration 2010b). According to Shuren, while some medical devices contain software components, others are composed solely of software. The FDA has largely refrained from enforcing regulatory requirements with respect to HIT devices. In 2010 he reported that in the past 2 years, the agency received 260 reports of HIT-related malfunctions with the potential for patient harm, including 44 reported injuries and 6 reported deaths. This reportage is largely voluntary.

The adverse events have fallen into four major categories: (a) errors of commission, such as accessing the wrong patient's record or overwriting one patient's information with another; (b) errors of omission or transmission, such as the loss or corruption of vital patient data; (c) errors in data analysis, including medication dosing errors of several orders of magnitude; and (d) incompatibility between multi-vendor software applications and systems, which can lead to any of the above (Seelman 2013). Shuren noted the unique characteristics of HIT devices which do not typically operate as stand-alone devices but are interconnected with one another into networks of varying degrees of complexity. He observed that regulation is necessary to assure patient safety which is an indicator of non-maleficence. His guidance focuses on HIT device manufacturers as responsible agents for correcting safety issues. The FDA would conduct post-market surveillance or track selected high risk devices. Information would be shared with vendors and others. Another approach involves focusing on manufacturing quality and post-market safety and on requiring manufacturers to adhere to FDA's Quality Systems Regulation.

This regulation establishes procedures to assure the quality and consistency of products on the market. He strongly recommends that manufacturers and users be required to report adverse events and errors. While these are policy and regulation recommendations, they correspond to some of the ethical dimensions of the software design and adverse event problems. Biomedical and computer ethicists could draft criteria for software design and guidelines for processing adverse events. They could work with the FDA the Office of the National Coordinator and CMS to develop guidance for the certification of medical and clinical software.

7.5 Conclusions

The purpose of this chapter is to explore the ethical dimensions of a cutting-edge technology, e-Health, in order to identify its impact on clinical conduct and propose modest ameliorative strategies to address barriers to ethical clinical performance in an e-Health clinical environment. We have argued that the public has an important role in adoption of e-Health and therefore, the public must be well-informed about the issues. Therefore, we have laid out the chapter as a comprehensive introduction to e-Health. We have analyzed problems using a socio-technical system concept and a Common Morality approach to ethics that assumes human beings are the basis for authority and are ethical agents. Common Morality contains action guiding norms and specific "privileged norms" which are constitutive of morality itself such as autonomy, beneficence, non-maleficence, and justice. While these privileged norms are content thin, coupling them with case studies has provided a rich medley of analytic tools and material. Common Morality also charges human beings to use their best considered judgment to examine problems and to make judgments about their amelioration, even to the extent of recommending mid to lower level adjustments in norms or supplemental guidance.

A brief summary of findings appearing below indicates that problems that impact on the ethical conduct of clinicians exist in each component of the socio-technical system as well as in practical ethics. In keeping with the responsibility of using a Common Morality approach, modest ameliorative guidance is provided followed by the identification of seemingly intractable problems which are beyond the purview of this chapter but require further inquiry.

7.5.1 Problems Which Generate Barriers to Ethical Clinical Practice

The socio-technical system and its components create problems for clinicians practicing in an e-Health environment. Performance in each component of the socio-technical system has been found to impact on ethical clinical conduct and individual clinical self-efficacy.

HIT and Internet and Broadband

HIT and Internet and broadband performance problems involve reliability, interoperability, safety, effectiveness, security, and confidentiality. They also involve consensus about semantic interoperability ensuring common meaning of exchanged information by any system or application and the development of an e-Health information infrastructure which has a common foundation. The ethical dimensions of these technical problems involve decisions about design and implementation. Some of the most serious problems involve quality criteria in the design of e-Health, safety, availability of information about HIT performance, and protection of privacy. Software designed to make medical decisions in place of human authority strikes at the core of bioethics. A second design problem involves authority for decisions as in device control options. Who should participate in deciding technological design in order to meet the criteria for patient autonomy as well beneficence? Without mandatory reportage by vendors and health entities, information about safety is relatively anecdotal; patients and citizens are harmed. Privacy concerns are pervasive across the various HIT activities including database management and system interoperability. Privacy concerns relate to individual anonymity, the security of privileged information, as well as freedom of expression and currency and accuracy of information. E-Health is global and many different interests must be involved in decisions involving ameliorative strategies. Ameliorative strategies are located in national and international governance (law and regulation) as well as in global industry and non-profit standards organizations. Considered judgment suggests developing indicators of quality for technical specifications and standards and benchmarking to set control and interoperability.

Vendor and E-Health Entity

The U.S. health system, unlike that of Europe, is profoundly influenced by tensions between two often conflicting sets of ethics, bioethics and business ethics and their respective personnel. Europe's e-Health initiatives, for example, may be less influenced by business ethics because the European health delivery system providers are not-for-profits and health care is universally available. Patient-centered service and the authority of medical personnel are not challenged by profit motivated vendors of e-Health and health service providers. In the U.S., when an adverse event occurs, its reportage depends on a decision about whether or not information about the performance and functioning of an e-Health system is proprietary or is judged primarily a matter of public interest. Decisions about the design of software introduced into clinical settings such as in-patient cardiology may be made by a range of experts such as the developer, the knowledge company and/or the clinician. Health entity management policy and practices for the design of workflows would benefit from best practice examples of quality management and change management. Application of indicators for quality management, change management, and accessibility would be useful for data collection to determine whether or not hospitals, clinics, and other health entities are pursuing practices that serve the interest of patients, clinicians, and the public. The authority base for standards of performance for vendors and health entities is dispersed among government, industry, and professional groups. Considered judgment would suggest the need to create incentives to benchmark quality management and best practices.

Law and Regulation (Governance)

The problem of releasing cutting edge technology into society without sufficient demonstration of value and safety is not new. Therefore, the resulting lags in norms, law, and regulation are not unique to e-Health but are nonetheless of considerable ethical concern. Within the governance structure, one of the most serious problems is the absence of anticipatory tools such as a comprehensive Technology Assessment (TA) capability in the federal government which might create policy options for the executive and legislative branches based on evidence-based studies of HIT performance. Because the ethical dimensions of e-Health are within the realm of bioethics, regulation would ideally involve governance units involving the health professions but aligned with the FDA. Still another primary problem is availability of information about e-Health and in particular, adverse events on which to base research, best practices, and policy. For clinicians and health entities to be more willing to report adverse events, questions about liability must be addressed. Guidance must include availability of information to the public. If e-Health is to serve people with disabilities across the age span, a huge proportion of those in the health sector, accessibility must be elevated to a level of importance given to meaningful use standards such as privacy. These problems involve the ethical distributions of cost, benefits, and risks. Considered judgment would suggest that the IOM move forward on a supplementary study to advise the government on these pressing issues.

Individual Health Professionals, Clients/Patients and Citizens

Problems identified in this chapter are within the professional jurisdictions of the fields of informatics and clinical informatics, clinical professions, and ethics. They are also important to citizens. The distribution of responsibilities for decisions about the use of e-Health among health professionals, patients, and citizens is a compelling problem that involves sometimes contending ethical principles such as patient autonomy and professional beneficence.

Health professionals are educated within accredited university programs and usually pursue continuing education throughout their careers. They are licensed and routinely are members of professional organizations that generate codes of ethics and standards of practice. Accreditation of university clinical and informatics programs, licensure, and professional organizations are entry points for introducing education and training in e-Health. As professions gain maturity, the nature of their ethical codes must change. The function of the code is not to protect the profession but to establish standards of trust required in fiduciary relationships, in this case involving clinician, client, and public trust in e-Health. Clinicians and their professional organizations can exert leadership in providing guidance about e-Health standards of practice and models for risk management to address the problem of risk to clinicians resulting from liability in e-Health system failures. On the individual level, guidance would include advancing competencies and enhanced conscientiousness in e-Health system safety.

Clients and citizens are not well-represented in e-Health policy and implementation. For the patient or client, problems include developing a reliable, safe, private, accessible PHR which meets his or her needs. However, assignment of self-management responsibilities must be carefully allocated to maximize autonomy and minimize harm. For citizens, problems may include quality standards for health and medical information on the web. Guidance would include factors such as transparency and honesty, authority, privacy, currency, accountability, and accessibility.

Ethics: A Modest Proposal

Ethicists, like health professionals, seem to operate in silos. In the case of the problems of interest in this chapter the silos are bioethics, computer ethics, and machine ethics. Problems generated by e-Health cross-cut these silos. However, bridges between human beings and their technology-mediated activities are needed. As a modest proposal, we suggest creating indicators of principled HIT performance, vendor and health entity management, law and regulation, clinical conduct, and citizen participation. These indicators appear as Table 7.3.

Table 7.3 presents basic principles in biomedical ethics used in this chapter and the corresponding practical standards indicating "right" performance for the components of the socio-technical system: e-Health technology (HIT), health-related entities, law, and regulation. It also presents character traits which correspond to "right" clinical conduct. Internet and broadband and HIT are subsumed under the technology performance column. Vending companies are folded into the health-related entity column because vendors and users often have overlapping responsibilities such as for software clinical decision system support system failures.

Indicators for standards of clinical conduct are drawn mainly from Common Morality moral character traits or virtues which have roots in Western ethical traditions and clinical practice standards such as truthfulness and fidelity are traditional virtues valued in clinical conduct, while consciousness of system performance is a new standard.

Indicators of standards for the other components of the socio-technical system are more problematic. There is no widely adopted ethical referent in biomedical ethics for technology that is equivalent to human beings and human action. Indicators for reasonable standards of performance for technology have been derived mainly from scientific reports, industry reports, and disability studies. Certain standards for technology performance such as safety and effectiveness, security, interoperability,

Table 7.3 Indicators for socio-technical system performance and clinical conduct

Principles	Technical performance	Health-related entities	Law	Regulation	Clinical conduct	Client, patient, public
Autonomy	Accessibility, usability, universal design	Security, privacy, quality management, education and training, trust	Privacy, accessibility	Authority for safety and effectiveness compliance	Competence; training; respect for confidentiality and privacy, and promise keeping, truthfulness, honesty	Education, training, information; prudent use of health information
Non-maleficence	Reliability, safety, effectiveness, interoperability	Contracts, policies to disclose, report, take responsibility for adverse events; error and risk management, transparency	Privacy, safety and effectiveness; adverse event reportage; anticipatory and regulatory policy; transparency	Scientific competence, risk management, testing and evaluation; collect and analyze adverse events data, reportage, recalls and compliance guidance	Veracity and fidelity; consciousness about system safety, efficiency, confidentiality and error reportage, risk management	Participation
Beneficence	Adaptable, flexible; usable; compatible with assistive technology	Change management; clinical standards, best practices; patient-centered care, training	Access, available, affordable; education of patients and staff training requirements	Continuous quality improvement	Caring, lovingness, kindness, non-malevolence	Self-management prevention
Justice	Tracking and monitoring reporting of system errors	Technology assessment; accessibility, availability, affordability; risk management	Equitable distribution of health benefits and costs/risk; accountability, technology assessment	Risk management; standards for user-centered design	Patient advocacy, accessibility, availability and affordability	Participation in policy development technology design

and usability are repeatedly named in the scientific, industry, regulatory, and patient literature (Cheng 2003; U.S. Food and Drug Administration 2010a; Institute of Medicine (U.S.). Committee on the Public Health Effectiveness of the FDA 510(k) Clearance Process 2011). Likewise, organizations such as the American Medical Informatics Association (AMIA) and the IOM have made valuable recommendations for guidelines for vendors, users, and regulators. They include reportage of adverse events, capacity for testing and validating software, best practice guidelines and other quality control responsibilities, risk management, and change management which involves leadership, workflow, and training (Battat 2012; Leviss 2010). The disability, patient, and consumer literature have attached value to technology development processes and outputs such as user-centered design, universal design, and health care distributional guidelines of affordability, availability, and accessibility (U.S. National Council on Disability 2009). Indicators for client, patient, and public are derived from various sources including the European Commission (European Commission 2012).

Intractable Problems and Future Inquiry

From the viewpoint of Common Morality, imbuing technology with authority for making decisions is not acceptable. Therefore, bioethicists and computer ethicists, along with technologists and informatics experts, lawmakers and regulators, and citizens who are committed to human beings as the source of authority are among those responsible for mapping out ICT system boundaries and identifying decision points which would lead to the identification of morally responsible agents. Still other problems await the development of science and technology and clinical solutions. However, as this chapter illustrates we do not lack for problems but perhaps only the willingness to take them on. Problems and challenges in pervasive computing proliferate, as illustrated in Chap. 8 which introduces ethics and pervasive augmented reality. Chapters 11 and 12 reflect our continuing effort to identify and develop a consensus on responsibilities that accrue to people who design, develop, deploy or use these computing products – and the enduring value of ethical principles in pursuit of this objective.

Acknowledgments Daihua Xie Yu designed Fig. 7.1, e-Health Model.
    Dr. Valerie Watzlaf made invaluable contributions by her review of the chapter.

References

Abdelhak, Mervat, Sara Grostick, and Mary Alice Hanken. 2012. *Health information: Management of a strategic resource*. St. Louis: Elsevier Saunders.
AHIMA. 2012a. *Avoiding medical identity theft. My PHR*. www.myphr.com/Privacy/medical_identity_theft.aspx. Accessed Mar 2012.
AHIMA. 2012b. *Code of ethics*. http://www.ahima.org/about/ethicscode.aspx. Accessed Mar 2012.

Allen, C., et al. 2006. Why machine ethics? *IEEE Intelligent Systems* 21(4): 12–17.

American Academy of Audiology. 2012. *Update on communications between the American Academy of Audiology (AAA), the Academy of Doctors of Audiology (ADA) and United Health-Care (UHC)/hi HealthInnovations (HI)*. http://www.audiology.org/advocacy/Pages/Update_Comm_AAA_ADA_UHC_HI.aspx. Accessed 6 Apr 2012.

American Telemedicine Association. 2009. *Telemedicine standards & guidelines: Policy and guidance for the establishment of telemedicine standards*. http://www.americantelemed.org/i4a/pages/index.cfm?pageID=3311. Accessed Mar 2012.

Anderson, Michael, and Susan Leigh Anderson. 2007. Machine ethics: Creating an ethical intelligent agent. *AI Magazine* 28(4): 15–26.

Andersora, Michael, Susan Leigh Anderson, and Chris Armera. 2006. *MedEthEx: A prototype medical ethics advisor*. Boston: American Association for Artificial Intelligence.

Archer, N., U. Fevrier-Thomas, C. Lokker, K.A. McKibbon, and S.E. Straus. 2012. Personal health records: A scoping review. *Journal of the American Medical Informatics Association* 18(4): 515–522. doi:10.1136/amiajnl-2011-000105.

Arnrich, B., O. Mayora, J. Bardram, and G. Troster. 2010. Pervasive healthcare: Paving the way for a pervasive, user-centered and preventive healthcare model. *Methods of Information in Medicine* 49(1): 67–73.

Battat, Brenda. 2012. *HLAA's comments on the United Healthcare direct-to-consumer hearing aid program*. http://brendabattat.blogspot.com/. Accessed 2 Apr 2012.

Beauchamp, Tom L., and James F. Childress. 2009. *Principles of biomedical ethics*. New York: Oxford University Press.

Bergeron, B.P. 2001. The wireless web and patient care. *The Journal of Medical Practice Management* 17(1): 39–43.

Bergeron, B. 2003. Telemedicine. *MedGenMed* 5(2): 43. doi:452996 [pii].

Bergeron, Bryan P. 2004. Wireless local area network security. *The Journal of Medical Practice Management* 20(3): 138–142.

Bhaskar, R.K., and G. Somu. 2011. Adoption of Information Technology (IT) in healthcare delivery – experience at a tertiary level hospital. *The Internet Journal of Medical Informatics* 5(2). www.ispub.com.

Birmingham, William. 2008. *Towards an understanding of artificial intelligence and its application to ethics*. Pittsburgh: American Society for Engineering Education.

Brennan, Patricia Flatley, Rupa Valdez, and A. Joy Rivera-Rodriguez. 2011. *Consumer health information technology in the home a guide for human factors design considerations*. http://www.nap.edu/catalog.php?record_id=13205. Accessed Mar 2012.

Centers for Medicare & Medicaid Services. 2012. *HHS proposes HIPAA standard for a unique health plan identifier*. http://www.cms.gov. Accessed 9 Apr 2012.

Cheng, Michael. 2003. *Medical device regulations: Global overview and guiding principles*. Geneva: World Health Organization.

De Moor, Georges, John O'Brien, Doug Fridsma, Carol Bean, Jos Devlies, Caitlin M. Cusack, Meryl Bloomrosen, Nancy Lorenzi, and Pascal Coorevits. 2011. Policy brief on the current status of certification of electronic health records in the US and Europe. In *Transatlantic cooperation surrounding health related information and communication technology*, Studies in health technology and informatics 170, ed. Georges J.E. de Moor, 83–106. Amsterdam: Ios Press.

DeLone, W.H., and E.R. McLean. 2003. The DeLone and McLean model of information systems success: A ten-year update. *Journal of Management Information Systems* 19(4): 9–30.

Duquenoy, Penny, George Carlisle, and Kimppa Kai. 2008. *Ethical, legal, and social issues in medical informatics*. Hershey: Medical Information Science Reference.

ECRI Institute. 2012. *Worst medical technology dangers for 2012*. http://www.ecri.org. Accessed Mar 2012.

EHR: Experience from the Field. 2011. *EHR & EMR insights industry updates*. http://ehrinsights.srssoft.com/2011/06/ehr-experience-from-the-field/. Accessed Mar 2012.

European Commission. 2012. The right prescription for Europe's ehealth. http://www.europa.eu. Accessed Mar 2012.

Falas, T., G. Papadopoulos, and A. Stafylopatis. 2003. A review of decision support systems in telecare. *Journal of Medical Systems* 27(4): 347–356.

Gearon, Christopher J., and California HealthCare Foundation. 2007. *Perspectives on the future of personal health records*. San Francisco: California HealthCare Foundation.

Goodman, K.W., E.S. Berner, M.A. Dente, B. Kaplan, R. Koppel, D. Rucker, D.Z. Sands, and P. Winkelstein. 2010. Challenges in ethics, safety, best practices, and oversight regarding HIT vendors, their customers, and patients: A report of an AMIA special task force. *Journal of the American Medical Informatics Association* 18(1): 77–81.

Haghenbeck, K.T. 2005. Critical care nurses' experiences when technology malfunctions. *The Journal of the New York State Nurses' Association* 36(1): 13–19.

Harman, Laurinda B. 2006. *Ethical challenges in the management of health information*. Sudbury: Jones and Bartlett Publishers.

Harrison, M.I., R. Koppel, and S. Bar-Lev. 2007. Unintended consequences of information technologies in health care–an interactive sociotechnical analysis. *Journal of the American Medical Informatics Association* 14(5): 542–549. doi:10.1197/jamia.M2384.

Haux, Reinhold. 2006. Individualization, globalization and health – About sustainable information technologies and the aim of medical informatics. *International Journal of Medical Informatics* 75(12): 795–808.

Health IT Policy Committee. 2009. "Meaningful use: A definition" recommendations from the meaningful use workgroup to the health IT policy committee June 16, 2009. Washington, DC: Department of Health and Human Services.

Honarvar, Ali Reza, and Nasser Ghasem-Aghaee. 2009. *An artificial neural network approach for creating an ethical artificial agent*. Daejeon: Institute of Electrical and Electronics Engineers Inc.

Hosmer, Larue Tone. 1995. Trust: The connecting link between organizational theory and philosophical ethics. *Academy of Management Review* 20: 379+.

Hsieh, T.C., G.J. Kuperman, T. Jaggi, P. Hojnowski-Diaz, J. Fiskio, D.H. Williams, D.W. Bates, and T.K. Gandhi. 2004. Characteristics and consequences of drug allergy alert overrides in a computerized physician order entry system. *Journal of the American Medical Informatics Association* 11(6): 482–491. doi:10.1197/jamia.M1556.

Institute of Medicine (U.S.) Committee on Planning a Continuing Health Care Professional Education Institute. 2010. *Redesigning continuing education in the health professions*. Washington, DC: National Academies Press.

Institute of Medicine (U.S.). Committee on Patient Safety and Health Information Technology. 2012. *Health IT and patient safety: Building safer systems for better care*. Washington, DC: National Academies Press.

Institute of Medicine (U.S.). Committee on the Public Health Effectiveness of the FDA 510(k) Clearance Process. 2011. Medical devices and the public's health the FDA 510(k) clearance process at 35 years. vol 2011. Washington, DC: National Academies Press (Orig. Pub.).

Iserson, K.V. 2000. Telemedicine: A proposal for an ethical code. *Cambridge Quarterly of Healthcare Ethics* 9(3): 404–406.

Jasanoff, Sheila. 1995. *Handbook of science and technology studies*. Thousand Oaks: Sage Publications.

John and Mary R. Markle Foundation., Robert Wood Johnson Foundation., & Connecting for Health (Organization). 2004. *Connecting Americans to their healthcare: final report, working group on policies for electronic information sharing between doctors and patients*. New York, MY.: Markle Foundation: Robert Wood Johnson Foundation.

Johnson, S.B., and R.A. Friedman. 2007. Bridging the gap between biological and clinical informatics in a graduate training program. *Journal of Biomedical Informatics* 40(1): 59–66.

Johnson, Deborah G., and Keith Miller. 2009. *Computer ethics: Analyzing information technology*. Upper Saddle River: Prentice Hall.

Karulf, Eric. 2008. *Body area networks (BAN)*. St. Louis: Washington University.

Kluge, E.H. 2007. The need for global certification in the field of health informatics: Some ethical issues. *Medinfo. MEDINFO* 12(Pt 1): 233–236.

Kluge, E.H. 2011. Ethical and legal challenges for health telematics in a global world: Telehealth and the technological imperative. *International Journal of Medical Informatics* 80(2): e1–e5.

Koppel, Ross, and David Kreda. 2009. Health care information technology vendors' "hold harmless" clause: Implications for patients and clinicians. *The Journal of the American Medical Association* 301(12): 1276–1278.

Kraemer, F., K. van Overveld, and M. Peterson. 2011. Is there an ethics algorithm? *Ethics and Information Technology* 13(3):251–260. doi:10.1007/s10676-010-9233-7.

Landro, Laura. 2008. For patients, a list of hospital hazards. *Wall Street Journal – Eastern Edition* 252(148): D2.

Layman, E. 2003. Health informatics: Ethical issues. *The Health Care Manager* 22(1): 2–15.

Lee, Sharon. 2010. Contemporary issues of ethical e-therapy. *Journal of Ethics in Mental Health* 5(1). http://www.jemh.ca/issues/v5n1/documents/JEMH_Vol5_No1_Contemporary_Issues_of_Ethical_E-Therapy.pdf.

Leviss, J. 2010. *H.I.T. or miss lessons learned from health information technology implementations*. Bethesda: American health Information Management Association Press.

Manders-Huits, N. 2011. What values in design? The challenge of incorporating moral values into design. *Science and Engineering Ethics* 17(2): 271–287. doi:10.1007/s11948-010-9198-2.

mHealth Regulatory Coalition. n.d. http://mhealthregulatorycoalition.org/. Accessed Mar 2012.

Michalowski, W., R. Slowinski, S. Wilk, K.J. Farion, J. Pike, and S. Rubin. 2005. Design and development of a mobile system for supporting emergency triage. *Methods of Information in Medicine* 44(1): 14–24.

Miller, R.H. 2012. Satisfying patient-consumer principles for health information exchange: Evidence from California case studies. *Health Affairs (Millwood)* 31(3): 537–547. doi:10.1377/hlthaff.2011.0531.

Nickel, P.J. 2011. Ethics in e-trust and e-trustworthiness: The case of direct computer-patient interfaces. *Ethics and Information Technology* 13(4): 355–363.

Oregon Health & Science University. 2011. *CPOE.org computerized physician/provider order entry*. http://www.cpoe.org/. Accessed Feb 2012.

Pearson, Dave. 2011. Beware the ghost in the machine: Software-related recalls on the rise. *Healthcare Technology Management* 1(6). http://www.healthcaretechnology.com/index.php?option=com_articles&view=article&id=30568:beware-the-ghost-in-the-machine-software-related-recalls-on-the-rise.

Kelly, D. 2012. Pittsburgh Post-Gazette. Tech distractions a worry for hospitals. 5 Apr 2012.

Poon, E.G., A.K. Jha, M. Christino, M.M. Honour, R. Fernandopulle, B. Middleton, J. Newhouse, et al. 2006. Assessing the level of healthcare information technology adoption in the United States: A snapshot. *BMC Medical Informatics and Decision Making* 6: 1.

Rybynok, V.O., P.A. Kyriacou, J. Binnersley, and A. Woodcock. 2010. Development of a personal electronic health record card in the United Kingdom. *Conference Proceedings – IEEE Engineering in Medicine and Biology Society* 2010: 4431–4435. doi:10.1109/IEMBS.2010.5626004.

Schopp, L.H., J.W. Hales, G.D. Brown, and J.L. Quetsch. 2003. A rationale and training agenda for rehabilitation informatics: Roadmap for an emerging discipline. *NeuroRehabilitation* 18(2): 159–170.

SearchHealthIT.com. 2010. *How the HITECH act changes HIPAA compliance*. http://searchhealthit.techtarget.com/tip/How-the-HITECH-Act-changes-HIPAA-compliance. Accessed June 2012.

Seelman, Katherine D. 2013. Health information management and rehabilitation: moving toward an adequate ethical framework for telerehabilitation. In *Telerehabilitation*, ed. Sajeesh Kumar and Ellen R. Cohn. London: Springer.

Sidorov, Jan, and Disease Management Care Blog. 2011. *More on the impact of health information technology on medical practice: Errors of omission. Disease manage-*

ment care blog. http://diseasemanagementcareblog.blogspot.com/2011/07/more-on-impact-of-health-information.html. Accessed 11 Feb 2012.

Simborg, D.W. 2009. The limits of free speech: The PHR problem. *Journal of the American Medical Informatics Association* 16(3): 282–283. doi:10.1197/jamia.M3069.

Simpson, Jenifer. 2010a. *CMS on 'Meaningful use' in regard to electronic health records,* ed. Centers for Medicare & Medicaid Services. Washington, DC: American Association of People with Disabilities.

Simpson, Jenifer. 2010b. *To HHS on certification criteria for health record technology,* ed. Office of the National Coordinator for Health Information Technology. Washington, DC: American Association of People with Disabilities.

Singer, Peter. 1991. *A companion to ethics.* Blackwell companions to philosophy. Oxford/Cambridge, MA: Blackwell Reference.

Sittig, D.F., and H. Singh. 2011. Defining health information technology-related errors: New developments since to err is human. *Archives of Internal Medicine* 171(14): 1281–1284.

Snyder, L. 2012. American college of physicians ethics manual: Sixth edition. *Annals of Internal Medicine* 156(1 Pt 2): 73–104. doi:156/1_Part_2/73 [pii] 10.1059/0003-4819-156-1-201201031-00001.

Stahl, Bernd Carsten. 2004. Information, ethics, and computers: The problem of autonomous moral agents. *Minds and Machines* 14(1): 67–83.

The Joint Commission. 2012. *Joint commission topic library.* http://www.jointcommission.org/topics/default.aspx?y=2012&ps=25. Accessed Feb 2012.

Tonkens, Ryan. 2009. A challenge for machine ethics. *Minds and Machines* 19(3): 421–438.

U.S. Department of Health & Human Services. 2010. *Health information technology: Initial set of standards, implementation specifications, and certification criteria for electronic health record technology; Final rule,* ed. Office of the Secretary. Washington, DC: U.S. Department of Health & Human Services.

U.S. Department of Health & Human Services. 2012. Medicare and medicaid programs; electronic health record initiative program–stage 2, ed. Office of the Secretary. Washington, DC: U.S. Department of Health & Human Services.

U.S. Department of Veterans Affairs. 2012. *Blue button.* http://www.va.gov/bluebutton/. Accessed Mar 2012.

U.S. Food and Drug Administration. 2010a. Health Information Technology (H-IT) Safety Issues.

U.S. Food and Drug Administration. 2010b. Testimony of Jeffrey Shuren, Director of FDA's Center for Devices and Radiological Health. In *Health Information Technology (HIT) Policy Committee Adoption Certification Workgroup.* Washington, DC. http://hcrenewal.blogspot.com/2010_02_01_archive.html.

U.S. National Council on Disability, 2009. *The current state of health care for people with disabilities.* Washington, DC: National Council on Disability.

U.S. The Office of National Coordinator Health Information Technology. 2011. *PHR model privacy notice.* http://healthit.hhs.gov/portal/server.pt/community/healthit_hhs_gov__draft_phr_model_notice/1176. Accessed Mar 2012.

UnitedHealth Group. 2011. *UnitedHealth group business makes major breakthroughs in helping people assess, address hearing loss.* http://www.multivu.com/mnr/51966-healthinnovations-unitedhealth-group-launch-suite-low-cost-hearing-devices. Accessed Mar 2012.

Vital Wave Consulting. 2009. *mHealth for development: The opportunity of mobile technology for healthcare in the developing world.* Washington, DC/Berkshire: UN Foundation – Vodafone Foundation Partnership.

Wagner, P.J., S.M. Howard, D.R. Bentley, Y.H. Seol, and P. Sodomka. 2010. Incorporating patient perspectives into the personal health record: Implications for care and caring. *Perspectives in Health Information Management* 7: 1e.

Waser, Mark R. 2009. *A safe ethical system for intelligent machines.* Arlington: American Association for Artificial Intelligence.

Watson, Marcia L. 2005. *Can there be just one trust? A cross-disciplinary identification of trust definitions and measurement.* Coral Gables: University of Miami.

Zhang, Joy Y., Claire Marris, and Nikolas Rose. 2011. The transnational governnance of synthetic biology: Scientific uncertainty, cross-borderness and the "art" of governance. In *BIOS working paper.* London: London School of Economics and Political Science.

Zoubul, Carrie S. 2009. Healthcare institutional ethics: Broader than clinical ethics. In *Health care ethics*, ed. Eileen E. Morrison. Sudbury: Jones & Bartlett Publishers.

Chapter 8
Ethics and Pervasive Augmented Reality: Some Challenges and Approaches

Bo Brinkman

8.1 Augmented Reality, and Its Philosophical and Ethical Challenges

More than any previous technology, augmented reality has the potential to fundamentally change what human beings are. Like virtual reality, augmented reality puts a computer between our senses and the real world, directly disrupting our ability to know what is real. Unlike virtual reality, augmented reality has the potential to become pervasive. Virtual reality stops us from living our day-to-day lives of cooking, caring for children, commuting, and so on. Augmented reality is compatible with day-to-day living. As a result, the effects of augmented reality will be both stronger and less obvious than what we have seen with virtual reality. Foreseeing these effects is demanded by *anticipatory ethics* (Johnson 2010, 2011) and the principle of *extended consequences* (Pimple, Chap. 11, this volume).

The time is ripe for philosophers, including ethicists, to tackle the challenges of augmented reality. To begin, I will introduce and define augmented reality, and provide several examples of ways it is already being used.

8.1.1 Augmented Reality

Augmented reality is a technology that makes virtual objects appear to be a part of the real world. The most familiar example of this technology for most readers will be the yellow "first down" marker used on telecasts of American football games.

B. Brinkman, Ph.D. (✉)
Computer Science and Software Engineering, Miami University, 205-D Benton Hall,
Oxford, OH 45056, USA
e-mail: Bo.Brinkman@MiamiOH.edu

K.D. Pimple (ed.), *Emerging Pervasive Information and Communication Technologies
(PICT)*, Law, Governance and Technology Series 11, DOI 10.1007/978-94-007-6833-8_8,
© Springer Science+Business Media Dordrecht 2014

Fig. 8.1 The user must sort cards into two bins while wearing a special pair of goggles connected to a computer. In the *left image* the augmented reality system is turned off. In the *right image*, when the user looks at a card, the system adds a bright highlight (*a blinking neon square*) to the correct (in this case, *right-hand*) bin

Fig. 8.2 Simulated heads-up display, showing speed, date, and temperature projected onto car windshield. This is not an example of augmented reality, however, because the data being displayed is not kept in alignment with the real world

The white lines on the field are real, painted-on lines. The yellow first-down line is virtual, added by a computer in real-time during the game. (See Fig. 8.1 for an example of a similar technology.)

The software is designed to make the line look as realistic as possible. When the camera moves, or changes its view of the field, the line is moved automatically so that it stays in sync with the view of the field. The line is also drawn so that it covers up grass, but does not cover up the players as they run across it. This enhances the realism.

For the purposes of this chapter, it is important to see the distinctions between augmented reality, virtuality,[1] and heads-up displays. Heads-up displays (or HUDs) overlay data on top of the user's view of the world, and are a key component of many augmented reality systems. Some cars, for example, project speedometer information onto the windshield of the car (see Fig. 8.2).

---

[1] From this point on I use the term "virtuality" as a synonym for "virtual reality." I do this, as do many other authors, because I wish to emphasize that "virtual reality" is not really reality at all, but something different, which exists in its own right.

Fig. 8.3 A visualization of the continuum of mixed realities, based on Milgram et al. (1995)

This is not augmented reality, however, because the data being displayed is not kept in alignment with the real world. A technology is only augmented reality if the augmentations (that is, the virtual objects added to the scene) are positioned (or aligned) relative to the real objects in the scene.

Augmented reality is also very different from virtuality. In virtuality, the user's entire sensory input is replaced by input from a computer. This type of virtuality has been portrayed in successful movies, such as *The Matrix*, and is in wide use for applications like military training. In their influential paper on the definition and classification of augmented reality technologies, Milgram et al. (1995) propose viewing augmented reality as one point along a continuum between reality and virtuality (see Fig. 8.3).

I will return to a critique of their definition shortly, but their main idea is sound. In augmented reality, it is the real world that is the basic environment, and all virtual objects are layered on top of, and kept in alignment with, the real world. The user's real world position and point of view matter in augmented reality.

With this in mind, I define **augmented reality** to be the use of technology to present virtual objects to an individual's senses, aligned with the real world in some meaningful way.

The phrase "to the senses" may seem needlessly verbose, but the wording is intentional. Though most work in augmented reality focuses on vision and visual augmentations, there has been work in augmenting the senses of touch, smell, and hearing as well.

8.1.2 Current Examples of Augmented Reality

It is helpful to have some examples in mind before starting to think about the ethical and social implications of augmented reality. I distinguish between experimental augmented reality technologies and those that are in wide use by consumers.

Visual Augmented Reality

Augmented reality browsers are applications for smart-phones that display location-based data overlaid on top of video captured by the phone's camera. The user views the world by looking at the screen of the phone (see Fig. 8.4).

Popular augmented reality browsers include LayAR, ARgon, Wikitude, and Yelp Monocle. Most smart-phones include a built-in compass, rotation sensors, and

Fig. 8.4 A simulated view of an augmented reality browser for a smart-phone. The user looks at the screen of the smart-phone, and sees helpful information overlaid on the world, including the names of landmarks and directions to food and lodging

a GPS (Global Positioning System) receiver. Using the information from these features, the phone can tell where the user is, and which direction he or she is looking. The smart-phone can then contact online map providers like Google maps or Yelp for information about local businesses, and can add this information to the user's view of the world. The most common current application of this technology is to help users find restaurants or tourist destinations. Another impressive use of such a browser is to add real estate listing information to the scene. This allows the user to visually browse for properties for sale and do research on property values. This is particularly effective in dense urban areas.

In addition to these general-purpose browsers, there are many special-purpose applications of augmented reality on smart-phones. Google Skymap, for example, allows you to view the night sky and see augmentations with the names of stars and constellations. It also provides an arrow to guide you if you are searching for a particular celestial body. There are augmented reality storybooks that draw animated 3D graphics when used to view a physical book. Several video game companies, including Nintendo and Sony, have created augmented reality games where a hand-held game device, similar in capability to a smart-phone, can be used to view virtual pets that appear to live in the real world. Museums, college campuses, and historical societies have created augmented-reality tours. In addition to guiding the user, these applications can also show the user historical images overlaid on top of the current one, so that one can see what a place looked like in the past.

To achieve widespread adoption by consumers, augmented reality apps must run on a smart-phone, tablet, or handheld gaming device. These are the only devices currently on the market that are inexpensive enough for consumers, but powerful enough to do the visual processing necessary for augmented reality. For industrial applications, however, head-mounted displays have been used very successfully. Several groups of researchers, including teams at Columbia University and at BMW, have succeeded in creating augmented reality applications that guide mechanics through vehicle repairs. The augmented reality system can show you exactly which bolt to tighten or loosen. It can also show you visual cues, like a rotating screwdriver, to indicate the necessary action. This is particularly useful for military mechanics because military hardware is not mass-produced. Since each system is slightly different, military mechanics should not be expected to memorize the tasks they need to perform. The augmented reality system significantly cuts down the time spent referring to manuals.

One final example is the integration of augmented reality into passenger cars. BMW, GM, and several other auto manufacturers are working to create systems that can help drivers by highlighting important information like lane markings or animals in the road. This could greatly enhance the safety of driving at night, or in foggy or rainy conditions where road glare interferes with the driver's ability to see the lanes of the road.

Augmenting the Other Senses

Technology that interacts with our sense of touch is called haptic technology. One common form of haptic technology is the vibrate function of phones and video game controllers. Touch-screen phones will usually vibrate just a little each time you press a "button" on the screen, letting you know that the phone detected your button-press. This simulates the physical "click" that you used to experience with physical buttons.

Many devices used in industrial training allow the simulation of picking up or moving physical objects. These systems work by attaching a motorized exoskeleton to the user, which simulates the pressure or force you would feel if the simulated situation were real. For example, if you were wearing a glove (designed for haptic feedback) with rigid pieces of metal and motors and your hand closed on a simulated object, the motors would lock up, preventing you from closing your hand further. It would feel as if your hand had closed on a real object.

Electrical engineers and materials scientists are also experimenting with simulating the physical textures of objects. Using vibration and electric pulses they can create touch-screens that feel sticky, or smooth, or like various weaves of cloth, all at the programmer's whim. The goal is to make these technologies inexpensive enough to include them in consumer devices.

One particularly interesting project in the area of touch-based augmented reality is the directional belt created by Udo Wächter of the University of Osnabrück in Germany. As reported in *Wired* (Bains 2007), Wächter's belt included 13 vibrating pads. Whichever pad was pointing north would vibrate. While wearing the belt Wächter gained an infallible sense of direction thanks to his augmented sense of touch. Others have experimented with touch-based prosthetic devices that allow them to detect electromagnetic or ultrasonic fields.

Work on smell and taste is less advanced. Researchers in Japan have used smell emitters to change people's perceptions of food, for example, but it is hard to see how this technology could become pervasive.

The use of computer-generated auditory signals is already pervasive, but this is not the same as auditory augmented reality. Augmented hearing is the direct manipulation of an individual's sense of hearing through a computational medium. Some examples of interesting technology in this area include hearing aids that can distinguish between foreground and background noise, and audio processors that can artificially simulate the acoustics of a large concert hall in a small space. Another inventor created a device for color-blind users that translates colors into sounds (Akst 2012).

8.1.3   Technologies Often Mistaken for Augmented Reality

Because augmented reality uses, and is used by, several other popular technologies, it is easy to get confused and lose focus. It is important, when thinking about augmented reality, to be able to distinguish it from:

- A heads-up display (HUD), which is when the display screen is always in front of the user's eyes, so the user does not have to look down or away from the real world in order to see the computer interface. HUDs are often used in vehicles (as in Fig. 8.2), with information being projected on the windshield of the vehicle. There are also many varieties of head-mounted displays, which have display screens built into a pair of glasses that the user wears (such as Google's recently announced Project Glass). HUDs are often used to display information (such as speed or mileage in a car), but it is not augmented reality unless those virtual objects (the text of the speed display, for example) are aligned with the real world in some meaningful way.
- Location-aware computing, which means creating applications that need to know the user's location in the world in order to work. One popular example of this is the Google Maps application on smart-phones. Using GPS and compass functions of the phone, the Google Maps app can show the user how to walk from one place to another. This is not augmented reality, however, because it uses a map view, not a view of the real world. Again, there is not any meaningful alignment between the virtual objects and the real world. Some companies have tried to make a true augmented reality walking directions app (which would draw a path for you to follow on the sidewalk), but with only limited success.

- Image processing, which means computer applications that can look at an image or video feed, and make sense of what it sees. One example is the "pet mode" on some digital cameras. The camera does not take the picture when you press the shutter button; Instead, it waits until the pet turns to look at the camera before it takes the picture. In this case the camera is learning something about the real world, but it isn't presenting this information to the user in the form of virtual objects that are aligned to the real world. This is an example of automation, but not augmented reality.

All three of these technologies play important roles in the creation of sophisticated augmented reality applications, but to be augmented reality, the application must create augmentations that are perceivable by our senses (usually vision), and which are aligned to the real world.

8.1.4 A Friendly Critique of the Continuum

Let me return to Milgram et al.'s continuum of mixed realities, as presented in Fig. 8.3. While their work is useful, and not incorrect, I find that it can be misleading to those new to augmented reality. By presenting their continuum as a straight line between reality and virtuality, they give the impression that augmented reality is somehow the average of those two things – that when you mix a little bit of virtuality into reality, you get augmented reality, which is pretty close to being the same as reality.

This is a logical fallacy (and, I'm sure, not something Milgram et al. meant to encourage). Sometimes mixing things together creates a compound that has completely different characteristics than the components: Charcoal, bat guano, and sulfur, in the right combination, make gunpowder. This discovery completely transformed human culture. Augmented reality is not a mixture of reality and virtuality, like a mixture of salt and pepper; it's a compound in which the combined elements have new and powerful properties.

Part of the goal of this chapter is to justify this claim. If I am correct that augmented reality is something new, with properties that make it unlike both reality and virtuality, then I ought to be able to demonstrate some concrete situations where this is the case. In Sects. 8.3.1 and 8.3.2 I will introduce two such examples, both of which involve property rights.

8.1.5 A Manifesto for Studying Ethical Implications
of Pervasive Augmented Reality

The comparison of augmented reality to gunpowder, in the previous section, is not hyperbole. Augmented reality strikes right at the heart of philosophy, particularly epistemology. Epistemology is the study of knowledge – what is knowable, what we know, and how we know it. Most philosophers (though not all) agree that the evidence and data that we collect through our senses is our primary means of acquiring knowledge. We use reason (both inductive and deductive) and abstraction to extend this knowledge, and apply it to new situations.

Augmented reality works by allowing a computer to pre-process all input before it is provided to our senses. Because augmented reality mediates our experience of reality, it has the potential to completely remake our social institutions and our selves, how we know, and what we do.

Of course, it was not so long ago that such claims were made about virtuality, that it would completely remake what it means to be human. During the 1980s and 1990s, especially, philosophers and ethicists wrote extensively about virtuality. Hundreds of articles and book chapters have been written about the philosophy of virtual reality. And yet, so far, virtuality has had little impact on our everyday lives, beyond a passing fascination with Keanu Reeves' 1999 movie, *The Matrix*.

Augmented reality and virtuality are different because virtuality can never become pervasive. Michael Heim, in *The Erotic Ontology of Cyberspace* (Heim 1993), argued that people are not drawn to virtuality for aesthetic, sensual, or utilitarian reasons. Those that come to it for those reasons usually do not stick. He argues that those that come to stay in virtuality come because of a sense of Eros, a sense that virtuality provides something that they lack. Virtual worlds like Second Life and Minecraft, in particular, help satisfy our need to explore, extend our knowledge, and build, propagating our ideas and works into the future. Most people satisfy these needs in other ways, through work and family.

The movie *The Matrix* showed the only way that virtuality could become pervasive; we would all have to permanently give up our bodies, and plug into the computer. As long as we have to eat in reality, care for children in reality, and so on, virtuality can only be a limited, specialized, occasional, and place-bound[2] tool for entertainment, and the realm of a few die-hards and addicts.

Augmented reality, on the other hand, will (at first) make reality easier to cope with. It will become pervasive not by replacing reality, but by becoming an indispensable medium for doing the things that we already need to do. For this reason augmented reality deserves study by philosophers, ethicists, and social critics. We need to sit up and pay attention. While a cursory search of humanities research indexes will turn up hundreds of papers on virtual reality, I found less than 20 on issues of augmented reality. Augmented reality is not a new field; the Association for Computing Machinery's flagship magazine had a special issue on augmented reality nearly 20 years ago (Special issue on computer augmented environments: back to the real world 1993). We have simply failed to give it due attention.

---

[2] Virtuality is place-bound due to the technologies that make it possible, such as desktop computers and Computerized Automatic Virtual Environments (CAVEs). In CAVEs, free movement is often constrained due to safety concerns, because the user cannot see the real world (Waller et al. 2007).

8.1.6 Recent Events add Urgency

When I started this project I did not know whether or not I was writing science fiction. Both my students and the press would ask me how far off we are from consumers being able to buy a wearable augmented reality platform at the store. My answer has been "anywhere between 7 months and 15 years."

The reasoning was that the technology we need for this already exists. The iOS, Android, and Windows Mobile platforms are all capable of doing everything we need for augmented reality. The battery packs, screens, operating systems, and so on, are all available. The only thing we needed was for a large company (such as Apple, Google, or Microsoft) to make a product.

In the February 22, 2012 edition of the New York Times, technology writer Nick Bilton claimed that Google's top-secret X lab was working on just such a product, and that it might be available by the end of 2013 (Bilton 2012). Google's recent confirmation of this project, code-named "Project Glass" seems to downplay the augmented reality capabilities of the product, instead focusing on the capabilities of the heads-up display (Google 2012). The promotional video, however, clearly shows that the glasses can record video based on what the user is seeing, and this means the glasses have all the necessary features to support AR. Augmented reality systems that consumers can afford, and will want to use all the time, may be very close.

8.2 Augmented Reality, Property Rights, and Governance

Though it is my position that the social and philosophical implications of augmented reality deserve intense scrutiny (and thousands of pages of scholarship), I can only hope to start the dialogue here. My goal is to find a setting where augmented reality challenges some existing widely accepted school of moral, legal, or political thought. I believe I have found a rich vein of material in looking at property rights, and the public and private use of space.

Until now there has been little interaction between the computing world and the sphere of local governments. Most of the issues discussed in computer ethics textbooks (privacy, intellectual property, safety and liability) are the domains of federal and state governments. Land use and law enforcement, on the other hand, are mostly local issues.

8.2.1 Other Writing on the Topic

This chapter is meant to introduce the main ideas of augmented reality, and to demonstrate some of the important ethical problems it poses. As such, I will not present an extensive "related works" section. Nevertheless, it is helpful to see what kinds of people (if not ethicists) are writing about augmented reality, and what they are saying. So far, most of the work focuses on advertising and/or intellectual property.

For example, AdAge commentator Matthew Szymczyk (2010) points out that we need some rules for determining which parts of augmented reality belong to a person or company. A restaurant owner might not want a "competing restaurant from a few blocks away" to be able to post "a virtual advertisement and coupon" in front of her store window. He suggests one solution, geo-fencing – the idea that real-world property boundaries should also define the property boundaries in the virtual or augmented world. Szymczyk points out one important question about this approach: how high should one's property rights extend? Would advertisers need to buy advertising rights from property holders if they showed ads to airplane passengers flying overhead? In a later section I will point out some further questions about the geo-fencing approach to augmented reality property rights.

Google is clearly already thinking about these issues. As reported in Read-WriteWeb (Lardinois 2010), Google has filed a patent on a technology that would allow them to replace billboards in their "street view" product with new billboards. For example, the owner of the billboard could get it updated to reflect the current content of the billboard, not what was on it at the time the picture was taken. But should Google be able to sell that ad space to other advertisers, not just the owner of the physical billboard? What if a billboard (or other advertising space) changes hands?

Intellectual property lawyers are also becoming aware of the issue. Attorney Benjamin Wright points out augmented reality will affect the intellectual property rights of the owners and architects of famous buildings (Wright 2011). While U.S. copyright law explicitly permits two-dimensional portraits of buildings without the permission of the building's copyright holder, augmented reality applications are very different from two-dimensional portraits.

With augmented reality we can fundamentally change the user's perception and experience of the real building. For example, scientists have already created augmented reality systems that erase portions of a building from view to allow drivers to see traffic coming to a blind intersection. Artists have used light projection to make the walls and rooms of a hotel move around, and fall down. In the language of copyrights this is creating a derivative work, and the right to create derivative works is reserved for the copyright holder, not the public. This also affects museums that wish to use augmented reality to re-interpret or annotate artworks in their collections, because it is not entirely clear whether copyright law allows for this.

8.2.2   Definition and Philosophy of Property in This Work

Though the legal issues discussed above are fascinating, it is important to understand that this work is primarily about ethics, not law. That new technologies might require new laws and regulations, and impact existing laws, is not surprising. Much of what the law contains is not about right and wrong, but about setting up rules of the road so that everyone has a fair chance to pursue their life and desires. The law tends to be built on a foundation of ethical theories, but goes far beyond ethics.

I intend to show that augmented reality has the potential to disrupt law and policy, and what's more, it can also disrupt the ethical foundations on which our current law and policies are built. I contend that our current ethical understanding of property rights will be disrupted. Before I can make this argument I need to define and explain which rights I am talking about, and the ethical reasoning behind them.

Locke's Theory of Private Property

The most popular theory that supports the private ownership of land and property is John Locke's labor theory of property. Locke (1632–1704) wrote in many areas of philosophy, and had many influential ideas, but his *Second Treatise on Government* has been particularly influential in modern politics. I paraphrase Locke's arguments of chapter five of the treatise (Locke and Gough 1956):

1. Every person has an absolute right to labor however they wish, and to benefit from their own labor. (This implies, for example, that slavery is wrong, which is why the word "freedom" will come up very shortly.)
2. Things that are initially un-owned, like wild berries, or pasture land, are a common resource for all people. We often call this "the common," that is, the set of all things that are un-owned, or jointly owned by everyone.
3. If you use your labor to acquire part of the common, and make it productive, then anything so acquired becomes your own individual property, and no longer part of the common. If you gather berries from a public place, they become your berries. If you till a vacant field and condition the soil to make it suitable for planting, it becomes your own personal land.
4. This works so long as you acquire only as much as you can reasonably use, and there is enough left for others. You should not collect wild berries and then allow them to spoil, or fence off farmland and then leave it unused. If the berries are very rare, and there aren't enough for everyone that wants them (perhaps they cure a terrible disease), then the argument does not apply.

In short, the labor theory of property says that commons become private property when we expend labor to make them useful and productive. Because we have a natural right to our labor, we also have a natural right to the parts of the commons that we have improved by our labor.

Locke's argument is particularly appealing because it rests on the rights of individuals, not on arguments about the consequences of different land ownership policies. Most arguments about economic policy turn on our understanding of the economic consequences of those policies. This is particularly true with copyright, for example, which gives some rights to the public and other rights to the author based (apparently) on purely pragmatic reasoning; We want to maximize the public's benefits from creative endeavors, and so we need to encourage creators to create while simultaneously making sure that the public's use of creative works is not too restricted.

Locke's argument is not like this. It does not ask us to balance costs vs. benefits of policy decisions. It says plainly: The right to property is a natural right, which derives from freedom itself. Because we are free to work, and to benefit from our work, we must also be able to own property. Otherwise, the benefits of our work could not be stored up, and would evaporate as soon as we rest. Because it suggests that we deserve to own property if we have worked for it, some Libertarian political scholars cite Locke's theory of property, and count Locke as a "Libertarian Thinker."[3]

Though Locke's argument does not apply to scarce resources (like diamonds or gold), it fits well with our current concern, which is the ownership or control of small amounts of land by private persons and small businesses.

Public Ownership of Land

There are many critics of the idea that land can be privately owned by individuals or corporations. Locke's work implies that an individual can only take a commodity out of the commons if there will be enough left for everyone else, and that the portion that is left for others is just as good (in terms of quality) as what the individual took. It is almost always the case, however, that the most desirable land is scarce. Waterfront property in major cities, land with large gold deposits, and old growth forests are all examples of types of land where scarcity plays a role in the price.

But if such land is scarce, Locke's theory does not seem to apply to it. Instead, it is a race to get there first. Once someone discovers a gold deposit on a piece of land, anyone that comes there will be able to work the land to retrieve the gold. It isn't "mixing labor" that is the key factor here. Instead, the first person to arrive on the scene with armed guards, and the materials to build a fence, will get the land. This "you get what you grab" approach to managing scarcity seems, to many people, distasteful and unfair.

Of course, the main anxiety of our gold prospector is claim jumpers. Once you have found a mine, it is a race to get back to town, hire the guards, and get back to the spot before anyone else discovers it. Indeed, claim jumping is a good metaphor for something that is already happening on TV and the Web: advertisers using digital technology to overwrite the ads of competitors.

I will argue that augmented reality, if it becomes pervasive, will force a reformation of property rights and governance, because the metaphors on which current thinking is based will break down. Both the ethics and the law of the situation will change. Even if we take no legislative action, the introduction of this new technology will force the courts to re-evaluate and re-interpret our existing laws.

---

[3]See, for example, (Mack 2009), a book about John Locke in the "Major Conservative and Libertarian Thinkers" series.

8.3 Ethical Challenges of Augmented Reality

It is impossible to tackle the main topic of this chapter (the ethical implications of pervasive augmented reality) in a comprehensive way. The effects of pervasive augmented reality will be far ranging and numerous. Instead, I will present two concrete and practical examples of the ways that augmented reality will cause friction in society. Ethics comes in whenever we ask, "What is the *right* thing to do?" or "How *should* we respond?" I call these situations ethical challenges, because they cause us to re-think our currently accepted moral framework.

I'm not talking about the major questions of the definition of good and evil, or fairness, or justice. I'm talking about the everyday application of our morals to our own situation – what I call applied ethics or practical ethics. Applied ethics carries the connotation that we are applying ethical analysis to some particular concrete situation or context. And "practical ethics" does not imply that some areas of ethics are impractical. Instead, by practical ethics I mean ethics in practice or in action (as opposed to theory), or as ethics applies to some specific field of practice or study, such as the ethics of a particular profession.

The first example revolves around the rules of evidence and privacy as they will apply to smart-phones in the future.

8.3.1 The Smart-Phone and Its Metaphors

A metaphor is a figure of speech that represents something intangible or complicated by describing it in terms of a simpler concept. For example, the email client that you use every day was designed around the metaphor of physical mail.

Let us explore that example together. I could explain to you the system of mail servers, and the data file formats, routing, and so on that go into making email work, but as a user you don't usually need to know any of this. Instead, we (software engineers) use metaphors to describe what an email is: It has an address, a return address, and contains a message, just like real mail. It has a timestamp, similar to a postmark, that lets you know when the message was sent. Your email application has an inbox and an outbox (just as many of us had on our desks in the early 1990s). It is possible to "carbon copy" a message, so that you can give a copy to a supervisor or administrative assistant. I suspect that many people who use email every day don't know that the "CC" field on their email means "carbon copy."

Software engineers designed email so that it had many of the same features as regular mail, especially those features that were most needed by business users. By using terminology borrowed from physical mail (inbox, outbox, carbon copy, signature, address, etc.) we help the user understand how to use the new tool. It seems less frightening, less complicated, more comfortable. It makes it easy for businesses and individuals to use the new technology (email) in place of the old technology (physical mail) because we have already figured out how the old business processes should be adapted. For example, if the old process required carbon copies be sent to the client and to the boss, the CC field can now be used for this purpose. The email user doesn't have to think too hard about what to do.

There is a danger, however, in using a metaphor to reduce the apparent complexity of a new technology. Sometimes we can get confused and think that the new technology has features of the metaphor that it does not actually have. We overextend the metaphor. One example of this is email privacy: Most of my students assume that their email is private, because regular mail is private. Since regular mail is in an envelope that hides the message, they assume that the message of their email is also hidden. This is simply not true. As most of us now understand, our employers, or university personnel, can routinely scan our email messages if they wish.

Additionally, unlike physical mail, an email message exists in many places at once – on my desktop computer, my ISP's server, the recipient's ISP's server, the recipient's desktop computer, and potentially on many other servers. Physical letters can be intentionally copied, but email messages are automatically copied. It's often possible to destroy all traces of a physical letter by destroying one artifact, but deleting one instantiation of an email message only removes it from one virtual space (and even there, incompletely, unless extraordinary efforts are taken).

It is vitally important to understand the role that metaphor plays in the law and in applied ethics. Software engineers are not the only ones to use metaphors. Legislators, lawyers, and judges (especially Supreme Court Justices) routinely use metaphors to think through and explain tricky legal and ethical issues. Privacy of email is the canonical example of this.

When it comes to privacy, one important litmus test is "Do the police need a warrant to get this information?" If the police need a warrant, then the information was private. If they do not need a warrant, then it was public.

Applying this to the case of email is tricky, and can come down to a battle of metaphors. Is email more like physical mail, or is it more like shouting in a public square? The police need a warrant to open physical mail, but they do not need a warrant to write down whatever you are shouting in public.

I have asked my computer ethics students this question every year since 2005, and there is almost never consensus about which metaphor is more appropriate. Some students focus on the envelope: in email there is no direct analog to the envelope, which hides the message from prying eyes in regular mail. Hence, they say, the message is not private because the sender did not take the necessary action to keep it private (such as encrypting the email). Others point out that it isn't the envelope that really keeps mail private, but the fact that the U.S. Postal Service, and the laws of the United States, guarantee that the message will be kept private. Most (but not all) students eventually decide that email messages are private, and a warrant is needed if the police want to read them.

The point of this is that metaphors matter. I suspect that many of us that accept that emails should be private do so because of the "email is the same as regular mail" metaphor. The technical differences between the two systems are ignored because the metaphor is so persuasive, and because applying the metaphor to decide what to do (instead of creating new law) is comforting, easy, and enhances our trust in the existing system of laws.

And because metaphors matter it is crucial to look at the metaphors that surround a new technology, and question them. We must analyze them critically before they get a chance to settle in. Once our culture settles on a particular metaphor for a technology it is very hard to create policies, however well thought out, that fly in the face of the metaphor.[4]

The Smart-Phone as a "Container"

Are the contents of our smart-phones private, or public? In particular, can a police officer, during an arrest, confiscate a smart-phone and browse its contents without a warrant? The police, in order to protect their own safety and to preserve evidence, are allowed to confiscate and search the arrestee's immediate possessions, but does this extend to browsing through an arrestee's phone?

Several courts have said "yes," that the police may browse a smart-phone without a warrant, because "a smart-phone is a container." This is the metaphor by which some police departments and courts understand smart-phones.

This is important because, during an arrest, the police have the right to open and search any "containers" that are under the arrestee's immediate possession. This does not require a warrant. When arresting someone for reckless driving, for example, the police, for their own safety, may wish to search for hidden weapons. Because a warrant is not required, any weapons found in this search can be entered into evidence in court. The police may also search for and seize anything that might be used as evidence in a trial, to prevent the suspect from destroying or tampering with it. The police are allowed to open the glove compartment, any boxes that are in the passenger or driver area of the car, and so on. A "container" is defined (*New York v. Belton* 1981) as "any object capable of holding another object."

Based on this metaphorical understanding of smart-phones, many courts (though not all) have decided to treat a smart-phone on a car seat the same as a box of files. The arresting police officer is allowed to dig through the smart-phone, without a warrant, to look for threats to her safety and to preserve or discover evidence related to the case. When such warrantless searches are challenged in court the "smart-phone as container" metaphor is usually not challenged. Instead, the defendant will question whether or not there was a danger to the officer or any likelihood that evidence would be destroyed.

As long as everyone is working from the same metaphor (smart-phone as container), technologies tend not to be too disruptive to our way of life. If everyone is following the same set of metaphors with respect to a particular technology, then even if they disagree about the answer (whether or not a particular warrantless search

---

[4]One important and fascinating work on the role of metaphor in society is Susan Sontag's "Illness as Metaphor." She points out the difference between the romantic metaphors that surround tuberculosis and the military metaphors surrounding cancer, and how these metaphors affect the treatment of patients (Sontag 1977).

was justified under the law), we at least all agree on the important questions, and these questions get hashed out in court or through the legislative process. The real social upheavals, and ethical challenges, come when different groups are working from different metaphors.

In the case of email, for example, it is not unusual for computer science professors to teach students how to eavesdrop on email or chat messages flowing over the network. They may view this as non-troubling, ethically, because they view email as shouting in a public square. It might not even occur to an expert in network security that most people assume such messages are secret, because it is so obvious (to the security professional) that emails are wide open and easily intercepted. The clash of metaphors (computer scientists following one metaphor for email, ordinary users following another) is what leads to the ethical challenge of email privacy.

The Smart-Phone as an Extension of the Home

If augmented reality becomes pervasive, it will be natural for users to begin to view augmented reality, and the smart-phones that deliver it, as an extension of the home. This prediction is based in an analysis of the technology (pervasive mobile augmented reality) using Marshall McLuhan's tetrad methodology.

McLuhan's "tetrad" is a set of four questions designed to help us think through and predict the possible effects of a new technology on society. (The term "tetrad" means "set of four.") The tetrad is:

- What does the artifact enhance or intensify or make possible or accelerate? This can be asked concerning a wastebasket, a painting, a steamroller, or a zipper, as well as about a proposition in Euclid or a law of physics. It can be asked about any word or phrase in any language.
- If some aspect of a situation is enlarged or enhanced, simultaneously the old condition or unenhanced situation is displaced thereby. What is pushed aside or obsolesced by the new 'organ'?
- What recurrence or retrieval of earlier actions and services is brought into play simultaneously by the new form? What older, previously obsolesced ground is brought back and inheres in the new form?
- When pushed to the limits of its potential (another complementary action), the new form will tend to reverse what had been its original characteristics. What is the reversal potential of the new form? (McLuhan 1988, 129–130)

McLuhan encouraged students to write the answers to the tetrad questions in a 2-by-2 grid. I present one tetrad for pervasive mobile augmented reality in Table 8.1. In my tetrad I'm focusing on the effects of mobile augmented reality that will intensify our (already significant) confusion of "private" and "public" spaces.

Technology is already causing some confusion between private and public life. Many workers are confused about what they should do, or should not do, on company-owned laptop computers. The companies themselves are confused about how far their authority extends. In one widely publicized example, administrators of a high-school that provided students with laptop computers were remotely logging

Table 8.1 Tetrad for "pervasive mobile augmented reality"

Enhances	Reverses into
Privacy, secrecy, and individuality because others do not (necessarily) see what you see. This is particularly true in that it enhances the ability of children to define their own identities. If each member of the family has a different set of augmentations in the home, and these augmentations are not visible to other family members, individualism is enhanced. Customizability of the world. Just as we customize our computer's look and feel with a "theme," we will be able to select themes that affect the look of road signs, the walls of buildings, the walls of our house, and the sky and stars. These themes (just as with themes for computers or smart-phones) allow us to feel more ownership in the world, and to (semi-secretly) express our personal style and values.	Although AR enhances privacy and individuality, at first, it eventually reverses into paranoia and surveillance. This is because good AR systems require both video cameras and eye-tracking technology. The AR system has to be able to tell exactly what you are looking at. It is unlikely that this data will be kept private from corporations that provide AR software and services, because they will need it in order to provide us with the AR services we will want.
Retrieves	**Obsolesces**
A sense of "at-home-ness" in one's surroundings. Before the extreme mobility of the current age, people tended to grow up, live, work, and die in a single community. If one was lucky, there was a sense of knowing the surroundings and how to navigate them, and fitting in. With augmented reality this sense of fitting in can be retrieved. GPS devices have already started to retrieve this, by helping us always know where we are. AR will continue and intensify that process, while simultaneously working to change the appearance of the world to fit our tastes.	Non-AR information displays like billboards, prints of snapshots, digital photo frames, computer monitors, and televisions. All of these can be simulated in AR. The use of the "home" as an expression and confirmation of our personal identities. With mobile AR we will be able to bring our posters, snapshots, and wallpaper anywhere we go. If I choose, the extended stay hotel can be virtually redecorated any way I like. This virtual home (carried in AR) replaces the physical home as the primary anchor of my personal identity.

into the computers, turning on the cameras, and watching students in their homes (Martin 2010). The administrators, because they thought of the computers as an extension of the school, did not think of this as invading student privacy. The students, who thought of the computer as being "in the home" not "part of the school," were distressed, and filed a lawsuit against the district.

Pervasive mobile augmented reality will greatly increase this confusion. The main argument of Table 8.1 is that much of what is currently in the home (decorations, family photos, our personal sense of style) will be brought out into the world when augmented reality becomes pervasive. Because smart-phones (or smart-phone-like devices like Google's AR glasses) are the platform that delivers augmented reality, it is natural to think of the smart-phone as being part of the home. It is the part of the home that travels with us everywhere we go.

The Clash of the Metaphors

We have two metaphors for the smart-phone; "the smart-phone is like a container," and "the smart-phone is like the home." Members of the legal profession (including lawmakers, prosecutors, and judges) are working from the "container" metaphor, and will continue to do so for a long time, due to the natural inertia of the law. Smart-phone users, however, are likely to work from the "home" metaphor.

This has important ethical and legal implications because the "home" is such a special place. In their classic treatise on the right to privacy, Samuel Warren and Louis Brandeis (who went on to be a Supreme Court Justice) argued that "a man's house is his castle, impregnable, often even to [officers of the law]" (Warren 1890). They took this to be a point of settled law, and concluded from it that anyone whose "right to be let alone" is violated ought to be allowed to sue for breach of privacy.

This is an ethical philosophy; the home is a sacred and private space, into which the government should not intrude unless invited. (Noting that the government certainly may step in if invited by one of the occupants, for example to stop spousal abuse.) This position is supported by other well-known features of our legal system, such as the right against self-incrimination, and spousal privilege. (One spouse can refuse to testify against the other in court, and communications between spouses are protected from being entered into evidence in court.) But, in general, when a household is in harmony with itself, the government should butt out.

One fascinating example of this philosophy in practice was in the case of Stanley v. Georgia (*Stanley v. Georgia* 1969), which was heard by the United States Supreme Court. The government suspected Robert Eli Stanley of being involved in illegal betting, and his house was raided. They did not find the evidence they were looking for, but they did find three pornographic videos (reels of 8 mm film) in a desk drawer. Such materials were considered obscene, and therefore illegal, in those days. Stanley was convicted of possession of obscene materials.

The U.S. Supreme Court overturned his conviction. In his opinion, Justice Thurgood Marshall wrote that "The First Amendment as made applicable to the States by the Fourteenth prohibits making mere private possession of obscene material a crime," (*Stanley v. Georgia* 1969). This decision essentially legalized the private possession of pornography. "Private possession" referred to possessing these items in one's home. The decision did not legalize the production, transmission, sale, or transport of pornography because these activities all take place outside of the home. The court did not strike down all obscenity laws (and we still have many such laws today), but it did draw a bright line around the home. Personal possession of pornography, in the home, was outside the reach of the government.

This right, which is a privacy right, is something that most people have gotten used to. The home is not just a haven for exploring sexuality, but for all sorts of activities and opinions that we would not want publicly known. Our families can help us think through difficult issues of politics involving race, gender identity, class, abortion, and so on. These candid and safe discussions are key to our growth as individuals, and to developing our own political philosophies. As a result we often possess books, magazines, artworks, music, and the like that we would not necessarily want our work friends or church friends to see. We typically recognize the importance of the privacy right when it is violated: Facebook has recently started posting updates letting your friends know which news stories you have been reading, or products you have purchased, sometimes with embarrassing results.

If you hang a poster of Karl Marx, or a marijuana leaf, or Betty Page in your house, then the police are unlikely to ever find out. Certainly these could not be used as evidence against you in court unless a warrant was issued that specifically told police to be on the lookout for such items. If the poster is hung up in augmented reality, in your phone, there may be no such protection. If the smart-phone is merely a container, then the police are perfectly justified in rifling through your augmented reality, and entering everything they find into evidence. If you get used to thinking of your smart-phone as an extension of your house, then you may inadvertently fill your augmented reality with innocent but embarrassing artifacts.[5]

Blurring the Line

In this section I have argued that we need to pay attention to the role that metaphors play in our thinking about ethical issues of technology. In particular, pervasive augmented reality will lead to new metaphors for smart-phones that clash with the currently dominant metaphor. The bright line that protects our privacy in our homes, established in *Stanley v. Georgia*, will be blurred because augmented reality will cause us to bring our secret private selves farther out into public. We, as a society, will have to decide what this means for private life.

I leave this topic with three open questions. Will the use of augmented reality mean new powers for the police to snoop in our homes, or will it mean that our private space will actually extend outside the home? What is the ethical and philosophical basis for treating the home as a sacredly private space? Should this special status be extended to our augmented realities, and therefore to our smart-phones?

---

[5]Of course, some digital artifacts might also be illegal, such as child pornography.

8.3.2   The Importance of Methods of Foreseeing

The use of McLuhan's tetrad as a method for foreseeing the future merits additional emphasis as an important feature of my argument but also, more generally, as a tool for anticipating and grappling with impending technological change.

Throughout this volume, the authors return many times to the problem of foreseeing the future. Pimple, in Chap. 11, introduces anticipatory ethics. He points out (citing Johnson) that ethical analyses of issues often appear *after* a technology has already been taken up into the culture, when it is too late to affect meaningful change. Shilton, in Chap. 9, describes one way of practicing anticipatory ethics, through participating and embedding in a team that is inventing new technology.

Another example comes from "The Rules" (as presented by Miller in Chap. 10). Many of the rules only assign moral responsibility to a person if that person could "reasonably foresee" the outcome of their decisions. Ken Pimple, Katie Shilton, Deborah Johnson, and I are all signatories to these rules.

Because foreseeability of consequences is crucial in assigning moral praise or blame for an action, we need methods for making correct predictions about future effects of technology, and we need to teach these methods to all engineers. Perfect foreseeing is impossible, but it is a terrible mistake to completely give up, and to treat all forethought as hopeless. Science, government, and business all share an interest in predicting the future effects of possible actions, and predicting social change is just as important as predicting the trajectory of a projectile.

I have used McLuhan's tetrad because it is a very simple and concrete method for analyzing new technologies. It is particular helpful because it reminds us that the benefits of a new technology, when it is just being adopted, often reverse themselves as the technology becomes pervasive. McLuhan's method is also helpful because it was specifically designed for analyzing the impacts of new technologies and media, so it fits the kinds of challenges we face in PICT particularly well.

Practitioners and ethicists working with PICT need to build a toolbox of analytical and predictive methods that can be used in foreseeing the effects of new pervasive technologies. Otherwise, the rules and principles that we propose in this volume cannot be put into practice.[6]

8.3.3   Advertising as Extortion

In Sect. 8.2 I argued that our right to property interacts with our right to privacy, and that augmented reality will change those relationships. In this section I look

---

[6]The augmented reality research community seems very open to these efforts. I recently presented a poster about another of McLuhan's ideas, autoamputation, at the International Symposium on Mixed and Augmented Reality. The poster, which presented a McLuhan-inspired explanation for some unforeseen experimental results, won a best poster award (Brinkman 2012).

at another aspect of property rights: social control of how private property is used. I will start with a true story.

When I stepped out of the house that morning, there was a huge neon advertisement in my front yard. "Live nude girls," it said, in blinking neon letters, 40 ft tall. I went to tear it down, but quickly realized that I could not, because it was not really on my property after all, but in a tiny plot of land that had previously belonged to one of my neighbors.

Of course this did not happen in real life, but in an online game. In real life we have laws that allow us to regulate the visual appearance of our neighborhoods. Communities can pass and enforce rules that protect property values by preventing eyesores and blight. The micro-governments that enact and enforce these rules are called Neighborhood Associations or Home-owner's Associations. Examples of common Neighborhood Association rules include bans on the use of yard signs, limiting garage sales to certain specified weekends, regulating the shape and color of mailboxes, and banning vegetables from sidewalk gardens. Neighborhood Associations will often compel homeowners to undertake cosmetic maintenance (mowing lawns, in particular). Those that do not comply can, at least in some states, be evicted from their homes.

Neighborhood Associations are often viewed with skepticism. Many homeowners have stories about nosey neighbors using the Neighborhood Association as an excuse to stick their noses into the concerns of others. A national news story about a neighborhood association evicting a soldier's family from his house while he was on a tour of duty in the Middle East further stoked paranoia and criticism of these little local governments.

But on the day I stepped out of my virtual homestead and saw the giant and lewd ad in front of my door, I realized the critical function local governments play in stopping one neighbor from abusing another. We can learn a lot from this conflict, and its resolution. Even though it took place in an online game, the very same conflict is starting to play out in augmented reality. In augmented reality the stakes will be much, much higher.

A Story of Extortion

The first thing to understand about the giant neon sign in my yard is that it was never intended to actually function as an advertisement. My neighborhood in the virtual world only had 4–5 residents, with a very low amount of traffic. Usually advertisements are placed in areas of high traffic, so that they get many eyeballs and many clicks. Most advertisements in the game appear in dance clubs, or at the sites of various mini-games, places that thousands of people visit every day.

No, the ad was meant as an extortion attempt. In the game it was possible to see the ownership history of any piece of land, along with the prices paid when it changed hands. From this I could see that someone bought the piece of land at the going rate, then immediately put it up for sale at about 10 times the going rate. The purpose of the objectionable ad on this land was to entice me to buy the property at the greatly inflated asking price.

The obvious action to take, rather than giving in to this blatant extortion, was to contact the game masters of the game. They did not do anything, at least at first. After all, my new neighbor had lawfully purchased the land that he was using, and landowners are allowed to build anything they want on their land. There was no Neighborhood Association, and no local set of rules about what one could or could not build. The game had some global rules (no child pornography, no gambling), but very little local regulation. The game masters of the game simply did not have enough time to mediate every petty dispute between neighbors.

As a result of this experience I sold my land, and instead rented land from a landowner with a huge estate. Because the landowner could evict anyone at any time, he had the ability to set rules about content in his realm. The neighborhood was clean, had a consistent theme, and looked attractive. The people there were generally friendly and welcoming. There were no objectionable ads or extortion attempts, and whenever there was a dispute between neighbors the landowner could step in and mediate the dispute.

Extortion and Augmented Reality

What is to stop this extortion scenario from re-playing itself in reality, through the medium of augmented reality? Imagine if someone bought an augmented reality billboard in your front yard. What would you do?

In this case, reserving the "right to make an augmentation" for the property owner might actually work. Augmented reality systems could be designed so that only the owner of a piece of property could create an augmentation on her property. This idea is sometimes called "geo-fencing." If this were the case, then Neighborhood Associations would be an effective way to police augmented reality because any augmentation on a person's land is there with her permission. The Neighborhood Association would be able to use fines or legal action to force the homeowner to remove an objectionable augmentation. This approach did not work in the virtual world because there was no local government, but it could be workable in augmented reality.

Will augmented reality systems be designed to protect homeowner rights in this way? I believe they will, for the most part, because almost all "public" augmentations will be stored and provided by large companies like Google, Microsoft, and Yahoo. By a public augmentation, I mean an augmentation that can be viewed by anyone who is in the right place. Advertisements, road signs, and many other augmentations will have to be public to be effective. Users will want many augmentations to be public, because it is more convenient to discover augmentations through serendipity, rather than having to type in a web address. Most people will sign up for augmentation services from only a few companies at a time, and most people will only use augmentations from the big Internet companies.

So, if the big Internet companies implement the "only the homeowner can create augmentations on her property" rule, it will be fairly effective. It seems plausible that these big companies would indeed adopt such a policy if users ask for it.

In addition to satisfying customer expectations, it would also help the augmented reality services limit the number of complaints they get from users, and the amount of content policing they would have to do. Services like YouTube and Facebook get many complaints every day about objectionable content. Once a user flags an item as being objectionable, someone at the company has to investigate the complaint. This consumes time and resources, so reducing the number of complaints is an important goal for these types of companies.

Unfortunately, this rule is unlikely to be a complete solution to the problem, because augmentations that are fixed to a particular place in the world are not the only type of augmentation. Some of the most interesting augmentations must travel with the user.

Augmentations That Travel with the User

I previously discussed one example of this, a person's posters or wallpaper following them from room to room. We might also use augmented reality to give ourselves jewelry that is physically impossible, or to animate our tattoos. These augmentations are "attached" to the user, rather than to a point in space.

Private augmentations that follow the user are not ethically problematic, because they do not directly impact others. But private augmentation for animated tattoos would probably be rare: Insofar as an animated tattoo is intended to create a visible self-expression that others can see, keeping it private – out of sight of others – would be pointless. So consumers are likely to want augmentations that are publicly viewable, but which also follow them around.

For the most part, existing public obscenity and safety laws should be able to handle the problems associated with user-attached augmentations. It would not be hard to create a system that allows the user to find out who posted an augmentation, and/or flag a particular augmentation as objectionable. (This is similar to the system currently used by YouTube.) If a user posts a shocking image over another person's head in a café the other users nearby can flag it as obscene, and the user that posted it could have his or her account suspended.

A major difficulty crops up, however, because it will sometimes be hard for the user to know whether or not an augmentation is an attachment. Imagine a billboard in a public place that gets a lot of traffic. A shoe manufacturer has paid the billboard's owner to display an advertisement. It would be possible for the major augmented reality providers to re-sell that space. Because augmented reality works by drawing new objects over the real world, the real billboard could be completely covered up by a virtual one, and the user would never see the original. This erodes the value of the billboard for its owner, and the value of the advertisement purchased by the shoe manufacturer.

It might appear, at first, that the "only landowners can create augmentations" rule would prevent this type of abuse, but this is not the case. Using augmentations that attach to the user, the rule can be circumvented by drawing objects that pop up directly in front of the user's eyes, blocking the billboard.

Even worse, this can be done in a way that is very difficult for the user to detect. A single image of a fake billboard floated in front of the user's face would not be mistaken for the billboard itself. This is because our eyes are far enough apart that the billboard should look slightly different to each eye, and the single image would not give a realistic sense of distance. The trick is to create two very tiny copies of the inserted billboard, and float them directly in front of the user's eyes, oriented so that the user is fooled into thinking she is looking at a large and far-away billboard. As the user moves or turns her head, the augmented reality system would move the two mini-billboards to keep them lined up with the real life billboard.[7]

View Easements in Augmented Reality

This then is an ethical problem, not a technical one. Before we can decide what to do, technically, we must ask: Does the owner of a billboard have the right to expect that augmentations will not block the view of their ad? In general, is there some sort of right to expect the view of your property to be un-obstructed?

It is not immediately clear what ethics can say about this question, but from a legal point of view the answer is "yes." In many states, the government does indeed grant special rights to billboard owners. For example, many states have implemented "view easements" for highway billboards. These are zones between the billboard and the roadway that are kept free of visual obstructions, so that the billboard can be effective. Neither the government nor any private party can build anything in the easement, nor plant tall trees or other items that would block or de-value the billboard.

Imagine that we implement a view easement system for augmented reality. Here is one possible policy: *No augmentation may be placed in the 3-D visual region between the user's eye and a property that has an augmented reality view easement, unless the property is already visibly obstructed by a* real *object.* This last part comes into play if, for example, some people walk in front of an ad in a bus kiosk. We would not want all of their augmentations to be turned off just because they are standing in front of the ad, and turning off their augmentations won't make the ad visible anyway.

What if someone were to design an augmented reality ad blocker? Many people find ads and branding annoying or offensive. It may be possible to design an augmented reality application that automatically deletes all corporate logos, and also papers over any advertisements with pictures of the user's choosing. Should augmented reality view easements prohibit such an application? Many advertisers and web site owners are frustrated by "ad block" plugins for popular web browsers.

---

[7]Unlike in real life, augmented reality objects that are very close to the eye do not get "fuzzy." In real life, depth of field effects provide important distance cues to our brains – fuzzy objects are either very close or very far away. In a computer graphics system, making close items look blurry is actually much harder then making them look crisp and clear.

It can be argued that viewing a web page without viewing the ads is a form of "free riding," because the ads are what pay for the site's hosting fees. As far as I can tell there is no strong consensus about the ethical status of ad blockers for web browsers, and I suspect it will be very hard for governments to pass legislation that makes augmented reality ad blockers illegal.

Luckily, this is not a complete impasse. As long as the major Internet companies (Google, Microsoft, and so on) support augmented reality view easements, and the user is allowed to subscribe to smaller services that do not implement the easement rules, the system will be workable for everyone. Most people will not go to the trouble of subscribing to an ad-blocker augmented reality service, so the value of advertising won't erode too much. But everyone will have the freedom to ad-block if they wish.

The Unresolved Ethical Core

Is the concept of a view easement a matter of rights, or is it purely pragmatic? In the previous section I quoted Warren and Brandeis, who argued that the right *not* to be seen is, indeed, a basic right.

But is there a fundamental right to be seen, or at least a right to prevent obstruction of view to/from our property? This is the core ethical question of this section. For if there is a fundamental right to prevent obstruction of view, then this would prevent ad-blocking, and many other useful applications of augmented reality.

It may at first seem obvious that there is no such right, but case law involving "not in my backyard" initiatives argue for the opposite conclusion. Many landowners have successfully blocked developers from building wind turbines, new billboards, or high-rise apartments. Even though the developer may already own the land, the neighbors are often successful in stopping projects that would significantly change the view or visual character of the landscape. Many people seem to assume that once they buy a piece of land the character of the surrounding lands will not change significantly, and that this stasis is one of their rights. The fact that the courts do sometimes stop development on these grounds may indicate the germ of a rights-based argument for unobstructed views.

8.4   A Final Exhortation

Augmented reality is a technology with tremendous promise. Unlike virtual reality, augmented reality has a real chance of becoming pervasive. In the short term, Google's Project Glass promises to make high quality heads-up displays affordable for everyone. In the long term, such clumsy gadgets will likely be replaced by contact lenses or implants. Some university research labs have already started investigating building heads-up displays and wireless networking into contact lenses. Network connected contact lenses with one embedded LED already exist.

The time to start pondering the consequences of this technology is now. Marshall McLuhan and Ray Bradbury predicted technologies like Twitter and Facebook almost 50 years before they existed. As a result, scholars were, at least in some ways, prepared to understand and critique these new media. Who are the great thinkers who will help shape the way we think about and adopt augmented reality?

In this chapter I have attempted to make my own tiny contribution to this effort. I have shown two important areas for analysis of augmented reality. The first is to explore the metaphors of augmented reality. Metaphors do not just describe what a technology is like; they actually shape how we use the new technology, and the ethics surrounding it.

The second area is the lack of fit between the ways that our brains perceive information, and the ways that augmented reality systems present data. Optical illusions are (for most people) a source of idle entertainment. In the future they may be a vulnerability, like the pop-up ads and fake virus warnings of today.

I hope you will accept my invitation and join in this important project.

Acknowledgments My thanks to Julie Rogers and Brian Breitsch for their helpful feedback on early drafts of this chapter.

References

Akst, J. 2012. The sound of color. *The Scientist*. http://the-scientist.com/2012/05/01/the-sound-of-color. Accessed 11 June 2012.

Bains, S. 2007. Mixed feelings. *Wired* 15(4). http://www.wired.com/wired/archive/15.04/.

Bilton, N. 2012. Behind the Google Goggles, virtual reality. *New York Times*, p. B1. 23 Feb 2012.

Brinkman, B. 2012. Willing to be fooled: Security and autoamputation in augmented reality. In *The proceedings of the International Symposium on Mixed and Augmented Reality* (*ISMAR*). Nov. 5–8, 2012. Atlanta, GA.

Google. 2012. *Project Glass*. https://plus.google.com/111626127367496192147. Accessed 11 June 2012.

Heim, Michael. 1993. The erotic ontology of cyberspace. In *The metaphysics of virtual reality*, 83–108. New York: Oxford University Press.

Johnson, Deborah G. 2010. The role of ethics in science and engineering. *Trends in Biotechnology* 28(12): 589–590.

Johnson, Deborah G. 2011. Software agents, anticipatory ethics, and accountability. In *The growing gap between emerging technologies and legal-ethical oversight: The pacing problem*, ed. Gary E. Marchant, Braden R. Allenby, and Joseph R. Herkert, 61–76. Dordrecht: Springer.

Lardinois, Frederic. 2010. Google plans to upgrade old billboards in street view. In *ReadWriteWeb*.

Locke, John, and J.W. Gough. 1956. *The second treatise of government (an essay concerning the true original, extent and end of civil government), and a letter concerning toleration*. New York: Macmillan.

Mack, Eric. 2009. *John Locke*. New York: Continuum. http://amzn.com/1441123229.

Martin, John P. 2010. Lower Merion district's laptop saga ends with $610,000 settlement. *The Philadelphia Inquirer*, 12 Oct 2010. http://articles.philly.com/2010-10-12/news/24981536_1_laptop-students-district-several-million-dollars.

McLuhan, Marshall, and Eric McLuhan. 1988. *Laws of media: The new science*. Toronto: University of Toronto Press.

Milgram, Paul, Haruo Takemura, Akira Utsumi, and Fumio Kishino. 1995. Augmented reality: A class of displays on the reality-virtuality continuum. In *Proceedings of SPIE 2351* (Telemanipulator and Telepresence Technologies), 282–292. Boston, MA. Oct 31–Nov 1, 1994.

New York v. Belton. 1981. In United States Reports: U.S. Supreme Court.

Sontag, Susan. 1977. Illness as metaphor. In *Illness as metaphor and AIDS and its metaphors*. New York: Picador.

Special issue on computer augmented environments: back to the real world. 1993. (36)7, ACM: New York, NY. http://dl.acm.org/citation.cfm?id=159544&CFID=217319004&CFTOKEN=61499041.

Stanley v. Georgia. 1969. In U.S.: U.S. Supreme Court.

Szymczyk, Matthew. 2010. Your ad where? Defining virtual property rights in an augmented world. In *AdAge Digital*. AdAge.com.

Waller, D., Eric Bachmann, Eric Hodgson, and Andrew Beall. 2007. The HIVE: A huge immersive virtual environment for research in spatial cognition. *Behavior Research Methods* 39(4): 835–843.

Warren, Samuel, and Louis Brandeis. 1890. The right to privacy. *Harvard Law Review* 4(5): 193–220.

Wright, Benjamin. 2011. Augmented reality property protection. In *Wright's Legal Beagle*. legal-beagle.typepad.com.

Chapter 9
This is an Intervention: Foregrounding and Operationalizing Ethics During Technology Design

Katie Shilton

9.1 Introduction

Pervasive information and communication technologies can raise many ethical issues during their design. But as many chapters in this volume attest, ethical concerns are often supplanted by competing design values including efficiency, cost, and elegance (see Chaps. 2, 4 and 10 for explicit discussion of these issues).

This chapter explores these values tensions using data from a 2-year ethnographic investigation of, and intervention into, a pervasive technology design laboratory: The Center for Embedded Networked Sensing (CENS) (http://urban.cens.ucla.edu/) at the University of California Los Angeles. CENS was one of a number of academic and industrial research labs focused on designing and implementing systems for *participatory sensing*: an emerging form of research which coordinates mobile phones to collect data about people and their environments. A team of roughly 30 students, staff, and faculty worked on system design and implementation of participatory sensing technologies. A majority of the team members were computer scientists and electrical engineers. But because participatory sensing questions intersect with human and social science concerns, the team recruited researchers from outside of engineering, as well. In addition to partners from statistics, health sciences, urban planning, and ecology, the team recruited a researcher with a background in the social sciences—a *values advocate*—to do research on the challenges to ethics and social values posed by ubiquitous data collection systems.

I joined the CENS team in the summer of 2007 as that advocate. I was explicitly hired to deal with privacy challenges raised by team members and external advisors. Participating in the CENS design lab provided an opportunity to study the values

K. Shilton, Ph.D. (✉)
College of Information Studies, University of Maryland, Hornbake South Wing Room 4105, College Park, MD 20742, USA
e-mail: kshilton@umd.edu

K.D. Pimple (ed.), *Emerging Pervasive Information and Communication Technologies (PICT)*, Law, Governance and Technology Series 11, DOI 10.1007/978-94-007-6833-8_9, © Springer Science+Business Media Dordrecht 2014

built into an emerging technological infrastructure as designers embedded values in software, architecture, and practices associated with the new technologies.[1] This chapter reports on ethnographic data collected during 2 years of studying and intervening in design at CENS.

This chapter proceeds in three parts. Section 9.2 discusses the theoretical approach underpinning ethics-oriented interventions in science and technology laboratories. Section 9.3 describes how my own intervention developed at CENS. The final section (Sect. 9.4), builds on this description to suggest ways in which similar interventions might support ethics-oriented design cultures in other workplaces and laboratories.

9.2   Ethics-Oriented Interventions in Science and Technology

Because I was hired to advise the CENS team on privacy issues, my focus was not only observing design, but also intervening to help promote privacy and other ethical issues. I based my conception of, and methods for, an ethics-oriented intervention on two primary literatures: the study of social values in design, and the study of research ethics. Values in design (VID) investigates the social, ethical, and human factors that are built into technology systems (Knobel and Bowker 2011). Research ethics investigates what moral and human values are important when collecting data about people and animals (Herkert 2001). Both traditions are beginning to argue for social scientists and ethicists to conduct ethics-oriented interventions into science and technology laboratories.

9.2.1   Values in Design

Research emphasizing the human and ethical values incorporated into technologies falls under the rubrics of values in design or value-sensitive design. These similar traditions, developed in the information studies, media studies, and human-computer interaction literatures, explore the ways in which moral or social values become part of technological artifacts. For simplicity, I refer to both rubrics as the values in design perspective, or VID (Knobel and Bowker 2011).

VID emerges from simultaneous work in computer ethics (Friedman 1997; Johnson 2000), social informatics (Hara and Rosenbaum 2008; Kling and Iacono 1988), and participatory design (Schuler and Namioka 1993). VID posits that the process of designing something is about both interpretation and meaning (Latour 2008). As an individual or group designs an artifact, they construct its

---

[1] This work was an example of anticipatory ethics (Johnson 2010, 2011) in action. See also Chap. 11, in this volume.

uses and meanings. Values in design is primarily concerned with the moral values constructed during this process, or what Friedman describes as "values that deal with human welfare and justice" (Friedman 1997, p. 3). Friedman, Kahn, and Borning define these as "pertain[ing] to fairness, justice, human welfare and virtue" (2006, p. 13), encompassing a variety of ethical perspectives including deontology, utilitarianism, and virtue ethics. A values in design perspective recognizes that the values embedded in a technology are shaped endogenously, by their designers and their eventual technical affordances, as well as exogenously, by their users (Friedman 1997). Therefore studying both design of technology and uses of that technology are important to understanding the values implications of design.

9.2.2   Values Interventions

Values interventions focus on the endogenous embedding of values during the construction of technology. Constructivists argue that both social and technological pressures shape technology design decisions (Pinch and Bijker 1989). Embedding values debate and dilemmas among those pressures can potentially encourage the design of socially desirable or beneficial technologies. This is distinct from downstream approaches, such as regulation, which attempt to reform existing technologies to social goals. Johnson (2007) has suggested that adopting a socio-technical perspective within design can encourage scientists and technologists to explore the ethical implications of their work. Socio-technical perspectives can help engineers recognize their agency and responsibility, as well as the structural and technological limits on that agency.

A long tradition of embedded social science researchers includes some of the most notable work in science and technology studies, including the work of Suchman (1995, 2007) and Star (1999). Recent studies have added an interventionist agenda to description and analysis of design practices. For example, Guston and Sarewitz propose a method for social scientists to intervene in lab settings using what they call "real-time technology assessment" (2002). Manders-Huits and Zimmer (2009) served as values advocates in commercial design settings. Van der Berg (2009) relates mixed success intervening in a biotechnology design lab. An ongoing project lead by Fisher (2007; Fisher and Mahajan 2010) embeds social science and humanities graduate students in science laboratories to report on and influence ethical decision points. Rabinow and Bennett (2008) relate the ultimate failure of an intervention into bioethics. The embedded ethicist approach is formally codified in some research areas, thanks to National Science Foundation and National Institutes of Health grant guidelines that include "Ethical, Legal and Other Societal Issues" (ELSI) requirements (Hollander and Steneck 1990). Areas such as nanotechnology frequently invite a social science principal investigator to join projects to examine ELSI issues. Researchers involved in these intervention projects regularly report, however, that principal investigators and design team leaders see the ELSI functions as marginal to the major thrust of the research (Guston and

Sarewitz 2002; Manders-Huits and Zimmer 2009; Rabinow and Bennett 2008). This frequent finding highlights one of the major challenges in laboratory interventions—incorporating ethical discussions, challenges, and decisions as integral parts of design practice.

9.3 Intervening at CENS

This emerging focus on ethics-oriented interventions in the science and technology studies literature encouraged my experimentation with interventions in the CENS lab. CENS provided a complex case study in the challenges of encouraging ethics as integral components of design.

During my time at CENS, engineers worked on a variety of technologies for pervasive data collection. Mobile phones can record images, sound, location, and user-entered text, and with the right software, these functions can be coordinated for a variety of research projects. As an example, one CENS design project helped a mixed-income community in Los Angeles conduct research for a community revitalization project. Participants ran specialized software on their phones, which recorded GPS traces to document participants' routes to school and work. The phones also used location-based surveys to ask residents about the availability of healthy eating options and gathering places for youth, as well as less-desirable aspects of the community like safety hazards and poor housing conditions. At the end of the data collection period, the community group used annotated maps of community members' daily routines to contribute to a healthy community plan.

Another example is *Ohmage* (Hicks et al. 2011). *Ohmage* is a mobile phone application that helps participants work with a clinician or therapist to document health behaviors and activities, such as sleep quality, stress, eating habits, or risk behaviors, as well as places and times when those behaviors are triggered. *Ohmage* prompts users to input "experience samples" throughout the day (Csikszentmihalyi and Larson 1987). These experience samples ask users to sample and record elements of their experience, such as feelings of stress or trouble sleeping. Experience sample prompts might be triggered by the user's proximity to a location (e.g., a bar or fast food restaurant) or the time of day (e.g., upon waking). After a week of tracking and data analysis, users can see their experiences mapped to places and time, and work with a clinician or coach to plan interventions.

There are numerous ethical challenges invoked by collecting data about individuals using their mobile phones. Collections of personal data have wide potential for innovation and new knowledge creation, but they can also be invasive. Privacy is an immediate concern; how much data can participants share or hide? Consent is also complicated by devices that collect such granular data so close to our everyday lives. Persistent memory is invoked by this data collection—should all of this data be retained indefinitely (Blanchette and Johnson 2002; Bannon 2006)? Equity and power concerns arise as well: corporations and governments find it strategically advantageous to compile massive databases on people and their actions (Lyon 2002, 2006; Marx 2002). Who benefits from this kind of data collection? Participatory sensing, with its simultaneous pro-social potential and similarities to surveillance, serves as a complex case study into the shifting line between personal data collection and surveillance (Shilton 2010).

CENS leaders regularly engaged in deliberate discussion of these ethical issues. Concerns for privacy and equity were among the personal interests of lab leaders long before I joined the team. My intervention as a values advocate benefitted greatly from these interests among the CENS leadership, as well as personal fit and friendship with designers in the lab. While I watched and participated, the team debated thorny social issues such as consent, data retention limits, use of sensing systems by children, and the relationship between participatory sensing and surveillance. But values-sensitive design remained a challenge because of the simultaneous and sometimes competing needs of other values important in technology development, such as efficiency, productivity, and creativity. Embedding myself within CENS allowed me to explore these challenges and their resolutions.

My daily work at CENS was a combination of listening, talking, and writing. I attended daily meetings, both formal and ad-hoc. I tried to keep up with the technical conversation while asking pointed questions about features that might distribute personal data, lead to security problems or features, or complicate consent or user interactions. I conducted technical investigations such as analyzing existing applications for privacy sensitivity (Mun et al. 2009; Reddy et al. 2008). I helped write technical papers, while pointing my co-authors towards topics like data control and access, data legibility, or data retention policies. I worked with system designers to author data management and retention policies and I helped lab leadership implement data management procedures. I also cooperated with CENS designers to create both technologies and policies to protect values such as privacy and consent (Shilton et al. 2009). I used this opportunity for action research to explore the role of an advocate in articulating a set of values important to CENS design, and the work required to transform those values into concrete design decisions.

9.3.1   Values Levers

Over time, these daily activities that pried open conversations about anti-surveillance ethics in the midst of the rush towards software products and academic publications coalesced into a metaphor. I began to see that people and practices within the design setting that called attention to ethical problems functioned like levers by opening up new discussions and concerns. I began to label these people and practices *values levers* (Shilton 2012). The function of my intervention into design, as someone who couldn't build the software itself, was instead to draw attention to values questions and ethical challenges, and to help operationalize those challenges into design features. My intervention served as one among a number of such values levers.

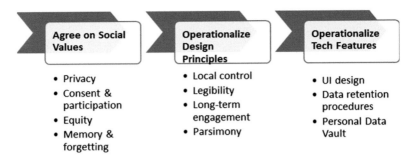

Fig. 9.1 From values to technology features

9.3.2 From Ethical Concerns to Technical Specifications

Serving as a values lever within design meant helping to drive the translation process from ethics of interest into design principles: goals for design. The process of moving from an ethical concern to a design principle can feel difficult to systematize. As one laboratory leader expressed:

> I want to say in the design process it's been ad-hoc. ... By the time that we're in a real project, [ethical] questions come up when people choose to raise them or when there are clear IRB issues. ... Ad-hoc isn't necessarily a criticism, because I don't know that structured ethical review of projects is reasonable in a university setting.

Ad-hoc as it was, the process of moving from ethical concerns to design principles and then to technological features was an important one to understand. The process of transforming social values like privacy into design principles was part political and part translational. It was a progression of recruiting people to ideologies, and then translating those ideologies into design principles. At CENS, the first step was identifying and justifying relevant ethical concerns, such as privacy, consent, equity, and forgetting (Shilton et al. 2008). The second was translating those values into design principles. I will illustrate how the CENS team defined principles of local control, legibility, long-term engagement, and parsimony to respond to anti-surveillance values. The final step is translating those principles into technology features, such as user interface considerations, data retention procedures, or secure data storage (Fig. 9.1).

The first step in this process—identifying and justifying relevant social values—was an ongoing advocacy process. Sometimes this involved giving presentations to spark discussions on troubling topics, such as surveillance powers enabled by participatory sensing or the undefined legal status of the personal data CENS collected. Justifying values frameworks to lab leaders was fairly easy; the majority of the laboratory faculty members held concern for privacy, participation, and social justice among their core values. Students showed more variable concern for these values, although most were receptive to their importance in ongoing discussions. I will illustrate the process, and the challenges, of moving from values to design principles by relating the story of CENS' first, and most thoroughly addressed, values challenge: that of privacy.

9.3.3 Defining Privacy

The first major challenge CENS faced in incorporating anti-surveillance ethics into design was defining what "privacy" would mean in CENS systems. Trying to operationalize an abstract ethic into principles that could be incorporated into our system required cross-disciplinary work to set definitions and then interpret these as designs. The definition of privacy we developed was the product of collaborative work with two center leaders, a faculty member in statistics, a law professor, and me. The team began with an "information privacy" approach, defining privacy as an individual process of decision-making about sharing and withholding information. Our approach fused perspectives from the technical and ethical privacy literatures into a framework we called *participatory privacy regulation* (PPR) (Shilton et al. 2009). PPR stemmed from the observation that negotiations of privacy occur in all phases of the research process. Control over capture was part of defining data collection requirements. Decisions about data resolution were part of presenting project results. Data sharing and retention were implicated in decisions about research outputs and goals. The process of negotiating privacy was indelibly a part of research. Privacy regulation as *participatory* therefore explicitly stated that decisions about personal disclosure boundaries were part of engagement in research or system design. Privacy regulation as a *process* meant that decisions to withhold or disclose information were more complicated than could be addressed by a single transaction, an on/off switch, or pre-set system settings. People controlled access to the self, or to information about the self, according to context. Such decisions were intimately tied to the identity a person assumes (e.g., parent, boss, friend) and the people and places with which she interacted. Privacy therefore acquired specific, variable, and highly individual meaning in specific circumstances and settings.

The team's PPR approach argued that participatory sensing systems should be designed so that people could negotiate social sharing and discretion much as they did in non-instrumented settings. Participation in the entire sensing process could help users understand a system's information flow, weigh the costs and benefits of sharing information, and make informed, context-specific decisions to disclose or withhold data. Allowing user discretion and autonomy in these functions could help researchers and participants build trust in each other and their technology.

Once we had a working definition of privacy, we needed to define how our systems would support that definition. We outlined four design principles that we hoped would encourage *participatory* approaches, fusing values of privacy, consent,

Fig. 9.2 Anti-surveillance
values and design principles

	Privacy	Consent	Equity	Memory
Local control	X	X	X	
Legibility		X	X	
Long-term engagement	X	X		X
Parsimony	X			X

and participation. These were developed over the course of writing several papers for computer science as well as policy conferences. After much iteration, the four principles were finalized as:

- *Primacy and empowerment of participants.* Participants should retain control over their raw data in addition to consenting to data collection.
- *Longitudinal engagement of individuals throughout the data life cycle.* Participatory sensing interfaces should encourage participants to engage with the data from the point of collection through analysis, long-term retention, or deletion.
- *Data legibility.* Participatory sensing systems should help participants make sense of, and decisions about, their data by providing visualizations of granular, copious data in ways individuals can understand.
- *Parsimony.* Captured data should be relevant to specified research objectives and the capture of peripheral information should be minimized.

As we developed these principles over time, we tried to ensure that our approach responded to each of the primary values concerns raised by surveillance. The following matrix of design principles shows the ways in which we mapped particular principles to the ethics of interest (Fig. 9.2).

We attempted to address privacy through attention to local control, long-term engagement, and parsimony. Similarly, concerns for consent were reflected in attention to local control, legibility, and long-term engagement. Equity was addressed by measures for local control and legibility, and memory by measures for long-term engagement and parsimony. Defining design principles helped the team to operationalize abstract ethics.

9.3.4 From Design Principle to Technical Specification

Transforming a design principle like participant primacy into a technical affordance was yet another interdisciplinary, translational process. It proceeded by using design principles to imagine tweaks to a system, a data flow, or an entirely new kind of software or architecture. In my role of values advocate, I could not move from principle to feature alone. Instead, I needed graduate students and staff to engage with the design principles, brainstorm, and then implement suggestions for realizing the principles.

Perhaps the most successful example of a system that responded directly to anti-surveillance values and the design principles of participatory privacy regulation was the effort to develop the Personal Data Vault (PDV). In early CENS systems, personal data flowed from a participant's phone directly to a sensing application provider (in this case, CENS servers). This positioned application developers as powerful personal data aggregators. That model struck the team working on privacy issues as problematic. We began work on the Personal Data Vault explicitly intending to democratize the process. The vault was built to sustain the participatory privacy regulation principles we had defined. We hoped that a vault architecture would help individuals foster a sense of ownership over their personal data, treating the data as resources to be collected, monitored, and shared judiciously (Shilton et al. 2009). We also intended that the vault provide a place for individuals to reflect on their data, transforming data collection from an outside gaze into a process of self-reflection, awareness, and identity building. We imagined an inference engine, which might help users understand what data the vault had shared, and what might be inferred about them by others from those shared data. In this way, the vault can serve not just as a data diary, but as a tool to track and peer into the data others may be holding about an individual.

A senior computer science graduate student assumed responsibility for the vault and tailored her dissertation to focus on advanced privacy filters that would allow data vault users to better match sharing preferences to their daily lives and realities. Both a postdoctoral scholar and a second graduate student started working on PDV-like implementations as part of their research. The leadership team also brainstormed systems that would allow vault users to negotiate with third parties to reveal less granular data, and vault mechanisms that would allow users to send replica (fake) machine-generated data for time periods in which they wished not to reveal real location data (Mun et al. 2009).

The conversations that helped the team translate between values such as privacy and implementations of the PDV often took place one-on-one, in person or over email, as we discussed concrete changes to a system. For example, some of the challenges to translate and implement data legibility played out in an email exchange between me and the lead PDV graduate student. She wrote:

> While the USC folks and I are working on PDV development, we're kinda confused about what roles the inference tool should have . . . The inference tool has to work for improving data legibility. But in what sense? We want to make it something more than just a data visualization. But we're having trouble designing it, especially from the user's point of view.
>
> So I went back to your paper [about design principles] and tried to re-think it. You mentioned something about totality: the tools must be capable of analyzing the totality of user's sharing decisions, to enumerate potential policy violations, and make what-if analyses about proposed data sharing policies. I understand what this statement means, but couldn't identify good usage scenarios . . . So I wonder if you had any good usage scenario in mind when you wrote this part.

I wrote back to try to clarify:

> Let's see. Usage scenarios for the inference engine. How about:
>
> A person is participating in both *PEIR* and *AndWellness* [two CENS projects], both using a data vault. She shares her commuting routes between 9 am and 5 pm with *PEIR*, and she shares her geo-tagged [experience samples] (but not routes) with *AndWellness*. The

basic visualization would of course show the routes shared with *PEIR*, and the locations shared with *AndWellness*. But the inference engine might mash these up, pointing out that non-commute routes could be inferred were *PEIR* and *AndWellness* to combine their data sets. ... A user running both would want to be aware of this possibility, and depending on their sensitivity, might want to change their [text input] sharing so that it was just between 9 and 5 too. ... A more complicated example might mash up Facebook status updates ("At Pizzeria Mozza for dinner!") against limited *PEIR* data and [experience sample] data to show inferred routes. ... The idea is to help people who are participating in multiple applications keep track of all of those different sharing scenarios ... Maybe we could brainstorm together a little more?

To which the student replied:

I like the example. Yes, it's a good start. We could come up with more examples and think about ways to generalize them to be implemented systematically.

The back-and-forth with the graduate student allowed us to continually translate from my concerns and skill set (operationalizing data legibility) to hers (designing filtering algorithms).

9.4 Fostering a Values-Oriented Design Culture

My intervention as a values advocate at CENS operated as a values lever—one of a number of forces within design which encouraged the team to transform ethical considerations into design principles and then technical specifications. The intervention was one of a number of levers that helped to support a values-oriented design culture at CENS (for discussion of values levers in addition to the ethics-oriented intervention, see Shilton 2012).

9.4.1 Characterizing Effective Interventions

One of the questions raised by my intervention at CENS was: How could I judge that the ethics-oriented intervention was successful at raising and embedding ethical issues in design? When analyzing field notes and interview data, I found three factors that characterized the intervention as successful. The intervention:

1. Changed the topic of conversation, making values such as privacy, consent, equity, and forgetting a part of regular design meeting discussions;
2. Contributed concretely to the process of technology development; and
3. Led to values-based modifications to the technologies under production.

The observation that effective values levers changed the topic of design conversation confirms theories posited by authors such as Los (2006) that, without the intervention of values levers, algorithms and databases are often discussed as if they are ethically neutral. As Los writes:

> The technicistic approach that prevails in global surveillance culture and likely affects
> programmers, managers and users of surveillance systems removes these systems' codes
> and scripts from the scope of moral reflection. These truncated, de-humanized and
> de-socialized scripts appear as 'given' and acquire a very positivistic air (Los 2006, p. 89).

By focusing on "neutral" code, developers risk neglecting ethical inquiry by placing values-based inquiry out of the scope of their design practice. Ethics-oriented interventions, however, change the focus of conversations, emphasizing moral values within discussions about systems.

Beyond changing the topic of conversation, an effective intervention concretely contributed to the process of technology development. This helped change the engineers' perception of the usefulness of social values to design. By making values something that directly applied to design and even opened up new spaces of creativity, values became agreed-upon design criteria. For example, privacy became a major driver for creation of the Personal Data Vault. Social equity became a driver for community-based campaigns.

The final indicator of an effective values lever was finding and documenting values-based modifications to the technologies under production. At CENS, these took a wide variety of forms. They were sometimes as simple as anonymization measures built into battery-use monitoring software. Sometimes values were engaged in a more complex way, such as in the complicated sharing filters developed as part of a graduate student's computer science dissertation. Finding these technologies at CENS confirms the VID perspective that social values can be inscribed into technological objects.

9.4.2 Engaging Inside Design

The success of the ethics intervention at CENS was due to a number of factors. Some were undoubtedly the good luck of my personal fit with, and the respect I received from, the leadership team. But some factors were easier to generalize and replicate. The most important of these was my effort to take the time, and do the work, to become a full member of the design team.

The importance of being able to shift from an outsider to an insider on the design team cannot be overstated. Indeed, many of the problems with values consultants or advocates explored in previous interventions stemmed from lack of acceptance by the scientific or technical team (Manders-Huits and Zimmer 2009; Rabinow and Bennett 2008). For values interventions by outsiders—social scientists, ethics boards, or even funding bodies—one persistent challenge is negotiating unequal power and design expertise. Outsiders, particularly social scientists, face a challenge that Rabinow and Bennett (2008) describe as the "hierarchy of power and privilege." These authors were involved in a bioethics collaboration with biologists and genetic scientists. As they wrote of the intellectual work of the lab:

> There was basically no effort made to do any of the background work that was required to
> make sense of some of our technical or scholarly terms. ... Despite the [funding] mandate,

there was an often polite, but unbending refusal to make this engagement mutual—it seemed
to be taken for granted as natural that members of the [social science] team were conversant
with the molecular biology and eager to learn more of the chemistry and engineering. No
reciprocity emerged nor was it encouraged (or discouraged) by the other PIs, it simply was
not considered. What remained therefore was a hierarchy of power and privilege (Rabinow
and Bennett 2008, p. 8).

The intellectual work of science and engineering, as Rabinow and Bennett found,
too infrequently includes values analysis, ethical debate, or humanistic conversation.
Rabinow and Bennett suggest that the solution to increasing values discussions in
science lies in "rethinking relations among the life sciences, human sciences, and
ethics" (Rabinow and Bennett 2008, p. 9).

I respect and understand Rabinow and Bennett's call for rethinking relations, but
I have taken a different approach. In many ways, my work accepted the hierarchy
of power and privilege between my field and that of CENS students and leaders.
I did this because I had a fundamentally instrumental goal. If outsiders from less
powerful social science disciplines want to change design, we need to work within
the existing realities of design.

At CENS, working within design meant joining problem-solving discussions
rather than simply observing; authoring papers with designers; making presentations
both to the designers in meetings and alongside the designers at conferences; and
otherwise participating in the academic work of the design lab. A byproduct of my
ethnographic method was the luxury of spending a lengthy amount of time at CENS.
Such a long (indeed, unsustainable) commitment, however, is not a requirement for
a successful values intervention. My primary motivation for a multiple-year stay
was ensuring validity of my ethnographic research methods. I began deploying
values levers (although I didn't think to call them that at the time) after an initial
stay of only a month or two, beginning almost immediately with an active role
drafting privacy policies for a carbon footprint calculator project. What was much
more important than the length of lab tenure was the *density* of time spent in the
lab: Regular attendance at weekly meetings, use of a work station in the lab, and
immediate availability for ad-hoc meetings and casual interactions. As the Director
responded when asked why the values advocate relationship worked:

It's a kind of respect. It's a kind of respect, but it's also engagement. There's a balance of
respect and engagement, because you gained respect by becoming engaged.

Ultimately, engagement was much more important than length of stay in the lab.
This finding suggests that the values advocate role could be adapted to the time
constraints of consultants or senior researchers with months, rather than years, to
spend on a project. But such advocates may need to rearrange their work, consulting,
or research schedules to allow total immersion in a design lab during those critical
months.

Beyond immersion in the lab, I made a concerted effort to take part in the
design work of the lab. Though I cannot code or design systems, I tried to find
ways to be useful to the daily work of the participatory sensing team. I helped

organize focus groups with users and suggested social science methods to bolster system evaluations. I coauthored a number of papers with other CENS students. And in addition to joining existing projects, I started CENS projects of my own. I spearheaded an ethics education grant that funded a course on values in design. I organized an ongoing exploration of legal implications of participatory sensing. I pursued grants with team leadership so that ethics projects might continue after I left. Fully joining the work of academic labor helped make me part of the team, instead of an outside values consultant. Such work also helped me maintain the support of lab leadership and the respect of coworkers.

9.4.3   Balancing Insider and Outsider Perspectives

At times, full membership in the design team seemed compromising for a values advocate. Indeed, the lengthy period that I spent in the design lab, necessary for ethnographic validity, heightened the problems of values compromise. There is a large literature in sociology discussing the relative advantages of insider versus outsider status, and the line between participant-observation and participation (Lofland et al. 2006). In my work as a values advocate, this tension was reflected in moments where my core anti-surveillance values began to slip. For example, I once surprised myself by suggesting a change to *Ohmage* to encourage continuous location tracking, rather than selective geo-tagging. Such a change hardly fulfilled the value of parsimony that I claimed to espouse.

While there were obvious problems with such ethical compromise, there were also benefits. Moments like these illustrated to designers that my principles were not rigid, and that sometimes other design values (in this case, a new, valuable outcome not possible without the continual location trace) outweighed anti-surveillance values. Such examples helped me avoid the label of a nag or hopeless idealist, and instead emphasized the cooperative nature of cross-disciplinary work.

But advocates must balance a lack of rigidity with strategies to ensure that core values are not compromised. One strategy stemmed from my experience reporting to my dissertation committee, comprised primarily of social scientists. Because I was beholden to this committee, I was careful not to let my core values slip too far. Advocates embedded in a design lab can benefit from external supervisors who are equally concerned with core values. This might take many forms, but would best be comprised of discipline-appropriate experts in applied ethics and values in design. In addition, advocates should cultivate a community of values-minded peers. Attending conferences or professional development focused on core values will reiterate their importance, help advocates find strategies for dealing with concerns, and help embedded researchers or consultants continue to be strong advocates. Finally, guidelines such as those developed in Chaps. 10 and 11 may be used not only as starting places for design principles, but also for ethical checks along the way.

9.5 Conclusion

My experience in the CENS design lab suggests that the goal of an ethics-oriented intervention into a science or technology laboratory should be to work as a *values lever*: A force that pries open discussion about ethical principles and helps the group achieve consensus about how to operationalize their values. Building technical systems may be outside the skill set of humanists and social scientists. But for those with a background in values, ethics, and socio-technical systems, it is quite possible to become a constructive participant in system design. Such interventions might be useful in a variety of design settings, ranging from public health surveillance as described in Chap. 3, to aging-in-place support technologies as described in Chap. 6.

I found that an effective intervention (a) changed the topic of design meeting discussions by introducing ethical principles, (b) contributed concretely to the process of technology development, and (c) led to values-based changes to the technologies under production. The intervention achieved these goals by helping to translate ethical concerns into design principles, and then participating in the work of the lab to build these principles into technical specifications. And while *engagement* with the design team is vital, long-term engagement is less important than *dense* engagement. Though such dense engagement had a tendency to weaken my outsider point-of-view, ongoing discussions with other social scientists and humanists provided an intellectual check and kept my work balanced.

Social scientists and humanists need not become technologists to contribute to the design process. Operationalizing values is our skill set for design.

Acknowledgments This work is based on material from my doctoral dissertation, "Building Values into the Design of Pervasive Mobile Technologies." Many thanks to my committee: Jeffrey Burke, Deborah Estrin, Christopher Kelty, Ramesh Srinivasan, and chair Christine Borgman. Their ideas, feedback and guidance have shaped this work immensely. This work was funded by the National Science Foundation under grant number 0832873.

References

Bannon, L. 2006. Forgetting as a feature, not a bug: The duality of memory and implications for ubiquitous computing. *CoDesign* 2(1): 3–15.
Blanchette, J.-F., and D.G. Johnson. 2002. Data retention and the panoptic society: The social benefits of forgetfulness. *The Information Society* 18(1): 33–45.
Csikszentmihalyi, M., and R. Larson. 1987. Validity and reliability of the experience-sampling method. *The Journal of Nervous and Mental Disease* 175(9): 526–536.
Fisher, E. 2007. Ethnographic invention: Probing the capacity of laboratory decisions. *NanoEthics* 1(2): 155–165.
Fisher, E., and R. Mahajan. 2010. Embedding the humanities in engineering: Art, dialogue, and a laboratory. In *Trading zones and interactional expertise: Creating new kinds of collaboration*, ed. M.E. Gorman, 209–230. Cambridge, MA: MIT Press.
Friedman, B. (ed.). 1997. *Human values and the design of computer technology*, CSLI lecture notes. Cambridge/New York: Cambridge University Press.

Friedman, B., P.H. Kahn, and A. Borning. 2006. Value sensitive design and information systems. In *Human-computer interaction and management information systems: Applications*, vol. 6, ed. D. Galletta and P. Zhang. New York: M.E. Sharpe.

Guston, D.H., and D. Sarewitz. 2002. Real-time technology assessment. *Technology in Society* 24(1–2): 93–109.

Hara, N., and H. Rosenbaum. 2008. Revising the conceptualization of computerization movements. *The Information Society* 24(4): 229–245.

Herkert, J. 2001. Future directions in engineering ethics research: Microethics, macroethics and the role of professional societies. *Science and Engineering Ethics* 7(3): 403–414.

Hicks, J., N. Ramanathan, H. Falaki, B. Longstaff, K. Parameswaran, M. Monibi, D.H. Kim, et al. 2011. *Ohmage: An open mobility system for activity and experience sampling* (CENS Technical Report No. 100). Los Angeles: Center for Embedded Networked Sensing.

Hollander, R.D., and N.H. Steneck. 1990. Science- and engineering-related ethics and values studies: Characteristics of an emerging field of research. *Science, Technology & Human Values* 15(1): 84–104. doi:10.1177/016224399001500109.

Johnson, D.G. 2000. *Computer ethics*, 3rd ed. Upper Saddle River: Prentice Hall.

Johnson, D.G. 2007. Ethics and technology "in the making": An essay on the challenge of nanoethics. *NanoEthics* 1(1): 21–30.

Johnson, D.G. 2010. The role of ethics in science and engineering. *Trends in Biotechnology* 28(12): 589–590.

Johnson, D.G. 2011. Software agents, anticipatory ethics, and accountability. In *The growing gap between emerging technologies and legal-ethical oversight: The pacing problem*, ed. Gary E. Marchant, Braden R. Allenby, and Joseph R. Herkert, 61–76. Dordrecht: Springer.

Kling, R., and S. Iacono. 1988. The mobilization of support for computerization: The role of computerization movements. *Social Problems* 35(3): 226–243.

Knobel, C.P., and G.C. Bowker. 2011. Values in design. *Communications of the ACM* 54(7): 26–28.

Latour, B. 2008. A cautious prometheus? A few steps toward a philosophy of design (with special attention to Peter Sloterdijk). In *Proceedings of the 2008 annual international conference of the Design History Society*, ed. F. Hackne, J. Glynne, and V. Minto, 2–10. Presented at the 2008 annual international conference of the Design History Society. Falmouth: Universal Publications.

Lofland, J., D. Snow, L. Anderson, and L.H. Lofland. 2006. *Analyzing social settings: A guide to qualitative observation and analysis*. Belmont: Wadsworth/Thomson Learning.

Los, M. 2006. Looking into the future: Surveillance, globalization and the totalitarian potential. In *Theorizing surveillance: The panopticon and beyond*, ed. D. Lyon, 69–94. Devon: Willan Publishing.

Lyon, D. 2002. Everyday surveillance: Personal data and social classifications. *Information, Communication & Society* 5(2): 242–257. doi:10.1080/13691180210130806.

Lyon, D. 2006. Why where you are matters: Mundane mobilities, transparent technologies, and digital discrimination. In *Surveillance and security: Technological politics and power in everyday life*, 209–224. New York/London: Routledge.

Manders-Huits, N., and M. Zimmer. 2009. Values and pragmatic action: The challenges of introducing ethical intelligence in technical and design communities. *International Review of Information Ethics* 10: 37–44.

Marx, G.T. 2002. What's new about the "new surveillance"? Classifying for change and continuity. *Surveillance & Society* 1(1): 9–29.

Mun, M., S. Reddy, K. Shilton, N. Yau, P. Boda, J. Burke, D. Estrin, et al. 2009. PEIR, the personal environmental impact report, as a platform for participatory sensing systems research. In *Proceedings of the international conference on mobile systems, applications, and services*, 55–68. Presented at the international conference on mobile systems, applications, and services. Krakow: ACM.

Pinch, T.J., and W.E. Bijker. 1989. The social construction of facts and artifacts: Or how the sociology of science and the sociology of technology might benefit each other. In *The social construction of technological systems*. Cambridge, MA/London: The MIT Press.

Rabinow, P., and G. Bennett. 2008. *Ars Synthetica: Designs for human practice*. Houston: Rice University Connexions. Web site. Retrieved from http://cnx.org/content/col10612/1.2/

Reddy, S., K. Shilton, J. Burke, D. Estrin, M. Hansen, and M.B Srivastava. 2008. Evaluating participation and performance in participatory sensing. In *UrbanSense workshop, SenSys 2008*. Presented at the Sensys, Raleigh: ACM.

Schuler, D., and A. Namioka. 1993. *Participatory design: Principles and practices*. Hillsdale: Lawrence Erlbaum Associates.

Shilton, K. 2010. Participatory sensing: Building empowering surveillance. *Surveillance & Society* 8(2): 131–150.

Shilton, K. 2012. Values levers: Building ethics into design. *Science, Technology & Human Values*.. doi:10.1177/0162243912436985.

Shilton, K., J. Burke, D. Estrin, M. Hansen, and M. Srivastava. 2008. *Participatory privacy in urban sensing*. Presented at the MODUS 2008, St. Louis, MO.

Shilton, K., J. Burke, D. Estrin, M. Hansen, R. Govindan, and J. Kang. 2009. Designing the personal data stream: Enabling participatory privacy in mobile personal sensing. In *The 37th research conference on communication, information and internet policy (TPRC)*. Presented at the 37th research conference on communication, information and internet policy (TPRC), Arlington, VA.

Star, S.L. 1999. The ethnography of infrastructure. *American Behavioral Scientist* 43(3): 377–391.

Suchman, L. 1995. Making work visible. *Communications of the ACM* 38(9): 56–61.

Suchman, L. 2007. *Human-machine reconfigurations*, 2nd ed. New York: Cambridge University Press.

van der Burg, S. 2009. Imagining the future of photoacoustic mammography. *Science and Engineering Ethics* 15(1): 97–110.

Chapter 10
Applying "Moral Responsibility for Computing Artifacts" to PICT

Keith W. Miller

10.1   Introduction to "The Rules"

This chapter and The Rules have their genesis in the March 2010 workshop entitled "Ethical Guidance for Research and Application of Pervasive and Autonomous Information Technology" (a.k.a., PAIT) and described in the Introduction to this book. A detailed history of the development of The Rules can be found at https://edocs.uis.edu/kmill2/www/TheRules/history.html (Miller 2010). In brief, participating in this workshop inspired me to start a collaborative effort to develop principles for computing artifacts in general. Over the course of several months, the number of collaborators grew from a handful of the participants at the PAIT workshop (notably Deborah Johnson, Chuck Huff, and Joe Herkert) to a group of 50 and the number of revised versions reached 27.

The project and document are designed to be a continuing work-in-progress, under the control of people willing to sign on to the document. The process uses a "coordinator," myself at the moment, who is in charge of receiving suggestions for changes, combining these suggestions into new versions, and sending the versions out to the people currently "signed on." In order to simplify citations to the document, the "signers" are now called "The Ad Hoc Committee for Responsible Computing." The latest version of The Rules is available at https://edocs.uis.edu/kmill2/www/TheRules/.

By the nature of their work, academics in general and philosophers in particular do not always emphasize things on which they agree. This document, inspired in part by Beck et al. (2001), started as an attempt to go against that trend, at least for a moment, in order to make what we hope is a useful statement about the moral responsibility for computing artifacts.

K.W. Miller, Ph.D. (✉)
University of Illinois Springfield, Springfield, IL, USA
e-mail: kmill217@gmail.com

K.D. Pimple (ed.), *Emerging Pervasive Information and Communication Technologies (PICT)*, Law, Governance and Technology Series 11, DOI 10.1007/978-94-007-6833-8_10, © Springer Science+Business Media Dordrecht 2014

This chapter brings the Rules project back into focus with PICT. In the next few sections, I will look at how the (more general) Rules can be applied to the more specific case of PICT.

10.2   Our Assumptions About PICT

The volatile, evolving nature of "pervasive ICT" is reflected in the plethora of terms that are often used as synonyms for individual devices and systems of devices that are being referred to as PICT in this book. Another popular term for technology that is often called "pervasive" is "ubiquitous computing." (For example, see Oladimeji 2011.) In this chapter I'll assume that PICT refers to socio-technical systems (hardware and software embedded in a particular context) that are designed to be integrated into devices and everyday life in such a way that they become nearly transparent to users. A catchy slogan for such systems is "everyware" (Greenview 2006).

I do not assume that all PICT developers are intentionally hiding the existence of their systems. Often, PICT artifacts are designed to blend into the background not to deceive users, but to serve users in a way that becomes invisible through convenient reuse. Many of us can remember when a desktop computer was used to respond to explicit user commands. Users turned on the computer, did a specific task, and turned the computer off. But today computing has become far more common, pervasive, and expected. Many people leave computers on continuously, and use computing for many different aspects of their lives, on multiple devices, throughout the day. A smartphone is an example of how computing is taking on characteristics suggested by "pervasive" and "ubiquitous."

When clean water was hard to find, fetching water was an explicit chore. In most homes in the U.S., fetching water is done by turning on a tap. Water taps aren't hidden, but we normally do not take much notice of them. As computing devices become ubiquitous and pervasive, we tend to take less notice of them as well. I expect that this tendency will accelerate for specific PICT devices that become cheaper, smaller, and widespread. It is exactly these devices that will have the most profound impact on the way we live, and the most profound ethical significance.

10.3   Applying "The Rules" to PICT

In this section, I examine each of the five rules in The Rules in turn. I will explore how characteristics of PICT interact with the letter and the intent of each rule.

10.3.1   *Shared Responsibility*

> Rule 1. The people who design, develop, or deploy a computing artifact are morally responsible for that artifact, and for the foreseeable effects of that artifact. This responsibility is shared with other people who design, develop, deploy or knowingly use the artifact as part of a socio-technical system.

PICT devices and socio-technical systems are designed to be useful in a way that is broad and accessible. This general usefulness may make it difficult to predict exactly how PICT devices will be used by different members of the public.

Rule 1 requires that PICT producers embrace moral responsibility for the PICT artifacts they design, develop, and deploy. This responsibility includes responsibility (in some way) for the effects of the artifacts. And Rule 1 then includes users in this general sense of responsibility.

But what is the nature of this moral responsibility when discussing PICT? If a company and individuals in that company implement PICT, are they to be accountable and blameworthy for every act done by anyone using that PICT artifact? That seems like over-reaching. As The Rules were being revised, it became clear to the signers that the word "responsibility" had many interpretations and nuances. In Rule 1, is seems clear that something short of blameworthiness for all uses is being described here.

Let's return to our analogy of clean water on demand as a technology that has (for many of us) become pervasive. If I am in charge of a municipal water system, it seems straightforward that I am morally responsible for delivering clean water to my users at a reasonable price with high reliability. If I am careless about the purity of the water delivered, I am ethically accountable for that lapse. If I am negligent in securing sufficient supplies of water, and my customers suddenly find their taps are dry, that is my moral responsibility. But if one of my customers, unbeknownst to me, uses some of the water I delivered to waterboard his adolescent son as punishment for not cleaning his room (which for the sake of argument we will take to be a moral harm to the son), it seems unfair to ascribe any moral blame to anyone connected to the municipal water system. Is the use of the water for torture "foreseeable?" Surely yes; but just as surely, the delivery of clean water to the depraved father should not be thought of as directly enabling the waterboarding in any morally significant way.

However, let's imagine a hypothetical manager of a different utility in a fictional country perpetually at war. This utility delivers napalm in 5-gal jugs for its (frequently hostile) residents, including people who are not trained in its use nor under military discipline. Now the moral calculus changes considerably. The purpose of the napalm is unambiguous, and delivering it widely and indiscriminately clearly invites mayhem. Now the moral responsibility for foreseeable effects appears to be far more appropriately described as blameworthiness when the ready availability of napalm results in needless deaths.

An engineer who facilitates the delivery of water or napalm is morally responsible for that delivery, and for the foreseeable effects of that delivery. But being "responsible" means different things for different delivered products. Being responsible does not mean that the engineer is blameworthy for all effects of any delivered product.

Clean water and napalm then fix the ends of a continuum: on one end, we have a utility that we can consider beneficial in its intent; at the other end, we have a utility that is designed to deliver a means of destruction. Clearly there are different expectations of the moral significance of delivering something at each end of that continuum.

How do individual instances of PICT relate to this continuum? Like so much of computer ethics, the best, most candid answer we can muster is "it depends." In order to illustrate that dependence, I'll look at two potential PICT devices, and their possible effects.

Consider the following fictional (but realistic) scenario: An engineer named Penny is brought into a project that has been described as a PICT development. After signing non-disclosure agreements and obtaining top secret clearance, Penny learns that she is to help develop nanobots. These tiny robots are to be the size and weight of pollen. When released, they can be dispersed by the wind. They are small enough to be breathed into human lungs without detection.

Penny's job is to develop a mechanism that will enable the remote activation and deactivation of the nanobots using wireless communications. Penny is not told what the nanobots' ultimate purpose is, and she can imagine different applications, including some in medicine, surveillance, and inventory. But for several reasons, Penny is confident that these nanobots are being designed for warfare, to injure or kill enemy combatants.

Although she is not a pacifist, Penny is concerned that weaponized nanobots could have catastrophic predictable effects, and significant potential for unanticipated bad effects. She expresses her concerns to her supervisor, and her supervisor suggests that she should either dismiss these unpleasant thoughts from her mind or quit the project. Penny quits the project, and is assigned to a completely different and unrelated project.

Consider a second fictional scenario: Roger is working on software for a radio-frequency identification (RFID) tag. The software is designed to be used on a wide range of small, simple tags for multiple applications. Roger's manager wants this software to be as simple as possible in order to minimize power requirements. Roger suggests, and then insists, that any RFID software they develop should include a protocol for disabling the tag. Roger points out that the capacity for turning off an RFID tag should be a requirement, not an option, because there are potential misuses of tags (misuses that threaten privacy, for example) that can be minimized if the tags are disabled after their original purpose has been fulfilled. Roger's manager agrees, and the disable feature is designed in to all RFID tags the company produces.

Although their approaches differed, both Penny and Roger took seriously their responsibility to consider the effects of artifacts they were helping to develop. They exhibited behaviors that Rule 1 encourages. Notice that the nature of PICT applications is significant in both these stories. In the case of the weaponized nanobots, Penny's concerns about unforeseen consequences are intense because the pollen-sized nanobots are easily distributed, but not easily controlled. Pervasive computing devices often have this quality. RFID tags raise similar concerns; the tags are inexpensive, and are already common. They may become ubiquitous. Roger was appropriately concerned that these devices should include the capability for tighter control before and after deployment because their widespread distribution would invite abuse if it were inconvenient or expensive to turn them off when appropriate.

10.3.2 Individual Responsibility

Rule 2. The shared responsibility of computing artifacts is not a zero-sum game. The responsibility of an individual is not reduced simply because more people become involved in designing, developing, deploying or using the artifact. Instead, a person's responsibility includes being answerable for the behaviors of the artifact and for the artifact's effects after deployment, to the degree to which these effects are reasonably foreseeable by that person.

When responsibility for computing artifacts is discussed, the "problem of many hands" often surfaces. Rule 2 is, in part, a response to the notion that because computing artifacts are developed by large, inter-disciplinary teams, sometimes distributed globally, no one in particular is accountable for the artifact and its effects. Nissenbaum (1994: 80) discusses this problem for all computing artifacts, and writes, "the call for accountability remains a standard worth restoring;" she contends that the problem of many hands must not allow us to abandon the idea of accountability. Rule 2 is consistent with Nissenbaum's call for accountability.

Rule 2 was written for all computing artifacts. But it seems especially important for PICT artifacts, especially for PICT artifacts that are mass-produced and widely distributed. When the number of copies of a PICT artifact increases, the number of people involved in the deployment and use of that artifact increases dramatically. Rule 2 emphasizes that these numbers do not mean that responsibility is diluted for developers or users. Even if "everyone uses X," that does not mean that anyone can use X without taking responsibility for that use.

Notice that the ubiquity of PICT is a crucial aspect of how Rule 2 applies to PICT. A technology that is "pervasive" and/or "ubiquitous" is vulnerable to the problem of many hands in ways, for example, a supercomputing mainframe is not. Developers and users of a rare supercomputer (like those of the best telescopes) are carefully selected, and tightly controlled. There are fewer hands "on" a supercomputer, and those hands are generally knowledgeable and professional.

Despite the brevity of The Rules and the document in which The Rules are explained, the signers of the document have crafted the language with some subtlety. The nuances are important when applying Rule 2 to PICT. There is a good deal of discretionary judgment implied by these words: "to the degree to which these effects are reasonably foreseeable by that person." In this and other rules, the idea of a foreseeable effect adds complexity to the assigning of responsibility.

"Foreseeability" in PICT is complex. Developers of a particular device have a completely different perspective on the technology than someone who casually uses the developed device. Some users are sophisticated and knowledgeable about PICT, and others may use the same technology without being aware of that use at all. So despite the brevity of Rule 2, the assigning of responsibility for PICT artifacts is not shown to be automatic, simple or straightforward. This does *not* mean that responsibility for PICT is therefore waived or diminished. Indeed, Rule 2 and all The Rules exist to emphasize the importance of acknowledging and embracing responsibility. However, we need to recognize the inherent challenges of understanding the complexities of these moral obligations in order to meet those challenges responsibly.

In each individual instance of PICT, the number of people responsible and their interactions will be complex. But Rule 2 encourages all of those people to understand and embrace their responsibility for using that technology ethically. Determining what their specific responsibilities are is part of what Rule 2 requires.

10.3.3   User Responsibility

Rule 3. People who knowingly use a particular computing artifact are morally responsible for that use.

Rules 1 and 2 focus our attention on computing professionals who design, develop, and deploy computing artifacts. Users are mentioned in Rules 1 and 2, but they are featured in Rule 3. The message of Rule 3 is straightforward, but the rule's reach is considerable. The inclusion of users in The Rules is a trait that distinguishes The Rules from codes of ethics; codes of ethics are generally written for professionals, and can focus on the role responsibilities of a narrow subset of people; The Rules have a grander ambition that is far more inclusive.

To illustrate the importance of Rule 3 to PICT socio-technical systems, consider the following fictional scenario: Imagine a future in which there are inexpensive wireless PICT devices that can capture a wide angle view of what is in front of you, and that these devices are commonly integrated into clothing. The devices are sufficiently inexpensive so that they become a normal part of many people's wardrobe. Assume that there are several competing service providers that will collect the resulting "life movies." Most of these providers charge a small fee, and make the movies available to the subscriber only. But one provider will collect the movies free of charge, as long as you allow the company to use your films in a project designed to generate income for the provider. The provider is compiling an immense database of information gleaned from all the films it collects and stores, and selling information from that database to commercial enterprises and government agencies.

When you make a decision of which provider will help you with your life movies, you are deciding how you will use your PICT devices. In this case, that use includes dealing with information not only about you, but also about all the people who wander into the range of the cameras you are wearing. If you choose the cost-free provider, you will be revealing information about friends, family and strangers to the provider, and to anyone who is a customer for the information the provider gleans from your life movies and from the life movies of others.

If you pick the provider who charges you nothing but takes control of your life movies, you might reason that your individual contribution to the database is relatively slight, and that it is not your fault if the company's policies are harmful to privacy. But Rule 3 stands in the way of such self-justifications. You are responsible for your use of the PICT artifacts you wear, and their effects. Despite the many hands involved, your hands get dirty too if you participate willingly in an enterprise that depends on those artifacts to do a moral harm.

Especially as PICT devices become enmeshed in common socio-technical systems, it may be that you are participating unknowingly in an enterprise with negative effects. For example, assume that you opted for a paid life movie collection service instead of the free one in order to *not* expose the people in your movies to a database that threatens their legitimate privacy concerns. But if the provider you choose secretly sells your movies to become part of that database anyway, then their deception is causing the harm, despite your attempt to prevent exactly that harm. Unless your ignorance of this deception is willful (you easily could have known, but didn't inquire because you did not want to know), Rule 2's use of "reasonably foreseeable" and Rule 3's use of "knowingly" mean that you are not responsible for this problem.

10.3.4 Context Awareness

Rule 4. People who knowingly design, develop, deploy, or use a computing artifact can do so responsibly only when they make a reasonable effort to take into account the socio-technical systems in which the artifact is embedded.

The life movie example nicely illustrates the importance of socio-technical systems when considering the ethics of PICT. In our example, the artifact and its output (camera and movies) were not the crux of the morally significant decision of the users. Instead, the crucial factor in that story is what the different service providers would do with those movies.

Rule 4 emphasizes the importance of socio-technical systems when assessing responsibility for computing artifacts. The Rules document defines a socio-technical system to include "people, relationships between people, other artifacts, physical surroundings, customs, assumptions, procedures and protocols."

The theme of "broaden your vision" animates much of applied ethics. Utilitarian analysis emphasizes a global view of consequences; deontologists urge us to think about responsibilities and intent, not just consequences; virtue ethics can be interpreted to consider the ideals we should aspire towards, not just a rational weighing of consequences and responsibilities. We can interpret an emphasis on socio-technical systems as another call to broaden our ethical vision; in this case, we want to avoid too narrow a focus on the artifacts. Instead, we are urged to also consider the broader context in which the artifacts are embedded.

The emphasis on this wider social perspective is useful with PICT. When a technology becomes ubiquitous, the systems in which that technology is embedded are particularly crucial to understanding the moral significance of the technology. Unfortunately, when a technology becomes commonplace and transparent, we may find it increasingly difficult to pay attention to the ethical significance of a technology that is disappearing because of its pervasiveness. An emphasis on analyzing socio-technical systems can bring PICT artifacts and effects back into a clearer focus.

As an example of a PICT socio-technical system, consider "smart meters" for electrical usage. This technology has a history that predates widespread use of the Internet, but smart meters are a common example of a ubiquitous computing device. Decades ago, some utilities, in exchange for a discount to the home owner on power bills, installed electricity meters that allowed the utility to automatically turn down water heaters at night. Those early smart meters communicated between the home and the utility over the power lines. Today smart meters can also use wireless Internet to enhance communications between the power company, the meter, and appliances in the home.

Individual smart meter devices are not particularly sophisticated or complex. But the socio-technical system in which they are embedded – the power grid – is sophisticated, complex, and value-laden. One indication of the significant value content of the power socio-technical system (and proposed changes to create the "smart grid") is the public reaction to smart meters. Smart meters have become highly controversial in many places where they have been deployed.

In the top six items returned by a Google search on the phrase "smart meters," we found the following titles of websites: "Stop smart meters: fighting for our health, privacy and safety," "Libertarian Florida house candidate comes out against smart meters" and "refusesmartmeters.com." Objections to smart meters are motivated by fears of adverse health effects of wireless transmissions, of increased utility costs, of invasions of privacy, and of remote appliance shut-downs (refusesmartmeters.com).

I do not take a position here on any of the objections to smart meters or the smart grid. But I contend that the breadth and intensity of public reactions to both indicate the importance of socio-technical systems in a civilization that relies so heavily on its technology. This importance has significant moral implications, and Rule 4 acknowledges this importance by pointing out that responsibility for computing artifacts includes explicit, conscious attention to socio-technical systems. Engineers and power utility executives who were enthused about smart meters might understandably think that such a relatively simple and straightforward PICT device would not have generated such opposition; but if they had thought more carefully about the socio-technical system in which the smart meters would be embedded, they might have been better prepared to integrate the devices in a way that did not enrage a significant portion of their customers.

Thinking ahead in this way is not only good business; it is also good applied ethics. If the protests against the smart meters are justified, then the installation of the smart meters constitutes a harm against people, a harm for which the smart meter producers and sellers are responsible. And even if the objections to the smart meters turn out to be mistaken, the furor itself is harmful to all involved; avoiding this friction would have been a moral benefit.

Rule 4's emphasis on large systems (and not just individual devices) makes this an appropriate place to comment on the role of policy makers in moral responsibility for PICT. Both corporate and governmental institutions are making policy and funding decisions that will largely determine the direction and scope of PICT developments and deployments. In order to make wise decisions, morally responsible decisions, about PICT, the decision-makers must be meticulously fair and well informed. Policy makers are "users" of technology, but in a way that is different from individuals who interact with devices on a day-to-day basis. The policy makers will use PICT to advance their own careers and (hopefully) to advance the public good. In doing so responsibly, they will have to make a good faith effort to predict and understand the effects, both intended and unintended, of projects that include PICT.

10.3.5   Transparency

Rule 5. People who design, develop, deploy, promote, or evaluate a computing artifact should not explicitly or implicitly deceive users about the artifact or its foreseeable effects, or about the socio-technical systems in which the artifact is embedded.

The philosopher Michael Davis pointed out that only Rule 5 of The Rules is given in the grammatical form of "People ... should ..." (Davis 2011). Rules 1–4 are instead written as descriptions of moral responsibilities associated with computing artifacts and socio-technical systems. Rule 5 stands out as the most prescriptive rule in tone. Indeed, it seems similar to a commandment: "Those shalt not lie about computing artifacts and socio-technical systems."

Earlier in this chapter I described how PICT devices and systems are designed to be unobtrusive and possibly "transparent" to users. When this invisibility is based on PICT applications becoming common and reliable, the disappearance is natural and benign, analogous to the everyday-ness of clean water on tap. But some PICT devices and socio-technical systems could be designed in order to deceive users and the public about the devices, systems, and their effects. Rule 5 explicitly forbids this sort of deception.

Rule 5 also embodies an objection to companies and individuals who exaggerate the capabilities or the positive effects of PICT devices in order to increase sales and profit. This kind of deception can occur on many levels: Researchers hoping to gain funding, managers hoping to curry favor for their units, salespeople deceiving customers, and public relations departments trying to fool the public. Because of technical details including size, complexity and sophistication, some PICT devices will be somewhat mysterious to all but the best informed technologists. This means the technologists have power, and Rule 5 demands that this power be used responsibly.

Many of those who object to smart meters accuse power companies of exactly this sort of deception. Opponents of smart meters are convinced that power companies and governments are colluding to hide the true effects of the meters on people, the true objectives of the smart grid, and the ultimate motivations of the people who are promoting the smart grid. If the opponents are right, smart meters are a prime example of a PICT application that has transgressed Rule 5. If the opponents are wrong, the controversies over the smart meters is still a potent reminder that professionals involved in PICT must strive for openness in dealing with a public increasingly dependent on socio-technical systems, and increasingly suspicious of the social effects of technology.

10.4   The Rules and the Searing's Three Cases

In Chap. 2 of this book, Donald and Elizabeth Searing present three "real-world examples" involving pervasive and communication technologies. In this section, I will briefly examine each of the three cases, and describe aspects of the cases that seem particularly relevant to The Rules.

10.4.1   Case 1. Lost in Death Valley

The details of this sad case are laid out well in Chap. 2; I'll only review a few main points here. In 2009 a mother drove her young son from Los Angeles to Death Valley National Park to do some camping. According to the mother, she faithfully followed the directions of her GPS device, and ended up stranded when her vehicle fell into a pit along a deserted mining track. There was no cell phone coverage where they were stopped, and they were too far away from civilization to walk out. The son died before the mother was rescued 5 days later.

GPS systems are mentioned explicitly in The Rules as a clear example of a socio-technical system: A GPS navigator is a computing artifact, but that artifact is useless without extensive infrastructure (e.g., the satellites that make location possible). Similarly, the use of the cell phone is also central to the case. There is also a considerable set of social practices associated with GPS devices. It is these social practices that are the focus of the Searings' analysis.

For example, a crucial factor in this case is the mother's apparent confidence as she continued to drive farther and farther from safety. There is a moment in the story when, prior to the final disabling accident, the rough road results in a flat tire.

The mother changes the tire, and continues driving ever farther from safety. Had she at that point turned around, disaster might have been avoided, but she pressed on.

With the advantage of hindsight, we can see this as a critical point in the story. Why didn't the mother take this as an ominous warning, and turn back? The Searings suggest that the pervasive socio-technical systems of cell phones and GPS devices were aspects of this (ultimately fatal) confidence. They write, "The technology works wonderfully, until it doesn't, and that transition can be sharp and unexpected." But who is morally responsible for the deadly consequences in this particular case?

Rule 3 states that "people who knowingly use a particular computing artifact are morally responsible for that use." Applied to this case of a GPS and cell phone user, the mother is a knowing user. I assume that in 2009 the mother knows that a GPS device is fallible, and that cell phone coverage is not universally available. Indeed, a resort inside the Death Valley National Park warns potential guests on its website: "Generally speaking, there is no cell phone reception in Death Valley. Depending on service provider and type of phone, some areas may have limited reception, but it is sparse and unpredictable" (Furnace Creek Resort 2013). I don't know if that web site warning was available in 2009, or if the mother saw it. But if she had seen and heeded such a warning, she might have turned back in time. Rule 3 designates that some of the responsibility in this case belongs to the mother because of the way she used the GPS device, and probably because of the way she relied on her cell phone.

Rule 2 emphasizes that "shared responsibility … is not a zero-sum game." The mother's responsibility for her overreliance on a GPS device and a cell phone does not automatically let other stakeholders "off the hook." For example, map data providers are a vital part of the GPS socio-technical system, and the Searings report that Death Valley National Park rangers "lobbied the map data providers to remove these old roads from these old maps of their park." Since the consequences of following a non-functional road can be dire in Death Valley, and since the map providers have been told about this problem, the map providers surely fall under Rule 1 and Rule 2, which assign responsibility to the people who design, develop or deploy a computing artifact for the foreseeable effects of that artifact. In this particular case, the danger of stranded motorists in a potentially lethal environment makes corrections to the maps (and perhaps to the path finding algorithms) literally a matter of life and death. Rule 4 emphasizes that those responsible for the creation and the maintenance of GPS devices should make a reasonable effort to take into account the socio-technical systems in which those devices will be embedded. Potentially life-critical uses of GPS devices should surely be part of the design and testing of these devices.

The timeliness of the map data used by GPS device manufacturers is one important issue; another important issue is how often users update their devices with revised maps. Some devices make this easy, and free; other devices require elaborate procedures, including charges that can rival the original cost. Both the users and the manufacturers share responsibility for this important aspect of how reliable and safe the GPS system becomes over time.

Rule 5 is also relevant to this case. The sellers of GPS devices are responsible for clear warnings of the limitations of the system. Many GPS devices include such warnings, but some do not. When clear warnings are given, it is the responsibility of users to behave accordingly.

The Searings do an admirable job of analyzing this case, and my brief discussion here is consistent with their more detailed work. In this case, a close reading of The Rules seems to complement their analysis.

10.4.2   Case 2. The Stuxnet Worm

The second case the Searings present in Chap. 2 is the apparent 2010 cyberattack against Iranian uranium enrichment systems. Subsequent analysis of what details were available led researchers to give the name Stuxnet to the worm used in the attack. The specific targets of this successful attack were computerized controlers for high-speed motors critical to the process of uranium enrichment (Gross 2011).

The writers of The Rules recognize the importance of military applications of technology. Some of the people who have signed The Rules explicitly oppose offensive cyber-weapons, but not all. Some of the signers are pacifists with respect to computing artifacts. The Rules do not advocate for or against such applications. Instead, The Rules merely advocate that those who design, develop, deploy and use cyber-weapons recognize their personal and professional responsibilities for those weapons and their effects, both positive and negative.

Given this understanding of The Rules, it is straightforward to apply them to the Stuxnet case, and to most cases involving cyber-weapons. Rules 1–5 insist that the people engaged in cyberwarefare must take moral responsibility for their actions, and for the effect of the systems they help to build and use. Thus, if you are convinced that all offensive military uses of computing artifacts are morally unacceptable, then The Rules suggest that you would hold blameworthy all those knowingly involved in the launch of Stuxnet. Similarly, if you think that the use of this cyber-weapon was morally praiseworthy, The Rules suggest that the praise belongs to all those involved. The Rules are a concise document about moral responsibility; they do not take positions on many important issues, including the issue of whether or not computing artifacts should be used as offensive weapons.

There are limits to how responsibility "flows" in analyzing incidents of cyberwarefare. Not everyone whose work is used to develop cyber-weapons can reasonably be held accountable for those cyber-weapons. For example, it is reasonable to assume that the developers of Stuxnet used compilers and computers that are easily available to the public while working on the worm. Does this mean that the people who produced the particular brand of PC and the particular compiler used to develop Stuxnet are personally responsible for the effects of the Stuxnet deployment in Iran? I think not. This is an example of why the word "foreseeable" appears in Rules 1, 2, and 5; why the word "knowingly" appears in Rule 3; and why the phrase "reasonable effort" appears in Rule 4. There are some causal paths that are just too long and indirect to be convincing arguments for moral responsibility.

10.4.3   Case 3. The Flash Crash

The third and final case in Chap. 2 explores a notable event in the American stock markets, an event that occurred on the 6th of May, 2010 (U.S. Commodity Futures Trading Commission (CFTC) and U.S. Securities & Exchange Commission (SEC) 2010). The Searings give a detailed account of the incident in Chap. 2; for the purposes of my analysis, a broad outline will suffice: One firm's software made what, in retrospect, were anomalous stock trades. These trades were the cause of other software trades that combined to push down the Dow Jones Industrial Average almost 1,000 points in a few minutes. Then, a few minutes later, the markets recovered most of those losses. This odd (and some would say frightening) fluctuation was nick-named the "Flash Crash."

In Chap. 2, the Searings give a remarkably clear analysis of the complex interactions that resulted in the Flash Crash. I will not attempt to either summarize or repeat their analysis here. Instead, I will choose one important point from their analysis, and discuss how The Rules relate to that point.

The Searings' analysis of the Flash Crash incident emphasizes "the complicated ecology of pervasive interconnected systems." They examine how financial professionals, software engineers, and market participants interact with the systems that make possible rapid, automated trading. After examining the ethical obligations of these stakeholders to each other and to the public, the Searings take a novel approach in asking "what is owed to the market itself?"

This last piece of analysis, and its associated question, are the single aspect of Chap. 2 that is the least reflected in The Rules. The question of "responsibility to whom?" is not explicitly addressed in any detail in The Rules. In the working definition of "moral responsibility," the following sentence appears: "'Moral responsibility' includes an obligation to adhere to reasonable standards of behavior, and to respect others who could be affected by the behavior." My experience with the evolution of the language used in The Rules convinces me that the moral responsibility the authors intend has to do most directly with the welfare of humans, not of computer artifacts, networks, or markets.

How then might The Rules be coherently applied to this case, if not by an appeal to responsibility for the markets themselves? I think a proper focus of an analysis based on the Rules would make the effects of the market on people the primary concern. The socio-technical system of automated trading – a system that includes automatic pieces, protocols for trading, laws and the absence of laws about what trades are proper, and how subsystems interact – has the potential for significant economic benefit to some, and for significant economic harm to others. Some of these benefit and harm effects are economically inevitable, and as incentives for wise investment, they may have overall laudatory outcomes.

But if overall harms result not from competition and legitimate market risks, but instead result from system problems, there is moral responsibility to the people responsible for those trading systems (including the markets within which they operate). These problems can include negative unintended side effects (errors, carelessness, or hubris about the systems) or negative intended side effects (unfair advantage-taking by insiders or external actors). Looked at from this perspective, harms from the Flash Crash (and from many other problems encountered in automated trading) can involve all five of The Rules. The kinds of safeguards and testing discussed by the Searings are things the designers, developers, and deployers need to be concerned with (Rules 1 and 2). Users who attempt to game the system, or use the system carelessly leading to system wide problems, are, according to Rule 3, responsible for that misuse and its effects. Rule 4 emphasizes that all the actors involved in the Flash Crash (including the three featured by the Searings) must be mindful of the entire socio-technical system, not only the piece or pieces they are most directly connected to. And Rule 5 prohibits using the financial trading system to deceive customers or fellow traders.

10.5   Conclusions

In this chapter, I've looked at how The Rules, written about moral responsibility for any computing artifact, might be applied to PICT artifacts, and the systems in which those artifacts are embedded. This exercise revealed some interesting facets of PICT. The Rules' emphasis on socio-technical systems and its strong condemnation of deception appear to be particularly useful in approaching the ethics of PICT in general, and in analyzing the three cases in Chap. 2.

The exercise also clarified some aspects of The Rules. Chuck Huff has characterized The Rules as something of a prophetic voice in computer ethics (Huff 2011). And Ken Pimple pointed out that besides being a document, The Rules are also the focal point of a community whose members have endorsed The Rules (Pimple 2011). Applying The Rules to PICT is one way that The Rules can encourage computing professionals and users to examine their moral responsibilities as they design, develop and deploy PICT socio-technical systems; this is the prophetic mission of The Rules in action. And if people involved in PICT become interested in the issues of moral responsibility, they may join the community of The Rules, adding their ideas to the next versions.

Codes of ethics for computing professionals can certainly be helpful in understanding how PICT should be produced and used. But the ambitiously broad scope of the Rules, as well as their relative simplicity, may also play a role in calling professionals, policy makers, and the public to account for their interactions with this emerging technology.

References

Beck, Kent et al. 2001. *Manifesto for agile software development*. http://agilemanifesto.org/. Accessed 22 May 2012.
Davis, Michael. 2011. *The authority of the rules: Why should anyone allow them to serve as a guide?* Paper presented at the Association for Practical and Professional Ethics, Cincinnati, OH, March 5.

Furnace Creek Resort. 2013. *Our most frequently asked questions.* http://www.furnacecreekresort.com/faq-s-531.html. Accessed 29 Jan 2013.

Greenfield, Adam. 2006. *Everyware: The dawning age of ubiquitous computing,* 11–12. Berkeley: New Riders.

Gross, Michael. A declaration of cyber-war. *Vanity Fair,* April 2011. http://www.vanityfair.com/culture/features/2011/04/stuxnet-201104. Accessed 24 Jan 2013.

Huff, Chuck. 2011. *The rules similarities and differences between IT codes of ethics and the rules.* Paper presented at the Association for Practical and Professional Ethics, Cincinnati, OH, March 5.

Miller, Keith. 2010. *A short history of the rules,* 10 July 2010. https://edocs.uis.edu/kmill2/www/TheRules/history.html. Accessed 21 May 2012.

Nissenbaum, Helen. 1994. Computing and accountability. *Communications of the ACM* 37(1): 72–80.

Oladimeji, Ebenezer A., Lawrence Chung, Hyo Taeg Jung, and Jaehyoun Kim. 2011. Managing security and privacy in ubiquitous eHealth information interchange. In *Proceedings of the 5th International Conference on Ubiquitous Information Management and Communication (ICUIMC '11).* ACM, New York, Article 26, 10 p.

Pimple, Kenneth D. 2011. *The rules: A bigger picture.* Paper presented at the Association for Practical and Professional Ethics, Cincinnati, OH, March 5.

Refusesmartmeters.com. 2011. *Stop smart meters, refuse smart meters, remove smarter meters.* http://refusesmartmeters.com/. Accessed 24 May 2012.

The Ad Hoc Committee for Responsible Computing. *Moral responsibility for computing artifacts: Five rules.* https://edocs.uis.edu/kmill2/www/TheRules/. Accessed 21 May 2012.

U.S. Commodity Futures Trading Commission (CFTC) and U.S. Securities & Exchange Commission (SEC). (2010). *Findings regarding the market events of May 6, 2010: Report of the Staffs of the CFTC and SEC to the Joint Advisory Committee on Emerging Regulatory Issues* 30 Sept 2010. http://www.sec.gov/news/studies/2010/marketevents-report.pdf. Accessed online 13 Oct 2010.

Chapter 11
Principles for the Ethical Guidance of PICT

Kenneth D. Pimple

11.1 Introduction

Information and communication technologies that are hidden, invisible, or often unnoticed are very common and, in all likelihood, will continue to proliferate at an increasing pace thanks to improvements in miniaturization, more efficient power sources, increasing capacity in wireless data transmission, and the like. At some point, these technologies will become, or have already become, *pervasive* or commonly found *over* wide physical areas, *within* particular places (offices, automobiles, human bodies), and *nested in* other technologies (GPS in mobile phones).

The benefits that PICT offer for health care, facilitating connections between people, sharing news and other information, enhanced safety, entertainment, science, art, and innumerable other applications cannot be denied. However, every positive change casts a shadow of possible, if not inevitable, negative change. The damage caused by new technologies is often unintended, but no less real for that. The core features of PICT suggest some potential dangers and how they can be inadvertently introduced.

First, it seems to me that most PICT devices and applications[1] pose very little danger on their own. Instead, their negative aspects appear, or dramatically increase, as they become widely used. One common concern about PICT is its threat to privacy. If only a few hundred people used Facebook or Google searches, the threat would not only be confined to those few people, but also unattractive to exploitation.

---

[1] I use the word "applications" here to cover both "how devices are used" and "software."

K.D. Pimple, Ph.D. (✉)
Poytner Center, Indiana University Bloomington, 618 East Third Street, Bloomington, IN 47405-3602, USA
e-mail: pimple@indiana.edu

K.D. Pimple (ed.), *Emerging Pervasive Information and Communication Technologies (PICT)*, Law, Governance and Technology Series 11, DOI 10.1007/978-94-007-6833-8_11, © Springer Science+Business Media Dordrecht 2014

There is not much incentive to pry into the private lives of a few hundred people at great effort, but when that same effort gives access to information on millions of people, there emerges a market. Of course the emergence of such markets is neither accidental nor incidental: Insofar as PICT is designed to collect, transfer, store, analyze, and use massive amounts of personal information, PICT sets the stage for massive privacy violation *by design*. Data mining pays.

Second, PICT's near invisibility makes it hard for most people to perceive its threats. This invisibility is sometimes physical, as with well-concealed cameras or listening devices. It is also often psychological. When a device provides a clear, welcome benefit through one or more of its functions, we often ignore, or are unaware of, other functions that are secondary to us but primary to others. Few of us are concerned that our mobile phones constantly broadcast our location. Facebook doesn't feel like a method of industrial surveillance. Most of us have no idea how many computers are embedded in our cars, kitchen appliances, and pacemakers, many of which can be programmed – or hacked – wirelessly.

Third, many PICT devices and applications are magnificently complicated. Many computer programs are too complex for any single person to understand; when a single physical device is constructed of several off-the-shelf components (camera, telephone, Wi-Fi), each with its own software, it's difficult to guarantee that no bugs remain.

For these reasons alone, it seems important to attend to the ethical issues that might be raised by continued development, deployment, and use of PICT. This chapter is divided into four sections following this introduction.

In Sect. 11.2, "Varieties of ethical guidelines," I consider several levels of abstraction at which ethical guidance can be offered and make a case for the utility of ethical principles in the case of PICT.

In Sect. 11.3, "The Belmont principles," I describe an undeniably successful application of ethical principles to a real-world problem – research with human subjects.

In Sect. 11.4, "The wider context of principles," I argue that principles cannot be effective in morally corrupt political and social contexts.

In Sect. 11.5, "Ethical principles for PICT," I offer eight principles for the guidance of PICT.

11.2 Varieties of Ethical Guidelines

The range of specificity of moral or ethical guidance is enormous. It is often said that all of the world's major religions teach some form of the Golden Rule – "Do unto others as you would have them do unto you." But all of those religions also have many other rules, some applicable only in very narrow circumstances. For a pair of examples, I will draw from my own tradition, Roman Catholicism.

In the book of Mark 12:28–31, Jesus is asked, "Which is the first of all the commandments?"

29 Jesus replied, 'This is the first: Listen, Israel, the Lord our God is the one, only Lord,
   30 and you must love the Lord your God with all your heart, with all your soul, with all
your mind and with all your strength.
   31 The second is this: You must love your neighbor as yourself. There is no commandment greater than these.' [*New Jerusalem Bible*][2]

Jesus' second commandment is clearly a variant of the Golden Rule, and its similar wording to and close association with the Great Commandment suggest that the two commandments are in a sense parallel, if not equivalent.

Of course, these are not the only rules honored by Catholics and other Christians. When my parents were growing up on farms on the plains of eastern Colorado, they were required by Church teaching to fast for 12 h before they could take Holy Communion. Because of the long fast and the normal sleep schedule of dry-land farmers, they typically attended the earliest service each Sunday. As part of this restriction, they were told that they should not brush their teeth before Mass for fear that they would swallow a bit of toothpaste, thus breaking their long fast.[3]

The toothpaste rule is clearly derived from the pre-Communion fasting rule, but I doubt that it would be possible to deduce the fasting rule, or even the Sacrament of the Eucharist (Holy Communion), directly from the Great Commandment.

11.2.1   Secular Foundations

The Golden Rule and the Great Commandment have secular analogs in (at least) Immanuel Kant's Categorical Imperative and Jeremy Bentham's Greatest Happiness Principle. The first of the three formulations of the Categorical Imperative is

Act only in accordance with that maxim through which you can at the same time will that it become a universal law. [Kant 1785]

Bentham summarizes the Greatest Happiness Principle as follows:

it is the greatest happiness of the greatest number that is the measure of right and wrong [Bentham 1891 (1776):93, italics in original]

Kant's ethical theory is called a *deontological* theory, from the Greek word "deon" (δεον), meaning duty or obligation. The focus is on the obligations of rational beings – humans. Rationality binds us to certain limitations in our thinking and our behavior. Any duty or rule we discern or create must apply to every rational being (no special pleading) and cannot be self-contradictory.

---

[2] See also Leviticus 19:18; Matthew 19:16–19; Matthew 22:36–40; Luke 10:25–28.
[3] Some readers will be aware that the length of the pre-Eucharist fast was reduced to 1 h. I do not know where the toothpaste rule lies on the continuum ranging from formal cannon law through a pastor's cautious offhand statement to a parent's well-intentioned advice.

An easily understood example of a Kantian duty is "keep your promises." Any duty created to circumvent the duty of promise-keeping, such as "keep your promises unless you can do a greater good by breaking your promise," will run afoul of the necessity of non-contradiction. The point of promising is to hold us to a particular course of action even when it is inconvenient, costly, unpleasant, or even dangerous. Our "faculty to make and keep promises," writes Hannah Arendt, is the "remedy for unpredictability, for the chaotic uncertainty of the future" (Arendt 1958: 237). Any formulation that justifies promise-breaking destroys the value of promising.

In contrast, utilitarianism is known as a *consequentialist* theory because the focus is squarely on the outcomes (consequences) of actions. Bentham argued that every action should be considered in the light of the amount of happiness is produced and the number of people made happy by the action. Whether this formulation seems reasonable or not, there is an undeniable appeal to the idea that the consequences of actions should influence our moral judgment of the action and the actor. Most people would sympathize with (and many would praise) someone who broke a minor promise because she was too busy saving lives at the scene of an automobile accident. From a utilitarian point of view, the promise-breaking would still be regrettable (because it would result in some degree of reduction of happiness), but perfectly morally supported by the greater good served in the process.

Kant and other deontologists do not ignore consequences, and utilitarians don't ignore duties, but the difference in emphasis can lead to very different evaluations of some actions in some circumstances. A hardline deontologist would forbid breaking a promise even to save a life, while a hardline utilitarian would approve of killing 10 to save a 100, but they would both accept certain principles as useful (if not absolute) guides to action, such as do no harm, be loyal, be fair, tell the truth, and keep your promises.

The comprehensive nature of foundational precepts also works against their universal acceptance. Basing all moral judgments and practices on the Categorical Imperative or the Greatest Happiness Principle is something like building a house on a foundation of mixed stone and sand. Some aspects of the resulting structure are clearly strong, while others are just as clearly weak, at least insofar as some of their logical and inescapable conclusions run counter to deeply ingrained moral intuitions and convictions.

11.2.2   *From Foundations to Principles*

The Golden Rule, the Great Commandment, the Categorical Imperative, and the Greatest Happiness Principle are all expressed in a single sentence; all can be seen as the foundation of a whole, complex moral system that conforms more-or-less well with most commonly held moral convictions and our strongest moral intuitions; and all make it clear that moral behavior is impartial – that is, all persons situated similarly must be treated similarly, *including the actor himself*. My suffering has no greater moral import than any other person's, but every suffering person has a stronger claim on the assistance of others than has any non-suffering person.

These foundational moral theories are also suspended in a web of tradition, interpretation, clarification, and elaboration ranging from additional broad commandments (don't kill, don't steal, don't lie) to narrow rules such as the toothpaste rule. Between the scope of Great Commandment and the toothpaste rule we find ethical principles – not too general, not too specific, but still potentially very useful, especially when they grow out of and are informed by a particular profession or set of social practices.[4]

Established social practices are not perfect guides to morally acceptable behavior, but they are ignored at our peril. They are imperfect because they are fluid, sometimes alarmingly so, following fads of the masses or the will of a charismatic leader. They are also fractured or multi-faceted in our pluralistic era. They cannot be ignored, however, because they are a gauge of how ordinary people behave and are willing to behave, what they find acceptable and unacceptable – the latter sometimes only with reference to *other people*, due to our all-too common tendency to ignore the universal character of all respectable moral codes.[5]

Unlike many rules, which are typically best understood within a relatively narrow temporal and cultural context, fundamental maxims seem to be (and possibly are) applicable to all humans, in all times, in all places. Principles again stand between the two because they focus on a slice of human behavior and experience situated in a fair-sized, but not universal, social and temporal context – such as that of the people and organizations who envision, develop, manufacture, sell, maintain, and use pervasive information and communication technologies.

Within relatively narrow social practices, such as the practice of law or medicine, the nature of the practice and its role in society help to constrain and define ethical boundaries: Lawyers intentionally breaking the law and physicians intentionally spreading disease are obviously acting against the purpose of their professions.

---

[4]The philosophy of W.D. Ross (1877–1971) has had a significant impact on ethical theory, particularly with regard to applied or practical ethics. As a methodological intuitionist, he maintained "that there is a plurality of first principles that may conflict, and that no explicit priority rules for resolving such conflicts can be provided. This means that principles of duty cannot ultimately be grounded in a single foundational principle as consequentialists and Kantians believe" (Stratton-Lake 2002: xii). What I am calling "principles," Ross called *"prima facie duties."* He lists the following in *The Right and the Good*: fidelity, reparation, gratitude, justice, beneficence, self-improvement, and non-maleficence (Ross 2002 [1930]: 21).

The principles that I offer below are not meant to be universal first principles, but do aspire to approach that status in the realm of PICT.

[5]It is beyond the scope of this chapter to make a case for how social conventions can be impartially determined to be corrupt, unjust, or otherwise unfit, but I believe it is safe to say that defending the morality or immorality of a practice solely on tradition (or "what we've always done") or human or written authority (human or divine) is always questionable. Such considerations can be *part* of a justification or rationale for particular practices, but they are indefensible as the *sole* rationale.

Of course while some of the boundaries demarking ethical professional practice are easily identified, some – especially those at the margins, such as physician assisted suicide – are highly contested.

Professional ethics and social convention constrain the behavior of practitioners, but they also provide a warrant – sometimes a monopoly – for some behaviors. Lawyers are allowed to protect some information to protect client confidentiality; physicians are allowed to injure people in certain ways (drawing blood, etc.) to serve their patients. For these professions, the boundaries are defined and upheld by professional bodies, such as the American Bar Association and the American Medical Association, with entry to the profession dependent on certification. Many other professions do not have such formal gatekeeping, including most occupations concerned with information and communication technologies. Nevertheless, their special training and skills, and in many cases their position in particular corporations or other organizations, enables them to do things beyond the ability and comprehension of the rest of us.

It is at this level that principles are of most use. They do not attempt to cover all possible contingencies in human life, nor are they so specific that they would have to be unusably detailed and cumbersome adequately to apply in all contexts.

11.3 The Belmont Principles

The Belmont Report is a concrete example of the utility of a principle-based approach. In 1974, responding to a number of scandals in biomedical research, the United States Congress passed the National Research Act, creating the National Commission for the Protection of Human Subjects of Biomedical and Behavioral Research. The Commission was charged, among other things, with identifying "the basic ethical principles that should underlie the conduct of biomedical and behavioral research involving human subjects" (National Commission 1979). Rather than suggesting specific regulatory recommendations to meet this charge, the Commission asked the Secretary of Health, Education, and Welfare[6] to adopt the Belmont Report in its entirety as official policy. Regulations were then constructed on the Belmont foundation.

The Belmont Report was published in 1979 and is a rarity among Federal documents in that it is short (about 5,500 words), readable, and relevant long after its publication. The report promoted three principles for the guidance of human

---

[6]The U.S. Department of Health, Education, and Welfare became the Department of Health and Human Services in 1980.

subjects research[7]: beneficence, respect for persons, and justice.[8] These principles have guided both biomedical research and biomedical practice with imperfect but impressive success for 30 years.

11.3.1   Beneficence

Beneficence is simply doing good, while its negatively-stated counterpart, *non-maleficence*, is refraining from doing harm. Together they could be understood as the whole of moral law, but only with some contortions, because *doing* is generally considered as physical actions. Many moral codes require certain attitudes and forbid some states of mind. Indeed, the Great Commandment can be interpreted primarily as concerning a state of mind, "love" sometimes being understood as an emotional state. However, we have two perfectly good words to cover good and evil attitudes – benevolence, wishing or willing good, and malevolence, wishing or willing evil.

In the Belmont Report, beneficence is emphasized and the word "non-maleficence" is not used, but the importance of protecting human subjects from harm is emphasized repeatedly.

I argue that it is important to recognize the asymmetry of beneficence and non-maleficence, and that the latter is a stronger and more comprehensive moral obligation than the former. This is because we are morally obliged to refrain from maleficent physical actions, such as striking someone with a stone, in almost all circumstances, but our moral obligation to perform beneficent physical actions, such as feeding the hungry, is situational rather than universal. Forbearing from harmful actions takes no time and nearly no effort, while beneficial actions, such as feeding the hungry, require both time and effort. If I lived under a strong, unconditional moral obligation to feed the hungry, I would never be able to do anything else. Of course, sacrificing some of my interests for the sake of others, as in altruism or charity, is morally praiseworthy, but doing so constantly is not demanded of us.

I assume that most developers, sellers, etc., of PICT intend to do good and not to do harm. However, considerable planning, insight, and care are required for their benevolent attitudes reliably to translate into actual beneficence and non-maleficence.

---

[7]The following characterization of the Belmont principles is rooted in the Belmont Report, but I have added my own interpretive nuances in an effort to broaden them from the context of human subjects research. No disrespect for the Belmont Report or its authors is intended.

[8]In the Belmont Report, respect for persons is discussed first, followed by beneficence and justice, but without any explicit statement that the order of presentation is intended to reflect the importance of the principles. I have chosen to discuss beneficence first because I believe that non-maleficence is arguably the most important of all moral principles. Ross writes, "it seems to me clear that non-maleficence is apprehended as a duty distinct from that of beneficence, and as a duty of a more stringent character" (Ross 2002 [1930]: 21).

11.3.2 Respect for Persons

In the Belmont Report, *respect for persons* primarily demands that researchers must receive informed consent from any potential human subjects. Emphasizing this principle was especially important in the 1970s following a series of revelations of cases in which researchers performed biomedical research on persons who did not consent to be research subjects.

I characterize respect for persons as the conviction that it is wrong to interfere with the ability of competent adults to make their own decisions, especially by deception, manipulation, coercion, or violence. It rejects *paternalism* of the sort that was rampant among physicians for most of the history of medicine, in which the physician simply told the patient to take this or that treatment, not offering choices or exploring the patient's values or wishes. That approach had some justification over the centuries-long span when the positive effects attributed to the efforts of physicians were mostly due to the placebo effect, but as more was learned about the causes and actual cures of disease, and alternatives became available, paternalism became gradually less acceptable.

Stated another way, respect for persons is about honoring the *autonomy* of competent individuals – their ability and right to decide the course of their own lives and to make their own decisions, including their own mistakes. Of course, my autonomy is limited by yours – I cannot ethically manipulate you for my own ends.[9]

Autonomy requires some degree of rationality, knowledge, and judgment, which together I will call *capacity*. Many people have limited capacity and thus limited ability to make their own decisions. Most children acquire capacity over time, but they rely on their parents or guardians to make many decisions for them. It would be unethical to allow a typical 4-year-old to decide whether to be vaccinated because she could not understand that the long-term benefit of vaccination outweighs the short-term pain involved.

Capacity and lack of capacity can sometimes be easily discerned, but not always. When an eccentric adult makes a non-typical decision about his own health care, a decision that most people would think unwise, it is tempting to conclude that his capacity has been impaired – that his understanding or judgment are inadequate. But if we take the moral value of autonomy seriously, at times we must allow people to make decisions that we, ourselves, think wrong. We should assume that people have capacity unless a limited number of criteria can be shown to apply, including broadly accurate assessment of incapacity based on age (infants have less capacity than toddlers, who have less capacity than preschoolers, etc.) and specifically accurate

---

[9]It is tempting to say that my autonomy is also limited by my abilities (I am not free to take a job for which I am unqualified) and circumstances (I am not free to take a vacation I cannot afford), but autonomy is a moral, not a practical, characteristic. My autonomy allows me to *choose* to become an airline pilot (it's a morally acceptable choice), but it does not ensure that my choice will be – or should be – realized.

assessment of capacity based on diagnosis or symptoms, such as a diagnosis of advanced dementia.

This assumption of capacity for autonomy must be honored in PICT.

11.3.3 Justice

Justice is a large and multi-faceted concept, but in the Belmont Report, "the question of justice" is presented as, "Who ought to receive the benefits of research and bear its burdens?" This formulation was inspired in part by the number of potentially harmful biomedical research projects that used captive populations, including hospital patients, prisoners, institutionalized "retarded" children, and already-oppressed racial minorities, often without any prospect that the research results would prove beneficial to similar populations in the future. It is morally objectionable to exploit the weak and few for the benefit of the powerful and many.

It is also objectionable when research funded by taxes neglects large swaths of the population. The glaring example is women, who were routinely excluded from participating in biomedical research for many years, meaning, for example, that for a while everything we thought we knew about heart disease reflected only heart disease *in men*. Women, of course, are not a numerical minority. True minority groups, including racial and ethnic populations, people with disabilities, and victims of rare medical conditions, were also ignored. The situation has improved significantly, but progress can still be made.

It isn't clear to me how PICT could differentially exploit the vulnerable, but it is clear that PICT can differentially *ignore* the vulnerable. There's a strong tendency in the design of many technologies to disregard physical differences and challenges, such as impaired eyesight, hearing, or mobility.

11.3.4 Other Principles

The Belmont principles are not the only important moral principles. Others include loyalty, respect for authority, reparation (making up for wrongs we have committed), and honesty. Not all principles are unqualified: Loyalty and respect for authority can both reasonably be tempered by the quality of the people who claim them. When our teammates, fellow party members, or relatives call on us to do evil, we are justified in refusing in spite of their claims of loyalty upon us, and illegitimate or corrupt authority figures merit no respect or deference. The principle of honesty derives much of its moral power from its relationship to beneficence and non-maleficence (dishonesty often results in harm) and respect for persons (autonomy is impaired when our actions are guided by lies).

Within the framework of the social practices enabled and demanded by PICT, principles stand a good chance of providing useful moral and ethical guidance.

11.4   The Wider Context of Principles

When fundamental aspects of a culture or community are corrupt, good rules and principles tend to be applied in a corrupt manner. For example, in the United States during the era of chattel slavery some human beings were understood to be property with limited protection under the law. Although slave owners recognized principles such as respect for persons and non-maleficence in regard to others of their kind, they systematically violated such principles in regard to their slaves. The exercise and, I believe, *understanding* of these principles were corrupted by the practice of chattel slavery.

On the spectrum of social organization, chattel slavery is quite distant from the social foundation I find most promising for a moral society, which I will call *liberal democracy*. By "liberal" I do not mean the hodgepodge of leftist positions currently associated with American liberals, but the older understanding of liberal as emphasizing the freedom of individuals to pursue their own ends with minimal interference from the government or each other. Liberal democracy also embodies the kind of liberty that is contrasted with "license," the former being constrained by moral obligations to individuals and communities, the latter referring to licentious – unrestrained and irresponsible – behavior.

Not all democracies are liberal because not all democracies guarantee human rights to all humans. In the birthplace of democracy, Athens, most citizens owned one or more slaves. Indeed, even the best democracies today are imperfect in securing and defending the equal rights of all due to racism, sexism, and other forms of bigotry that are commonly expressed in structural inequities.

Today's representative liberal democracy is built upon still more fundamental moral values, including at least some of the values of Judaism, Christianity, and Enlightenment humanism, and a complete exposition of its values is beyond the scope of this chapter. However, I do wish to contrast the values of representative liberal democracy – the values I endorse in this chapter – from some systems that I explicitly reject.

I reject the moral systems of dictatorial totalitarianism, technocracy, plutocracy, and consumer capitalism as unfit frameworks for the principles I propose. I doubt that many of my readers would defend the first three of these systems, but I will nevertheless briefly express my objection to them.

The value at the core of *dictatorial totalitarianism* is "might makes right," perhaps the oldest and least moral of moral precepts. Persons responsible for PICT should always bear in mind that any commercially available technology is available to dictators and would-be oppressors. It is irresponsible to assume that a technology will always and only be used wisely by people whose values are sound; we have to remember that there are and always will be violent, cruel, and destructive people who would be happy to use tools against us and against their own people.

Technocracy is the rule of (a) the skilled and (b) the possible.

The *skilled* are highly educated and intelligent people who can bring to bear on social and legal issues the latest scientific findings and forecasts. My sense is that technocracy was at the height of its appeal in the decades before and (especially) after World War II, the era when twentieth-century technology was born and took its first few halting steps. All babies foster hope and optimism, but few inspire confidence in their ability to craft social policy. Technological fixes (Weinberg 1966) of this era seemed to go wrong about as often as they went right. By the dawn of the twenty-first century, it seems that the bloom was off the rose of technocracy, if only because expertise has become so specialized and fractured. Rocket scientists and physicists are still recognized as smart people, but not very often as important social commentators.

Insofar as technocracy is the rule of the *possible* it is still dangerous. It's not just that technological fixes have too-narrow a focus combined with a too-broad impact, but also that technology demands to be used. Of course it's actually people who find it difficult to resist the allure of slick, shiny, new toys, but, after all, we create new things in part because we are driven to do so by our social and psychological predilections, which precondition us to be awed and inspired by our own creations into which we build features that we find attractive. That some of the features are intentionally dangerous does not make them unattractive; dangerous functions are particularly attractive to the military, the police, violent criminals, and terrorists.

The technical class have now and will inevitably continue to have tremendous influence over the development and use of PICT. Technicians also have important insights into the proper and improper uses of PICT. They are, and should be, leaders – but not the only leaders.

Plutocracy is the rule of money, or of the moneyed. A plutocratic society could take a number of forms, including dictatorship and technocracy, but not democracy. A plutocratic society could be quite benevolent (as can dictatorships), but would be unlikely to remain so. Money, like technology, tends to be its own highest value, and threats to money – such as social justice – are bound to take second place if they are not quashed altogether. Certainly no plutocracy can seriously espouse the value of equality.

In the end, dictatorship, technocracy, and plutocracy all are versions of might makes right, in which *the ability to act authorizes the action*. Liberal democracy alone enshrines as values qualities such as diversity, pluralism, fallibility, uncertainty, flexibility, and disagreement (non-conformity), which diffuse power when honored. These are among the fundamental characteristics of human and social life that can only be expunged along with humanity itself.

If for no other reason, liberal democracy is superior to dictatorship, technocracy, and plutocracy because people in power have a tremendous drive to consolidate, increase, and maintain their power. When any subset of the population achieves adequate control of power, imbalance and injustice are sure to follow. Insofar as liberal democracy is the rule of the people, power is dispersed and difficult to monopolize. All past and existing democracies are flawed, none have ever achieved a state in which the people do actually rule (and they never will), but they are still superior to the alternatives.

Consumer capitalism, or consumerism, provides an unacceptable moral foundation for rather different reasons. I take consumerism to be the collective, though not necessarily coordinated, effort of those who sell goods and services to convince a large section of the populace that their products are irresistible. Producers cannot attain even partial success in this effort without the tacit approval of the people, who must accept the premise that *buying* is a key (possibly the best) path to happiness, satisfaction, and a good life. Without this acceptance, advertising and marketing as we see it today would be so distasteful that it would not be endured.

The consumerist imperative is "if it can be sold, it must be produced." This imperative is more obvious than those of technology and money and its success can be seen in the innumerable trinkets, gadgets, shades of lipstick, variations of razors, and the rest of the mind-numbing variety of things that can be bought and sold. Apps for tablet computers and smartphones are the ideal consumer products; most of them are valuable only because of their novelty, and since novelty wears off (but is ever desired), more apps must be consumed regularly.

The potential for PICT to serve consumerism is virtually[10] unlimited. The danger is that the development and distribution of PICT will be justified simply by the fact that it can make money, with little or no consideration of the product's wider ramifications, including not only physical danger and intentional misuse, but also, possibly, the erosion of important social values. Salability is obviously an important consideration in a capitalist society (which need not be a consumerist society), but if salability is the prime consideration, important ethical considerations will tend to be overlooked or, worse, trumped.

11.5   Ethical Principles for PICT

The principles I offer to guide PICT are expressed in a somewhat less abstract and more specific way than are the Belmont principles. My list and discussion may well be incomplete and in need of improvement, but I hope they provide a fruitful starting point in fostering more detailed ethical guidance for PICT for policy- and law-makers; researchers, engineers, designers, and other technicians involved in the development, creation, and maintenance of pervasive information and communication technologies; PICT manufacturers, advertisers, marketers, vendors, and others involved in promoting and distributing PICT; corporate and individual purchasers and users; and individuals, communities, agencies, and others responsible for decommissioning, retiring, recycling, or disposing of PICT artifacts.

An end user or a manufacturer may be legally *liable* for the bad consequences of the use of a technology, but in an important sense the *responsibility* for the bad consequences might also redound to the government (lax oversight), higher education (inadequate training for engineers), professional associations, etc. Responsibility

---

[10]Pun noted, but not intended.

does not always imply blame; in many cases, having or taking responsibility for damage or harm takes the form of fixing the system that caused the problem. In this sense, responsibility is shared by many stakeholders and some errors cannot be easily rectified without common action.

Sects. 11.5.1 through 11.5.8 are organized as follows:

- The section title names the principle for ease of reference.
- The root principle(s) upon which the PICT principle is based is/are listed.
- A sentence summarizes the core of the PICT principle.
- One or more short paragraphs expand on the PICT principle.

11.5.1   Anticipatory Ethics

Root principles: Beneficence, non-maleficence, justice, and respect for persons

Ethical analysis and technological innovation should proceed hand-in-hand.

Anticipatory ethics, defined by Deborah G. Johnson as "ethical analysis aimed at influencing the development of new technologies" (Johnson 2010: 590),[11] a concept embodied as practice that is needed because ethical analysis too often emerges *after* technologies are developed and deployed, when the harm – if any – has already begun.

Anticipatory ethical analysis requires a number of groups to work together, including technicians, policy makers, ethicists, potential end-users, and potential non-users. Together they can endeavor to ensure that emerging technologies "are more attuned to social values" (Johnson 2010: 589) by foreseeing and forestalling ethical hazards. There is no guarantee that such efforts will always succeed, but certainly some of the time they will be better than our typical post hoc hand wringing.

11.5.2   Extended Consequences

Root principles: Beneficence, non-maleficence, and respect for persons

Developers (etc.) of PICT should account for effects of deployment and use beyond the local.

Like all other new technologies, PICT should provide benefits for its users and should not harm them. In addition, however, the potential reach of PICT makes a typical focus on the end user too narrow. When one person has his DNA analyzed,

---

[11] See also Johnson (2011).

all of his blood relatives are implicated whether they like it or not. The physical bond of genetics does not typically feature in PICT (although it could), but information about one person can be coupled with information about her friends, family, and colleagues with astonishing ease.

Insofar as possible, the unintended effects, positive or negative, of PICT should be anticipated. Such effects might redound to society, the economy, the environment, and the commons.

Consideration for the commons is particularly important because it is so often ignored. The commons includes everything that is owned by no one but needed by everyone, the most obvious examples being our planet's atmosphere and water, but also includes forests, landscapes, minerals and other natural resources, and, arguably, a view of the stars. When one or a few persons exploit and damage the commons for personal gain disregarding the public good, all are harmed and an injustice is done. It has been some decades – perhaps centuries – since humans could dump our waste in streams and gullies without suffering the consequences, but our social practices have not caught up with that reality. PICT already assails the commons by filling every heretofore quiet place with telephone conversations and threatening to usurp radio frequencies for the sole use of bandwidth hogs. We should be on guard to ensure that it does not do worse.

11.5.3 Anti-malice

Root principle: Non-maleficence

> Designers (etc.) of PICT should consider the possibility of and guard against malicious uses of the technology.

I do not know whether it is typical for developers of consumer or industrial machines (widely construed) to consider how their devices might be misused by criminals, terrorists, rogue states, and other people and groups with nefarious aims. Without adequate safeguards, some forms of PICT can be used to inconvenience or harm thousands or millions of people at one blow. Measures should always be taken to minimize such risks.

11.5.4 Proportional Safety

Root principle: Non-maleficence

> The safety of a system should be proportional (at least) to potential negative consequences of its misuse or failure.

Efforts to ensure the safety of PICT at all stages – design, manufacturing, marketing, use – should increase with (or beyond) the severity of potential negative consequences of misuse or failure. In some systems this principle requires serious ongoing involvement of the technology providers (developers, manufacturers, sellers); for example, in training persons responsible for using the technology.

An accompanying maxim:

> The safer and more nearly idiot-proof a system, the higher the collective responsibility for consumer education, training, and protection.

One strange side effect of creating a safer environment is that many people act as if it is entirely safe. Systems that are apparently safe for non-experts may be harmful when the safety features are cryptic, making it hard even to imagine how such a system might go wrong. When non-experts use complex but not perfectly safe systems, we need social changes, laws, and public education to counter the bad effects. Consider the case of texting while driving.

11.5.5   Transparency

Root principle: Respect for persons

> It should normally be possible for individuals to know what PICT systems do and where they are.

Hiding devices, processes, or functions from users should be frowned upon and avoided. Hiding them because the developer believes users will object to them is *prima facie* evidence of bad will. If developers fear users will object, they should find out how to achieve the same goal in an unobjectionable way, or abandon the project.

11.5.6   Informed Choice

Root principle: Respect for persons

> Individuals should normally be able to opt out of involvement with PICT.

Without transparency, informed choice is impossible. However, being able to opt out can be inadequate when a technology becomes so wide-spread that it is assumed that everyone has it. Parents should have the right to ban Internet access from their own homes, but schools that assign online homework make this difficult. If we respect freedom, we should avoid forcing people to use technologies when they do not want to, and we should not ask for explanations.

Furthermore, users should not be expected to opt in unless they can do so with adequate understanding, comprehension, and freedom.

11.5.7   Privacy

Root principle: Respect for persons

> Identifiable personal information is not a commodity.

Identifiable personal information should not be bought or sold, at least not by third parties (that is, I should not sell your personal information; selling my own personal information may be another matter); identifiable personal information should not be collected without the person's permission; and information gathered for one purpose should not be used for another purpose without further permission.

This principle also covers trading or sharing of (other people's) identifiable personal information even when money does not change hands.

Effective and widespread application of this principle would alleviate many problems with pervasive technology. Data mining would not be as profitable, but privacy would be better protected.

11.5.8   Maximum Access

Root principle: Justice

> The digital divide should not be widened.

Those who do not adopt PICT, for any reason, should not be deprived of useful or essential services or shut out of civil life due to technological advances. The underprivileged, including poor and disabled people, should not bear a disproportional share of the burden of technological and social changes.

It's one thing for some people to depend on GPS; it's another to make it impossible for anyone to function without it. The popularity of cell phones has led to the decline of pay phones; if pay phones disappear entirely, some people will be left without access to an essential service (they are already significantly inconvenienced).

Non-adopters include those who cannot afford to adopt the technology, those who choose not to adopt, and those who cannot use it because of disability. This principle also implies that legacy systems must be supported as long as they are in use; when the cost-benefit ratio of such support becomes excessive, technologists should buy out non-adopters rather than abandon them.

This is a democratic principle that falls upon civic society and government. It doesn't seem realistic to expect industry to honor this principle without incentives or mandates coming from somewhere besides normal market forces.

11.6   Conclusion

All of the chapters in this book provide ethical guidance of PICT in a variety of ways, some more overtly than others. For example,

- in Chap. 3, Lisa Lee provides a list of three mandates that should inform public policy and ten basic requirements for a national policy to protect the privacy of public health data (both in 3.4.3);
- in Chap. 4, Mark Andrejevik specifies four principles that might guide regulations on data collection and use (4.4); and
- in Chap. 9, Katie Shilton shares the four design principles she and her team developed to "encourage *participatory* approaches, fusing values of privacy, consent, and participation" (9.3.3, emphasis in original).

In this chapter, I have offered eight principles standing between foundational ethical theories and detailed rules in the hope of assisting the process of anticipatory ethics in the design and deployment of pervasive information and communication technologies. I hope that some of them will be adopted and prove fruitful. I will also be pleased if some are productive as negative examples that lead to corrective action. But my highest hope is that this chapter will stimulate conversations and actions that will inspire everyone involved with PICT to think carefully about what they do.

Acknowledgments   In addition to many of the people mentioned in the Acknowledgments for the entire volume, I am indebted to Katherine D. Seelman and Jennifer Livesay for critical comments on an earlier draft.

References

Arendt, Hannah. 1958. *The human condition*. Chicago: University of Chicago Press.

Bentham, Jeremy. 1891 [1776]. *A fragment on government,* ed. F.C. Montague. Oxford: Clarendon Press.

Johnson, Deborah G. 2010. The role of ethics in science and engineering. *Trends in Biotechnology* 28(12): 589–590.

Johnson, Deborah G. 2011. Software agents, anticipatory ethics, and accountability. In *The growing gap between emerging technologies and legal-ethical oversight: The pacing problem*, ed. G.E. Marchant et al., 61–76. Dordrecht/New York: Springer.

Kant, Immanuel. 1785. *The groundwork of the metaphysics of morals*. Various editions.

National Commission for the Protection of Human Subjects of Biomedical and Behavioral Research. 1979. *The Belmont Report: Ethical principles and guidelines for the protection of human subjects of research*. Washington, D.C: United States Department of Health, Education, and Welfare.

Ross, David. 2002 [1930]. *The right and the good,* ed. Philip Stratton-Lake. Oxford: Clarendon Press.

Stratton-Lake, Philip. 2002. Introduction. In: Ross, David. 2002 [1930]. *The right and the good*. ed. Philip Stratton-Lake. Oxford: Clarendon Press, ix–lviii.

Weinberg, Alvin M. 1966. *Will technology replace social engineering?* Alfred Korzybski Memorial Lecture.

Glossary

action research Collaborationbetween researcher and research participants to solve a problem or challenge through the research process. (9)

affordance A quality of an object or situation that makes an action possible, as the resilience of a rubber ball affords bouncing. (9)

Agency for Healthcare Research and Quality (AHRQ) United States agency set up to improve the quality, safety, efficiency, and effectiveness of health care for all Americans. http://www.ahrq.gov (7)

American Health Information Association (AHIMA) The worldwide professional association of recognized leaders in health information management, informatics, heath data technology, and innovation. http://www.ahima.org (7)

arbitrage Using the difference in the price of a financial asset between two markets to make money. (2)

augmented reality The use of technology to present virtual objects to the senses, aligned with the real world in some meaningful way. (8)

Clinical Decision Support System (CDSS) Any system designed to improve clinical decision-making related to diagnostic or therapeutic processes of care. Typically responds to "triggers" or "flags" – specific diagnoses, laboratory results, medication choices, or complex combinations of such parameters –and provides information or recommendations directly relevant to a specific patient encounter. http://psnet.ahrq.gov/glossary.aspx (7)

computerized physician/provider order entry (CPOE) System in which clinicians directly enter medication orders, as well as tests and procedures, into a computer system. The order is then transmitted to the pharmacy or pertinent department. http://psnet.ahrq.gov/glossary.aspx (7)

deidentified data Data from which identifiers are removed; identifiers are traditional data elements that lead to the determination of an individual person, e.g., name, date of birth, social security number, address, and zip code. (3)

Numbers in parenthesis correspond to the chapter(s) in which the term is used.

K.D. Pimple (ed.), *Emerging Pervasive Information and Communication Technologies (PICT)*, Law, Governance and Technology Series 11, DOI 10.1007/978-94-007-6833-8, © Springer Science+Business Media Dordrecht 2014

do not resuscitate order (DNR) A stipulation that a patient whose heart has stopped or who has stopped breathing should not receive CPR or breathing assistance and thus be allowed to die. DNR orders are generally requested by patients (or families of patients) who do not wish to have their lives prolonged artificially. (6)

e-Health or eHealth The use of information and communication technologies (ICT) for health. http://www.who.int (7)

Electronic Health Record (EHR) A longitudinal electronic record of patient health information generated by one or more encounters in any care delivery setting; includes patient demographics, progress notes, problems, medications, vital signs, past medical history, immunizations, laboratory data and radiology reports. http://www.himss.org (7)

E-mini A type of contract based on the expected future price of a stock market index designed primarily for smaller speculators. (2)

epidemiologist A public health professional who studies diseases, their effects, and their risk factors in populations. (3)

E-psychotherapy and counseling Delivery of psychotherapy and counseling via the internet through videoconferencing, chat, or email web applications. (7)

exchange-traded fund A type of investment which allows investors to hold a piece of a group of different securities, differing from a mutual fund in that they are actively traded daily in the market by automatic or manual means. (2)

fiduciary standard The legal requirement that financial analysts place the client's interests above their own interests, including disclosure of conflict of interest. (2)

haptic technology Technology that interacts with the sense of touch, such as vibrating mobile phones. (8)

heads-up display A computer display that is in front of the user's eyes, so the user does not have to shift attention down or away from the real world. (8)

Health Informatics The field involved with the analysis, use, and dissemination of health information by applying computer technology. (7)

Health Information Exchange (HIE) Electronic movement of health-related information among organizations according to nationally recognized standards; also sometimes referred to as a health information network (HIN). (7)

Health Information Management (HIM) The profession that focuses on health care data and the management of health care information resources; it addresses the nature, structure, and translation of data into usable forms of information. (7)

Health Information Technology (HIT) A broad range of products, including electronic health records (EHRs), patient engagement tools such as personal health records (PHRs), secure patient portals, and health information exchanges; excludes software for medical devices (Institute of Medicine). (7)

learning health system A health system that improves by learning from itself by establishing a system of quality improvement that combines health services research and comparative effectiveness analyses using routinely collected clinical data to improve the care of all patients. (3)

location-aware computing Computer applications that depend on the user's location, such as restaurant recommendation or driving direction apps. (8)

meaningful use The way in which EHR technologies must be implemented and utilized for a provider to be eligible for the EHR Incentive Programs and to qualify for incentive payments. http://www.hrsa.gov. (7)

m-Health or mHealth Mobile health; the provision of health services and information via mobile technologies such as mobile phones and Personal Digital Assistants (PDAs). http://www.who.int/goe/mobile_health/en/. (7)

Personal Health Record (PHR) Confidential, easy-to-use electronic tools that can help patients manage their health information, such as doctor or hospital visits, allergies, shots, or a list of medicines, all in one place. http://www.medicare.gov/Publications/Pubs/pdf/11397.pdf. (7)

sensor-effector system A system model comprised of elements which intake observational data about surroundings, employs a decision logic, and then takes action which impacts those surroundings. (2)

SPDR A proprietary group of exchange-traded funds which track the S&P 500 stock index. (2)

stub quote A price far from the market price of a security used to enable certain market trades or protect the owner from calamity; now regulated by the SEC. (2)

suitability standard The legal requirement that stock brokers find a satisfactory or acceptable financial instrument for their client. (2)

syndromic surveillance The ongoing, systematic collection, analysis, interpretation, and application of real-time (or near-real time) indicators for diseases and outbreaks that allow for their detection before public health authorities would otherwise note them. (3)

telehealth Delivery of health-related services (preventative, promotive, and curative) and information via telecommunications technologies. (7)

virtuality Preferred synonym term for "virtual reality," which is the use of computers and head-mounted displays to create a simulated world that feels real to the user. (8)

VIX The ticker symbol for the Chicago Board Options Exchange Market Volatility Index, which is used to measure volatility in the stock market. (2)

Contributors

Mark Andrejevic, Ph.D., is the Deputy Director of the Centre for Critical and Cultural Studies, University of Queensland, Australia. He is the author of *Infoglut* (2013), *iSpy: Surveillance and Power in the Interactive Era* (2007), and *Reality TV: The Work of Being Watched* (2004) as well as numerous articles and book chapters on surveillance, digital media, and popular culture. He is the chief investigator on the Personal Information Project, an Australian Research Council-funded research grant to study Australians' attitudes toward the collection and use of their personal information online.

Bo Brinkman, Ph.D., is an Associate Professor and the Graduate Director of Computer Science and Software Engineering at Miami University, in Oxford, Ohio, USA. He began his research career studying computer algorithms, but stumbled into computer ethics after being asked to take over the course for a retiring colleague. He has recently shifted his research focus to augmented reality because it is an area that leverages algorithm design while generating interesting ethical challenges. He has achieved national recognition in all three of his fields of expertise: His algorithms work has been published in the prestigious *Journal of the ACM*; his textbook on computer ethics, *Ethics in a Computing Culture*, was published in 2012 by Cengage Learning; and he recently won a best poster award at the International Symposium on Mixed and Augmented Reality (http://BoBrinkman.com).

Linda M. Hartman, M.L.S, A.H.I.P., is the Reference Librarian and Liaison, School of Health and Rehabilitation Sciences, Health Sciences Library System (HSLS), University of Pittsburgh, Pennsylvania, USA. She has more than 14 years of experience searching the medical literature and providing bibliographic instruction. She is the co-instructor of HSLS' multi-day class "Systematic Review Workshop: The Nuts and Bolts for Librarians." She is a Distinguished Member of The Academy of Health Information Professionals (http://www.hsls.pitt.edu/about/staff/profile?name=lhartman).

Francis Harvey, Ph.D., is an Associate Professor in the Department of Geography at the University of Minnesota, Minneapolis, USA. His research interests include

K.D. Pimple (ed.), *Emerging Pervasive Information and Communication Technologies (PICT)*, Law, Governance and Technology Series 11, DOI 10.1007/978-94-007-6833-8, © Springer Science+Business Media Dordrecht 2014 location privacy, spatial data infrastructures, geographic information and sharing, semantic interoperability, and critical GIS. He serves on the editorial boards of the *International Journal for Geographical Information System*, *Cartographica*, *GeoJournal*, and the *URISA Journal*. He published *A GIS Primer* with Guildford Press in 2008. He also contributed to the development of a model curriculum and resources for GIS ethics teaching (http://gisprofessionalethics.org; http://www.tc.umn.edu/~fharvey).

Cynthia M. Jones, Ph.D., is an Associate Professor of Philosophy and the Director of the Pan American Collaboration for Ethics in the Professions (PACE) at the University of Texas – Pan American. She has published in several areas of applied and professional ethics, especially medical ethics, animal rights, ethics and technology, and intelligence ethics, including recent publications in the *American Journal of Public Health*, *Teaching Ethics*, and pop culture and philosophy books. She regularly presents to professional groups such as counselors, attorneys, and social workers on ethical decision-making in the professions. She currently directs a grant-funded Campus Violence Prevention Project as well as a donor-funded Constitutional Scholars Program (http://utpa.edu/PACE; http://utpa.edu/CAVE; http://utpa.edu/Constitution).

Lisa M. Lee, Ph.D., M.S., Chief Science Officer in the Office of Surveillance, Epidemiology, and Laboratory Services at the Center for Disease Control and Prevention, Atlanta, Georgia, USA, is a public health ethicist and surveillance scientist with more than 20 years of experience in ethics of public health surveillance, scientific integrity, development and evaluation of surveillance systems, research on HIV and fertility, HIV/AIDS survival, HIV and tuberculosis, and data quality. She has published in numerous scientific publications and has served as a peer- and guest reviewer for many scientific conferences and journals. She serves on the Board of Advisors and is adjunct faculty at Georgia State University's Institute of Public Health. She served as lead editor of *Principles and Practice of Public Health Surveillance*, 3d edition (Oxford University Press, 2010).

Keith W. Miller, Ph.D., is the Orthwein Endowed Professor for Life-Long Learning in the Sciences at the University of Missouri-St. Louis College of Education, USA. Dr. Miller's research interests include computer ethics, software testing, and online learning. He received the 2011 Joseph Weizenbaum Award from the International Society for Ethics and Information Technology and was the inaugural Schewe Professor of Liberal Arts and Science at the University of Illinois Springfield. He helped to write a code of ethics for software engineers (http://seeri.etsu.edu/Codes/TheSECode.htm) and is the coordinator for "The Rules," a collaborative project concerning moral responsibility for computer artifacts (https://edocs.uis.edu/kmill2/www/TheRules/). He has more than 350 papers, talks, book chapters and presentations listed in his vita at https://edocs.uis.edu/kmill2/www/keith.pdf.

Kenneth D. Pimple, Ph.D., is an Associate Scholar and the Director of Teaching Research Ethics Programs at the Poynter Center for the Study of Ethics and

American Institutions, Indiana University Bloomington, USA. He has more than 20 years of experience in organizing faculty workshops on ethics, teaching ethics, and research ethics. He has made presentations on research ethics in several U.S. states as well as Norway and the Slovak Republic. He has published widely in journals and edited one previous book, *Research Ethics*, an anthology published in 2008 as part of Ashgate's International Library of Essays in Public and Professional Ethics (http://mypage.iu.edu/~pimple).

Donald R. Searing, Ph.D., is a co-founder and the Director of Research of the Center for Ethical Decision Theory and Practice and CEO of Syncere Systems, Lawrenceville, Georgia, USA. He is a practicing software architect who has extensive background in building automated and computer-assisted decision-making systems as well as autonomous agents (moral and otherwise) and their environments. He created Ethos System, the first commercially available ethical decision-making assistance software system and was involved in the development of the engineering ethics program at Texas A&M University. He has designed automated decision-making systems for regional and national-scale health insurance companies in the USA as well as working on the design and development of Rockmarsh, a large-scale multi-agent simulation environment. He has previously published works on automated ethical decision-making, ethics in engineering design and is currently focusing on defining the ethical guidance necessary for the creators of autonomous systems (http://www.synceresystems.com/people/donaldsearing.aspx).

Elizabeth A.M. Searing is a co-founder and the Executive Director of the Center for Ethical Decision Theory and Practice, Lawrenceville, Georgia, USA. She is currently pursuing her doctorate in public policy at the Andrew Young School of Policy Studies at Georgia State University in Atlanta, where her primary research and teaching emphases are nonprofit studies and social economy. She has conducted or presented research on three continents and has served as the Chief Operations Officer in multiple software companies involved in the field of decision research (http://www.decisiontheory.org/people/elizabethsearing.aspx).

Katherine D. Seelman, Ph.D., is the Associate Dean and Professor, School of Health and Rehabilitation Science, University of Pittsburgh, Pennsylvania, USA. Her secondary appointments include serving at the School of Public Health, the Center for Bioethics and Health Law, and Xian Jiatong University, China. Seelman is the Co-research Director of the NSF-supported Quality of Life Technology Engineering Research Center. She served as one of two from the USA on the WHO/World Bank guiding committee for the development of the first World Report on Disability for which she was a section author. Seelman served as the Director of the National Institute on Disability and Rehabilitation under President Clinton. She has published widely and is the recipient of many awards.

Katie Shilton, Ph.D., is an Assistant Professor in the College of Information Studies at the University of Maryland, College Park, USA. She is also a Senior Research Fellow at the University of Maryland's Information Policy & Access

Center. Her research explores ethics and policy for the design of information technologies. Her research has been funded by the National Science Foundation and published in both social science and computer science conferences and journals (http://terpconnect.umd.edu/~kshilton/).

Daihua X. Yu, M.S., is the Doctoral Candidate and the Graduate Student Researcher at the Health & Rehabilitation Informatics Lab, University of Pittsburgh, Pennsylvania, USA. She has more than 7 years of experience in system development and research. Her previous works include the latest transcoder gateway called AcceSS, which transforms web content into accessible presentations for visually impaired users, and iMHere, a rehabilitation platform to support self-management and care delivery for people with chronic conditions. She has published several studies on the accessibility of U.S. government and health-related websites. Yu contributed to the World Health Organization's first World Report on Disability.

Index

Printed in the United States
By Bookmasters